SUCCESSFUL
BASS FISHING

KEN SCHULTZ

ILLUSTRATIONS BY CHRIS ARMSTRONG

Ragged Mountain Press
Camden, Maine

D0166081

International Marine/
Ragged Mountain Press

A Division of The **McGraw·Hill** *Companies*

10 9 8 7 6 5 4 3 2 1

Previously published as *Bass Fishing Fundamentals,*
Second Edition

Library of Congress Cataloging-in-Publication Data
Schultz, Ken
    Successful bass fishing / Ken Schultz.
       p. cm.
    Rev. ed. of: Bass fishing fundamentals. Enl. and rev. 2nd ed.
1986
    Includes index.
    ISBN 0-07-057236-4
    1. Bass fishing. I. Schultz, Ken. Bass fishing fundamentals.
II. Title.
SH681.S36   1996
799.1'758—dc20   96-20765
                                CIP

Questions regarding the content of this book should be
addressed to:
    Ragged Mountain Press
    P.O. Box 220
    Camden, ME 04843
    207-236-4837

Questions regarding the ordering of this book should be
addressed to:
    The McGraw-Hill Companies
    Customer Service Department
    P.O. Box 547
    Blacklick, OH 43004
    Retail customers: 1-800-262-4729
    Bookstores: 1-800-722-4726

A portion of the profits from the sale of each Ragged
Mountain Press book is donated to an environmental cause.

Successful Bass Fishing is set in 9.5 point Adobe New Baskerville

♲ *Successful Bass Fishing* is printed on 60-pound Renew
Opaque Vellum, an acid-free paper that contains 50 percent
recycled waste paper (preconsumer) and 10 percent post-
consumer waste paper.

Photographs are by the author unless otherwise noted.
Illustrations by Chris Armstrong
Printed by Quebecor Printing, Fairfield, PA
Design and Production by Dan Kirchoff
Edited by John J. Kettlewell, Ellen Egan, and Pamela Benner

•

**To Virginia Schultz
and the late Edward
Schultz, my parents,
for giving me youthful
summers at Kirk Lake
and an exposure to
the outdoors.**

•

CONTENTS

PREFACE

Bass fishing has evolved into what may be the quintessential American angling form. It's a compelling scenario: aggressive and scrappy fish, widely distributed, ravenous predator; susceptible to a wide range of lures and fishing methods; pursued by people of all means, fishing as simply or as elaborately as their interests and wallets dictate. No wonder that bass are king in the collective heart of North American fishermen.

I've enjoyed bass fishing from Maine to Oregon, from California to Florida, and in Canada, Mexico, and Cuba. In some ways, the sport's the same in all those places. Some of the same lures that have caught fish for me on New York's St. Lawrence River, for instance, have also landed me bass on Lake Eufaula in Alabama and on Texas' Sam Rayburn Lake. But it's different in some ways, too. The techniques needed to fish for bass on tree-filled Truman Lake in Missouri, for example, are different from those required on New Hampshire's Lake Winnipesaukee, where the only tree in the water has fallen from the shoreline.

Successful Bass Fishing is not about bass fishing in one region or state. Because it contains important information about the principles of bass fishing, and about all of the tackle and its applications, you can use it no matter where you fish for bass.

Successful Bass Fishing has a simple premise: provide basic, useful, and thorough information that will help make you a better bass angler wherever you fish.

Because bass fishermen are as much interested in equipment, especially lures, as they are in the where-to-find and how-to-catch information, I've devoted a major part of this book to a detailed review of which equipment to use and how to use it. Furthermore, the practical aspects of what to use, and where and how to use it effectively, form the foundation for bass-angling success.

Perhaps it is worth noting that I've tried to give helpful information about tackle without being overly enthusiastic about any one manufacturer's goods. I'm not sponsored by any manufacturer, and owe no allegiances to anyone. But I've used most of what is on the market today, especially for reporting on fishing techniques and tackle trends for *Field & Stream*. Some of the things that bass anglers employ today will be out of favor tomorrow, and I've tried to keep the proper perspective on this so that the information here will stand the test of time.

I don't think I'll ever know everything about bass fishing, and it's probably best that no one ever does. This book, which is a revised version of two earlier editions of my book *Bass Fishing Fundamentals*, reflects the best I can offer at the moment, and I guarantee that it provides the foundation for becoming a good, knowledgeable bass angler.

At times it seems as though bass fishing has become more of a business than a sport. Where bass angling in the popular literature once meant reports on cane poles and bobbers, it now means reports on highly sophisticated equipment. Where it once meant leisurely rowing and casting, it now means selective bait presentation, problem analysis, structural-fishing adaptations, and time management. Where it once meant the enjoyment of a total outdoor experience, it now means the production of fish to justify the effort and investment.

Not that there's anything wrong with the use of highly sophisticated equipment; it's only natural that fishing techniques should become more complex as different forms develop. But to put this in perspective, it was less than a century ago that James Heddon created the first plugs, which were used for bass fishing. After some stupendous catches on these new lures, there was talk about banning them because they made catching bass too easy!

A preoccupation with size and stature is part of the American way—bigger is better and biggest is best—and in all honesty there is no form of angling in which you will not find importance attached to the catching of large fish. But don't be overly concerned with catching big bass, or a lot of bass, as a measure of a good experience.

It is a little alarming today that bass anglers on the whole have become a highly aggressive, intense bunch, with more emphasis on the catch than the sport. Whether you fish from the bank, from a jonboat, or from a turbocharged fishing machine, remember that this is fun, that it is a sport, and that the first question at the end of the day shouldn't necessarily be, "Did you get a big bass?" or "Did you catch a lot of fish?" but rather "Did you have a good time?"

Remember, too, that the future of bass fishing is tied in with effective management of all our natural resources. In addition to being good stewards of those resources, bass fishermen can help their sport by taking proper care of the fish they catch and by releasing most of their bass, especially those they will not eat, regardless of the size. Bass fishermen used to keep most of the big bass they caught. That is changing. Not only have attitudes altered, but today you can release your big bass and still have a trophy, thanks to the marvelous replica work being done by top taxidermists.

Use the information in *Successful Bass Fishing* to help you become a more proficient bass angler, but as you become more knowledgeable and successful, consider it your responsibility to take good care of the fish. That way, we will all continue to enjoy good times while pursuing America's favorite fish.

ACKNOWLEDGMENTS

My sincere thanks go to the anglers who are the subjects of these photographs and who graciously took time out from good bass fishing to accommodate me; and to all the fishermen who have shared their bass-angling moments, opinions, techniques, and favorite waters with me.

1 THE HOME

This is largemouth bass country. Shallow places with plenty of cover provide the casting and fish-catching challenges that make bass so popular.

OF THE BASS

Largemouth bass are the most adaptable of our popular gamefish. They are the only species that thrives in all states but Alaska; north and south of our borders; and in Europe, Japan, and Africa. Smallmouth bass, though not quite as extensively distributed, are found from the Mississippi River drainage east, most abundantly concentrated in areas with generally cool, deep-water lakes and free-flowing rivers. Cleaner waters, colder temperatures, and less turbid conditions characterize the smallmouth's domain.

Although largemouth and smallmouth bass coexist in many regions and in many individual bodies of water, and although their physiological makeup is essentially the same, they differ in habitat, spawning, and feeding requirements. To be successful, the bass angler must understand both their similarities and their differences. Their behavior is governed by their temperature requirements and desire for the protection and security afforded by cover. Their basic needs are met in a locale that offers cover, comfortable water conditions, and adequate feeding opportunity.

Water Temperature

Bass, like all fish, are cold-blooded—their body temperature corresponds to the temperature of the water around them. Largemouth bass are most active when the water temperature is 60 to 78 degrees Fahrenheit (F). Sixty-five to 72 degrees F is their optimum temperature, but they function well above and below this. Smallmouths like it a little colder, with 55 to 72 being their active range and 62 to 68 degrees F their optimum.

These temperatures are merely general guidelines. Smallmouths may feed actively when the water temperature is in the mid-40s, and largemouths may feed in shallow lakes where the water temperature is a scorching 92 degrees F. Both species can tolerate extremely cold temperatures, including those of well-frozen northern lakes and ponds. Largemouths survive in temperatures above 90 degrees F; but smallmouths are not well suited to waters over 80 degrees F, though they briefly inhabit such water on occasion.

Bass are opportunists. Within reason they adapt to the circumstances in any given body of water. Where they have the choice, they generally seek the water temperature most comfortable for them, provided they can find forage there. However, they often subsist in locales where the water temperature is above or below their preferred range. This may be mandated by environmental conditions, as in extreme southern lakes and ponds where the summer water temperatures are high, or it may be that this water provides the only available cover for feeding. Whatever the reason, bass can acclimate to regional conditions, and their adaptability adds to the difficulty of understanding them and contributes to the challenge of finding and catching them.

Every body of water goes through a cyclical transformation in the course of a season. In early spring the surface layers and shallows warm up first. As the surface water surpasses 50 degrees F, bass become a little active. When the shallows are warm enough, the bass spawn. Depending on locale, this occurs from mid-spring to early summer. Eventually the upper layers warm past the preferred temperature range, and the fish begin to go deeper, where water temperatures are lower. In the fall the upper layers and the shallows cool off. Bass react to these changes in accordance with the type of water they live in, the amount and location of food, and the availability of cover.

Water Types

Bass can be found in creeks, ditches, sloughs, canals, and many little potholes that have the right cover and forage, but they live principally in reservoirs, lakes, ponds, rivers, and streams.

Reservoirs, which are man-made bodies of water, have been created for water-supply, hydroelectric, and/or flood-control purposes. They usually have some features that many natural lakes do not, such as large coves, lengthy feeder creeks and tributaries, submerged timber and structural objects, and submerged river and creek beds. They are also subject to

Bass of all sizes are found in small bodies of water, which provide some of the most concentrated habitat and best fishing.

extreme fluctuations in water level and changes in the size of bass populations, and in some cases may be affected by current, either from tributaries or from water usage connected with water-supply and hydroelectric demands. There are lowland reservoirs, which are basically shallow and broad, and highland reservoirs, which are essentially deep, long, and relatively narrow. Some reservoirs are fairly uniform throughout, with the deepest water by the dam and the shallowest at the head of the lake by the main tributary. Other reservoirs feature a wide variety of bass habitats.

Natural lakes tend to have fewer good bass habitats in the open-water, midlake sections than do man-made bodies of water. They usually have more consistent bass populations, yet are prone to rapid aging. Found in all sizes, natural lakes feature many of the same characteristics as reservoirs and ponds.

Ponds, whether natural or man-made, frequently possess an abundance of bass cover and are some of the best and most reliable bass-fishing environments. I suspect there is more good bass habitat per acre in most ponds than in the average lake or reservoir, and that this is a prime contributor to anglers' success on these waters.

Rivers and streams are an altogether different type of home, and they vary considerably in size and type. Current is always the foremost factor here, but bass seek the protection of some type of cover in all flowages, just as elsewhere.

In any body of water bass make their homes in a variety of places, depending on water conditions at a given time of year and a number of other factors. But there is some, basic survival-related reason in their choice of residence, whether it be temporary or seasonal.

Cover

Both largemouth and smallmouth bass seek cover, usually toward bottom. Most of their preferred food is found in or near cover of some form, and cover provides protection from predation and sunlight, as well as an ambush point.

So this is a major factor in their specific habitat preferences.

Smallmouth bass have a much narrower habitat preference than do largemouth bass. In their northernmost range, where water temperatures are unlikely to exceed the low 70s throughout the summer, smallmouths may be found in shallow to mid-depth environs throughout the fishing season. But where water temperatures in shallow and near-shore areas exceed the low 70s for a long time, bass move deeper. Smallmouths are regularly found in lakes with at least modest depth, generally 15 to 25 feet or more. Usually, shallow lakes support these fish only if they are spring-fed lakes or if they're located in northern environments where cool summer evenings temper the effect of daily warmth.

Smallmouths typically inhabit rocky terrain. Their native range is typified by somewhat infertile, natural, rocky-shored northern lakes. Their expanded range now includes southern impoundments with shoreline and deep-water rock structure. Smallmouths don't inhabit lily-pad beds or grass fields, though they may be caught along the edges of such vegetation. They aren't found around stumps and timber with sandy bottoms, though they may use such objects as cover in rockier locales.

Smallmouths are located around rocky points, craggy cliff-like shores, rocky islands and reefs, and riprap shores. They prefer golf ball- to brick-size rocks if they have a choice, but larger rocks, including boulders, are also suitable. In the spring, prior to spawning, smallmouths in lakes that are completely rock-laden prefer to be near large rocks, and you may be able to work a shoreline quickly by keying on every big boulder in shallow water.

Perhaps the primary reason for the smallmouth's fondness for rocks is that they harbor crayfish. Certainly smallmouths eat whatever is most abundant in their environment, and they'll readily consume small fish when they are plentiful or when the proper opportunity presents itself. But crayfish are their staple.

Largemouth bass are found in all types of cover. We can roughly separate them into visible (that which can be seen in relatively shallow water) and nonvisible (existing entirely below the surface and usually in moderately deep or very deep water). Visible cover includes logs, stumps, lily pads, brush, weed and grass beds, bushes, docks, fence rows, standing timber, bridge pilings, rocky shores, boulders, and points. Submerged, nonvisible cover includes weed-line edges, stone walls, timber and stumps, creekbeds, house foundations, road-beds, points, ledgelike drop-offs, humps, shoals, and islands.

In some lakes bass may prefer one type of cover and in another, nearby lake, a different type. But they may be located in any of the types of cover mentioned, in any region where they are found. Good habitat consistently produces catches of bass. Large bass often inhabit the most desirable locations, but other bass move in not long after the former resident has been removed by an angler.

Water Conditions

Bass can, and do, thrive in water of marginal purity and quality. Largemouths are most toler-ant in this regard. Smallmouths are more apt to thrive in clear, fair-to-good-quality environs. In waters that have become stagnant through eutrophication, the lowered oxygen levels at the deeper, cooler sections may harm these fish, and such bodies of water may eventually become unsuitable for them.

Where chemical contamination is severe, chemical pollutants are found at various levels in the bass. Although this may have an adverse biological effect on the fish, such as reducing the viability of spawn, it does not seem to adversely affect their behavior.

The turbidity of bass water varies markedly from one lake to another across the country and even varies in a particular lake throughout the fishing season. Many of the larger lakes and reservoirs in northern areas are reasonably clear. Light penetrates deep there, and bass are either well secured in what thick cover might exist or are more likely deep enough to avoid

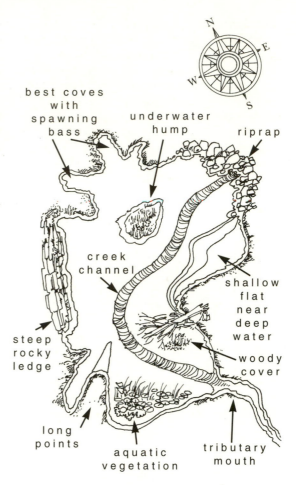

Bass favor locations that offer shade, ambush opportu-nities, and protection; and a typical bass lake provides many such locations. In the early part of the year, bass are found shallow and in areas that warm up early. Prime spawning sites are often coves or shorelines along the north shore, where sunlight and southerly winds help warm the water.

the discomfort of light. In such waters you can see a brightly colored lure 6 or more feet below the surface. Here, bass tend to be spooky, and a refined fishing presentation, utilizing small-to moderate-size lures and light line, is benefi-cial. Blue-green waters allow visibility for 3 to 6 feet below the surface—considered very clear by many southern anglers, who never see the ultraclear waters of mountain lakes.

Many bass waters are off-colored, allowing only limited visibility. Farmland runoff, sediment from tributaries, and bank erosion cause the muddy, milky, slate gray, and tea-colored water common in many reservoirs after heavy rains. You may not be able to see a light-colored lure more than a few inches below the surface. In some large lakes only the upper ends are so affected, while the lower ends remain relatively unchanged, or at least unaffected for several days. In still other bass waters, particularly in Florida, the high tannic-acid content gives the lake a blackish brown tint. In all these highly turbid waters, where visibility is limited, bass are likely to be relatively shallow and holding tight to cover, especially in the early part of the season and when water temperatures are not excessively high.

Turbidity is the only water condition some anglers ever see, and turbid water can be good for bass fishing. It does not require a stealthy approach or light line as clearer waters do. And certain types of lures, such as big spinnerbaits, crankbaits with good vibration qualities, and noisy surface baits, are well suited to angling under these conditions.

Because bass can adapt to such a wide variety of conditions, the odds are good that the next lake or pond you pass will hold some type of suitable bass habitat—another home for the most sought after gamefish in America.

2 BASS

This chunky largemouth has obviously been eating well. Where there is plenty of forage, bass can be almost gluttonous, and their aggressive feeding behavior is what makes them susceptible to lures like the crankbait shown here (see page 17). This bass, incidentally, is light in color because of the light coloration of the water and its habitat (deep structure as opposed to thick grass or timber).

BIOLOGY

Facts and Figures

The angler who understands something of the biology of his quarry and appreciates its implications for his fishing success, increases both his enjoyment and his productivity on the water.

Growth

One of the most fascinating aspects of bass biology is growth rate. Few anglers know the age of a given bass or comprehend how long it has taken for a particular fish to reach its current size. Nor do they realize that growth rates differ between largemouths and smallmouths, as well as between bass of different geographical regions and sometimes between bass in different lakes in the same region.

The growth of any bass is dependent on water temperatures, length of growing season, food supply, and the extent of competition in its particular body of water. As a function of climate, the growing season for bass ranges from year-round in the southernmost areas to barely four months in the northernmost locations. When water temperatures are low, the metabolic rate of a bass is low, and the fish is dormant. When temperatures are high, the fish's metabolic rate is high, but the fish doesn't necessarily get optimum benefit

from its food consumption. Bass, in fact, are usually sluggish at extremely high temperatures. When water temperatures are moderate, bass feed and grow. Obviously, the longer the water temperature is in the moderate range, the more growth there will be. This is why southern bass generally grow larger (but do not necessarily live longer) than northern bass.

Largemouths and smallmouths have a similar growth rate in their first three or four years in areas where both fish coexist. After that, however, the largemouths begin to outdistance their cousins because, overall, smallmouths have a slower growth rate. A typical smallmouth bass reaches sexual maturity when it is 9 to 11 inches long. In northern waters that fish will be between 3 and 4 years old. A 16-inch fish, which might weigh about 3 pounds, would probably be 8 years old in most northern environments. In the most northerly reaches of its range, it would be even older. A 5- or 6-pound smallmouth, recognized as a trophy everywhere, is obviously one of the elders of the bass world.

Largemouths, on the other hand, grow slightly faster. In the North, a sexually mature 10-inch bigmouth would be 3 years old. In some areas of the South, a largemouth can reach 10 inches in its first year. This difference in the size/age ratio is primarily due to the difference in growing season. A 19-inch, 5-pound largemouth in that northern area would be 7 to 8 years old. So, it is difficult to make comparative judgments about trophy-size bass from these geographical regions. The catch of a 7-pound bass in New York, for instance, where that fish is well over 10 years old, is akin to the catch of at least a 10-pounder (possibly a 12-pounder) in a southern area, where such a fish would also be 10 years old.

There is, moreover, a difference in growth rates between the *northern* and *Florida* subspecies of largemouths. A northern largemouth is any fish that is not a Florida bass. Floridas grow exceptionally fast in areas with a temperate year-round climate. The Florida strain, however, does not acclimatize well to the colder water of northern regions; and it may not adapt at all. However, transplanted Florida bass are doing well in some places, notably Texas and Southern California, where many huge bass in the 15- to 20-pound range are caught. Many people think the next world-record largemouth will be taken in California. (The current record—22 pounds, 4 ounces—has stood since 1932; the fish was caught in Montgomery Lake, Georgia.)

Growth rates also differ in geographically close waters. This does not occur frequently, nor is the difference often substantial. Such a situation indicates extraordinary circumstances in the population of one or both groups: perhaps one has too little forage, resulting in an overpopulation of bass and stunted fish, and the other has abundant forage and little competition, resulting in slightly faster-than-usual growth. The latter situation would most likely exist in a newly created lake, where bass grow fast and the population booms for a few years before the lake matures.

Life Span

Fish scales look like a cross section of a tree trunk, with definable annual rings. Within a year, the age of any fish can be determined by analyzing a scale under a microscope and counting the rings. Fifteen years is the longest reported life span for a bass. The older a bass, the harder it is to reliably determine age by checking its scales—the space between rings

Largemouth bass (above) and smallmouth bass (page 9) differ somewhat in their habitat and food preferences, and therefore require different angling tactics. Also, growth rate and life span within each species vary among geographic locales. They share a feisty temperament, however, wherever they are found.

decreases as the bass's growth slows. The large, trophy-class bass of both species are females. Males do not live as long, on average, as females.

Speed and Stamina

Bass have little reason to do any long-distance swimming; instead, their physical abilities allow high speeds for short distances. Fisheries biologists have calculated that bass can burst up to 12 miles per hour. That may not sound fast, but it's considerably faster than you can retrieve a swimming or diving plug. There is no question that an angler cannot retrieve a lure faster than a bass can swim; a bass can run it down. A bass may be alarmed by a speedy retrieval, however, and although capable of capturing the bait, may not be inclined to do so. Moreover, because bass are opportunistic fish, they're not accustomed to working extraordinarily hard for their meals.

Bass seldom make long, sustained runs during the course of a fight. They may make several speedy dashes, dive for cover, or leap in an attempt to throw the hook, but they do not

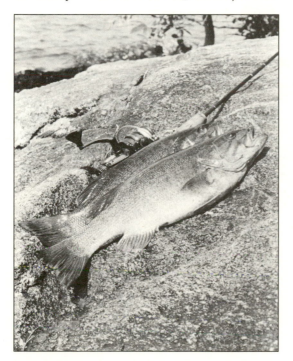

fight for a long time. Their stamina varies with the water temperature and the strength of your tackle.

Bass are generally sluggish fighters in very cold or very warm water, yet I have caught hard-fighting largemouths in 90-degree F water and in 45-degree F water. Stamina and fighting characteristics can vary within a particular lake, so I can make only general assertions about this characteristic. Some bass fight sluggishly even in optimum-temperature water, when you expect them to be aggressive, and others fight well when you expect them to be lethargic. Chunky fish have a tendency to be spirited fighters. Shallow largemouths usually fight well and jump more often than deeper bass. Furthermore, smallmouths are generally known for slightly better fighting abilities than largemouths.

Intelligence

Scientists have not pegged the intelligence level of bass, either objectively or relative to other gamefish. My observations lead me to conclude that bass generally recognize and avoid dangerous situations they have encountered before, and that they are therefore capable of learning. Heavy fishing pressure on many lakes has resulted in poor angling, in part because the easy-to-catch bass were caught off the banks long ago, but also in part because bass have become wise to the ways of anglers. Whether this is intelligence or not, I can't say, but I do think that bass become accustomed to seeing lures and quickly learn to avoid that which appears unnatural or threatening.

Laboratory experiments, incidentally, have proven that bass can differentiate between beneficial and hazardous conditions. This smidgen of evidence proves that bass have some learning ability, though how this relates to their natural environment is uncertain. Yet a bass can be caught repeatedly, even on the same lure it has fallen to in the past.

I once conducted a tagging and fishing study of largemouth bass on a small lake. Out of 470 bass tagged, I personally recaptured 39, and other anglers recaptured 38. Several fish were caught twice more after I tagged them, and one 13-inch largemouth was caught and released four times within a year. The soonest any bass was recaptured was five days. That fish fell for different lures and had migrated across the lake in that time. The longest recapture period during four years was three years, nine months; and that fish had gone from one end of the lake to the other. Most fish were recaptured in the same place or close by. Two-thirds of the fish succumbed to a different lure the second time around, though one that didn't was caught twice in 13 days on the same lure in the same place.

What this all means is that bass are often savvy enough to avoid capture, but not necessarily smart enough to avoid recapture. I noticed on this lake, however, that bass seemed to become conditioned to the lures I'd been offering them, and that, although the population had not apparently decreased, the fish were not as readily fooled as they were in the past. Were the fish just dumb, extra-hungry, or protective, or was the presentation of something that resembled food very good? An answer isn't always apparent. That's why I think presentation and retrieval technique are critical to bass-angling success.

Reproduction

Bass begin spawning about the time the water temperature reaches 60 degrees F. In very small lakes, all bass spawn at the same time. But in others, especially large lakes with arms where temperatures vary, spawning progresses over several weeks.

Bass generally reach maturity and are capable of reproducing at 10 inches. The male selects a nest site in shallow water and fans away debris. The female deposits the eggs with the help of the male, and then abandons the nest, leaving the male as sentry.

Guarding males can be effective against individual intruders but not against a school of fish, such as bluegills and perch. The well-being of the overall bass population demands that balanced fisheries populations exist in a given body of water. If a lake is overrun with panfish, they

will diminish the bass population through exceedingly heavy predation of eggs and fry. To maintain and restore the total fisheries balance, panfish must be brought under control.

The depth of a nest site is usually 1 to 4 feet for largemouths, but may be 6 to 8 feet if light and warmth can penetrate. Smallmouth nests are often at the deeper end of this range. The nests are dish-shaped and fairly large, usually at least 2 feet in diameter. Bass will not nest too close to other bass, and they like to have a large object—such as a stump, log, or rock—nearby, generally at the rear of the nest. Bluegill or sunfish nests, sometimes confused with bass nests, are smaller, close to one another, and sometimes in the open. Moreover, bass spawn before bluegills and sunfish have even constructed their nests.

Nest sites are usually found on shorelines and in coves, where the water is warmer than in other areas and where the nests are fairly well protected from strong winds. The north, northwest, and west banks of creeks, bays, coves, and the like are often favored by spawning bass because they warm up first.

Female bass can carry and deposit thousands of eggs. Prior to spawning, as much as 10 percent of a female's body weight may be egg mass. A large number, but not all, of these eggs will be deposited on the nest. One nest may contain the eggs of more than one bass, as a male will attempt to bring several or many females into the nest site to spawn. Older bass generally have more eggs than younger bass, and their eggs tend to be slightly larger. Unripe eggs are not deposited but form the beginning of the next egg mass. That's what you find in female bass caught in late summer and fall; they will carry those eggs throughout the winter. The presence of eggs does not necessarily mean the females have failed to spawn.

Environmental Influences

Only a fraction of the spawn survives beyond the fry stage, and fewer still become adults. Predation and environmental factors take their toll. If a particular *year-class* (young of that year) of fish has been subjected to particularly damaging ecological conditions, in subsequent years that generation of fish will be noticeably absent from the fisherman's take. A premature heat spell, for instance, warms the water early and prompts bass to take to their nests; if that is followed by a cold spell with lowered water temperature, the fish will be driven off their nests, jeopardizing that generation's survival. If the bass have already spawned, the colder temperature will seriously affect the fry. If the bass have not spawned, only some will later return to the nests.

Keep in mind that just because the water temperature is favorable and the time of the moon is right, there's no guarantee that bass will rush to spawn. A certain biological adaptation is in process, and bass instinctively know when the time is right—when their eggs are ripe and when their urge should be heeded—and they will not spawn until then, regardless of how "right" everything else seems to be.

Another common environmental factor that affects spawning bass is a sudden increase or decrease in the water level, as would occur in some hydroelectric or water-supply impoundments, and in the event of flooding. With receding water, bass will either be forced to leave nests already made, or will find a severely decreased number of suitable spawning habitats. Rising water may put the nest too deep, in colder water, which can also have a negative effect. In any case, the survival rate for that year-class-to-be will be severely impaired. Many bass that have made nests and then left them when the water level changed have simply absorbed their eggs instead of making new nests. This, too, can contribute to a missing age-class of bass.

Angling Influences

Anglers, by removing nesting bass, are also a factor in the survival of the fry. Because the female is on the nest for only a relatively short time to deposit eggs, and because the male builds the nest, fertilizes the eggs, and then stays on the nest site guarding the eggs and fanning silt off them, the male is the one that is usually caught on a nest. Some studies show that when the male bass is

It's pretty easy to catch bass, especially small males, off their shallow and near-shore nests in the spring. It is important to treat these fish carefully and release them.

caught and released, he generally returns to the nest. If the male bass is kept by the angler, however, this results in mortality of the unhatched eggs and near-total mortality of any newly hatched fry.

Spawning time is when big bass are most likely to be caught. Aggressive females loaded with eggs can be enticed into striking a lure before spawning. A male bass guarding the nest can be agitated, and both sexes can be caught (male first, though) during spawning. Bass don't eat at this time, but they will strike objects that come close to or threaten their nest site. A live baitfish, a plastic worm, a spinnerbait, and a few other lures can catch spawning bass, as long as they appear to be a threat to the nest and the eggs and are placed in the midst of the activity.

Bass will be eager to eat after spawning is completed, but don't look for them to be super-aggressive immediately afterward. They go into a withdrawal or recuperating stage and may take up to two weeks to get in sync and start striking terror among their prey.

The issue of fishing during the spawning period is a complex and controversial one. Some anglers have misgivings about fishing during that time. Yet, some fisheries biologists maintain that fishing during the spawning season is seldom detrimental to the bass population. This issue is influenced by such variables as the size of a given bass population, number of predators, growth rate and length of growing season, water temperature, and extent of fishing pressure. Ideally, each body of water should be evaluated on its own merits in this regard. In areas of high fishing pressure and in small bodies of water or where growing seasons are short, the removal of spawning bass can hurt the fish population.

Whether it is sporting, even if legal, to take bass off nests is another issue. I've caught a lot of bass in many states just before and during the spawning period, always with artificial lures and always releasing the fish. These fish have not been unduly damaged by the experience, so I feel confident in saying that where moderation is practiced, fishing for bass during the spawning season can be reasonably harmless. However, I seldom

go hunting for fish on beds or deliberately try to find beds. Because the fish are defending their nests, and strike only to remove an intrusion, they are fairly easy to catch and not particularly challenging. There's not much sport to that.

Sensory Abilities

Vision

Blindness does occur in fish, and they do survive. There have been many recorded instances of blind bass living to a plump old age, apparently by using other highly developed senses to avoid capture and to prey on food fish. Although hearing is the most dominant sense in bass, vision does play a major role. Bass have an extremely wide field of vision. Each eye is capable of 180-degree sight on offset planes, meaning the eyes cross and produce binocular vision in front of the fish. Although they cannot see through the surface, they can see overhead objects mirrored upon it, in what biologists call a *circular window*. Objects directly overhead appear proportionately largest. When an angler wants to get close to a fish in clear, calm water, he'd best keep a low profile.

In moderately clear and very clear water, the appearance of a lure, in addition to its action and vibration, plays an important role. This is where the size, shape, and overall look will influence a bass.

The ability of a bass to perceive color and its reactions to color stimuli are interesting aspects of its vision. Yes, bass can distinguish colors. No, they don't see them exactly the same way humans do.

The retina of a bass's eye contains both rods to receive light and cones to measure color. Because there are more rods than cones, bass see well in dim light and poorly in bright light. Some tests show that red is the most highly visible color to a bass, and that violet appears the same as red. Yellow and orange are also highly visible. Red, yellow, and orange have a greater intensity than blue and green, which have the lowest intensity and the least visibility. Remember, though, that any color's visibility is affected by the surrounding colors and by light penetration. Thus, saying that one color is more visible to bass than another may be an oversimplification. And, of course, a bass's ability to perceive color is significantly affected by the degree of water clarity.

Water acts as a filter, and colors with long wavelengths are more readily absorbed. Both above the water and underwater, fluorescent colors are highly visible (due to the effects of ultraviolet light) at considerably greater distances and depths than their fluorescent-deficient counterparts.

Color is clearly a big part of a lure's appearance. Sometimes, lure color that contrasts with the background is best. In my experience, dark colors are generally more useful in clear water and on bright days; light colors are effective in turbid water and on dark days. This contradicts the maxim "dark days/dark lures, light days/light lures." Again, lure color matters most in shallow and clear water. The deeper you fish and the more turbid the water, the less important the color. Chartreuse is an example of a successful bass color. Most popular with spinnerbaits and used with white, it is effective in moderately dirty blue-green water.

But don't be fooled into thinking that color alone accounts for your success. Obviously there are no red or blue baitfish swimming in our bass waters, and it is generally nature's way to camouflage, so remember that for bass, color is rarely more important than lure action and retrieval technique.

One final area where color and vision might play a role in bass behavior is with fishing line. If red, yellow, orange, and fluorescent colors are highly visible underwater, then bass should be able to perceive such colors and fluorescence in monofilament line. They can, and large-diameter line has a more pronounced underwater appearance. Researchers determined through laboratory tests that bass can distinguish line color and fluorescence, and that the most readily recognized line was fluorescent yellow.

Does this mean we should fish with the best-camouflaged line? Not necessarily. There are too many good anglers successfully using brightly colored or fluorescent lines to discount their effectiveness. And all lines lose visibility as turbidity increases. But to be safe, use clear lines or the least visible colors—green, blue-green, and blue. And remember that the stronger and thicker a line is, the more visible it will be, regardless of color.

Bass, like all fish, are sensitive to light, having no natural eye covering as humans do. But most bass waters are at least slightly turbid, and in these waters vision is of restricted importance to a bass, and appearance is of minimal importance in a lure.

Hearing

In waters of marginal to poor visibility, the most important features of a lure are its action and its vibration patterns, which appeal to a bass's most acute sense—hearing. This is especially true when vision is limited. Hearing is activated through two modes: the inner ear and the lateral line.

The inner ear, a complex structure of interlocking rings, is sensitive to high-frequency vibrations and plays a minimal role in the angler's efforts. The lateral line is a series of sensory pores that extend the length of the fish and enable it to detect and locate prey and predators and to detect vibrations in its environment. Though vibrations travel differently through water than through air, most of the vibrations detected by bass are of low frequency.

Underwater, sounds are pronounced. A jet aircraft takeoff, heard on land at a distance of 230 feet, is only 20 percent louder than the underwater sounds of a 25-horsepower outboard motor heard at 45 feet. And that motor sound is 25 percent greater than that of a loud automobile horn heard at a distance of 3 feet. Pretty noisy, huh?

The sound of a moderate conversation, as held by fishing partners, is not noticeably transmitted through the water and has little impact on bass. But sounds made in a boat, which are transmitted directly through vibrations to the fish, are noisy and alarming. Common sounds

Bass, like this largemouth, have a keen ability to locate prey—and lures—through their lateral line, which extends the length of the fish. This is particularly important when visibility is limited.

detected by bass include those made by outboard and electric motors, and shore noises. The vibrations generated by these sounds are picked up by the lateral line.

Some evidence indicates that bass become conditioned to these sounds, but the conscientious angler should minimize his noises. For instance, shutting down the outboard engine a considerable distance from the area to be fished is worthwhile. Also, sustained low-speed electric-motor operation is preferable to the more alarming start-up/shut-off operation.

At night and in conditions of limited visibility, bass detect lures—particularly surface lures—through the lures' vibrations. And they can detect plastic worms, other fish, and bait where they cannot be seen at all. Signals received through changes in water pressure produced by baitfish are relative to their shape and fin movement, so it is possible for bass to detect not only the presence of a fish without seeing it, but also to detect its approximate size and species.

For lures to be successful bass catchers, they must resemble bait in the way they're perceived by the lateral line of the bass. The action of a constantly moving lure is critically important. A tight, fast wiggle in a crankbait is more desirable than a wide, slow action because the former more closely mimics the body and tail movement of baitfish. This action and vibration, coupled with the introduction of BBs in the cavities of some lures to appeal to a bass's acoustic abilities, are the choice assets of good bass-catching lures. Manufacturers have realized this for some time and have worked to develop products that stimulate bass accordingly.

Interestingly, bass that have been deprived of their lateral-line function and their vision are still able to locate and capture prey in laboratory experiments, albeit with more difficulty than normal. This suggests some reliance on the other senses: smell, taste, and touch.

Smell and Taste

A bass's sense of smell functions through four small openings on the snout; water is drawn through the two forward openings, passed over smell-sensitive tissues, and ejected from the two rear openings. How important their sense of smell is to their feeding and general behavior is open to conjecture. Manufacturers of specialty masking or attracting agents claim that bass have a highly developed sense of smell and that they may choose to feed on some prey as a result of their odors. I am not convinced of this. It is largely speculative whether bass detect human or other unsatisfactory odors on lures. In my opinion odors are subordinate to visual stimuli and to lure action vibration patterns as sensory stimulation for bass.

It should also be noted that bass have taste-buds in their mouth and on the upper lip and tongue, although they are not well developed. It is possible that bass retain a lure longer than they might otherwise, or reject it quickly, because of how it smells or tastes.

Touch

The surface of a bass's body reacts to touch, and surface nerve endings are sensitive to temperature changes as well. Bass have been known to scratch and to chafe against logs as if to relieve an itch or scrape off external parasites. This sense is underdeveloped. It is evident that the two most developed senses of a bass are also the two most utilized in the eating, reproducing, and surviving process.

Feeding Behavior

The most dynamic aspect of black bass is their feeding disposition. Bass have large mouths and large stomachs and an appetite to match. They are not dainty, delicate feeders like stream trout, nor menacing choppers like pickerel and pike. When a bass eats, it goes to town. Under certain conditions it may attempt to stun its prey first, but usually it swallows the prey whole, either chasing and capturing it or simply sucking it in head-first unawares.

Bass, particularly largemouths, have vacuum-like suction. When they get near their prey, in one swift action they open their mouths wide,

This well-fed bass, living in murky, timber-filled water, was caught on a spinnerbait. Although it doesn't look like anything a fish would see in nature, the lure produces an appealing vibration that the fish was able to detect.

flare their gills, and force a tremendous suction that rushes water into their mouth and out their gills while directing the object of consumption right into their gullet. You may have had the experience, when using a surface lure, of watching the water around your plug suddenly open up and the plug disappear into the mouth of a fish; that was the powerful effect of the bass's feeding method.

Forage

Bass eat all kinds of creatures, but they have a marked preference for certain foods. Bass are meat eaters; they cannot digest vegetation. As fry, bass begin to eat zooplankton (small crustaceans), graduating to insects, fingerling fish (including each other), and then larger fish and crayfish as they grow. The primary forage for adult largemouth bass is baitfish and crayfish. Baitfish may take the form of shiners, bluegills (bream), shad, alewives (also called *sawbellies* or *herring*), minnows, and other small creatures, depending upon their abundance and accessibility. Smallmouths show a marked preference for crayfish. Their baitfish choice runs to the fingerling-size shiners and minnows, and, to a lesser extent, alewives and small panfish; in streams, insects may make up a large part of the smallmouth's diet as well. Fingerling-size fish, whether of forage or gamefish species, are probably the number one food item for largemouths.

When shad or alewives are abundant, bass will consume them, sometimes heavily. However, gizzard shad grow large and soon grow too big to be prey for most bass. Gizzard, threadfin shad, and alewives are open-water cruisers, sometimes found deep, but only occasionally wandering by the usual lairs of bass. At times, bass will corner a school of these fish and tear into them, or will take advantage of the passage of these fish into their domain. As a rule, though, bass are not constantly foraging on these species unless their regular fingerling-fish or crayfish quarries are unavailable, or conditions bring them into regular and frequent contact. The latter situation occurs on some impoundments where shad fol-low submerged creek channels and venture near the channels, flats, or points that attract bass.

Frogs, salamanders, water dogs, snakes, mice, baby ducks, worms, and tadpoles are some of the more exotic fare for bass. Much hype has centered on the bass's propensity for eating, including occasional mouthfuls like those. Such creatures, however, are just an incidental part of an opportunist's diet. In frog waters, frogs may be the most regularly consumed of these animals.

To maximize your fishing effectiveness, keep in mind the type of bait predominant in the diet of the bass you intend to catch, but don't feel that it is essential to match the forage explicitly. Lures resembling bait that is not part of a regular diet can fool fish. Plastic worms and spinnerbaits are prime examples. In clear water, close representation of the bait may be warranted. In turbid waters, where visibility is limited, or in tight cover, you will often be more successful with a suggestive lure rather than an imitative lure, capitalizing on the behavior of the bass.

What Motivates a Strike?

Bass strike a lure or attack prey for a variety of reasons. They sometimes exhibit specific feeding patterns, but that can vary from lake to lake and even among fish in the same population. Bass feed during the day and at night. They feed year-round, although less frequently in colder weather (and barely at all in frigid water). As you might expect, the rate of feeding corresponds to water temperature. The metabolic and feeding rates peak at the optimum temperature range. Below that they decrease. At 50 degrees F and below, feeding and general movement drop off significantly. During the winter, bass may feed as infrequently as every two weeks, and do not grow. At optimum water temperatures, however, a bass may digest its food in 14 to 24 hours.

Though I haven't kept records regarding the stomach contents of bass I have kept and cleaned, I estimate that 60 percent of the largemouths had empty stomachs and that 40 percent had one or more foods in their stomachs. For smallmouths, the breakdown is more even, with about half having some form of bait, primarily crayfish, in their stomachs. Indeed, I've caught bass that had just consumed large shad, that had the tail of a good-size catfish sticking out of their gullets, and that had recently filled their crop with other delectables. So it seems that bass strike not only when they are hungry but even when they are not.

All fishermen, and particularly bass anglers, are fascinated by lures. They have a greater interest in learning about a successful lure (its size, shape, or color) than about any other aspect of a catch: the habitat, the other tackle, the time of day, or other conditions.

This preoccupation with lures is sparked by the many questions surround the feeding behavior of bass. For instance, why would a bass strike a lure when it can easily see the lure, its color, and the color of the line extending through the water to the lure? Why does a fish strike something (a spinnerbait, for example) that does not look, smell, or feel like its accustomed prey? Is it because the skill of the angler, imparting life to a lure, is just as important as the lure's appearance and the vibrations it emits? Is it because the bass is in a feeding mood and is indiscriminate about its meal? Could it be that it is upset about the intrusion of what it perceives as a subordinate creature into its domain? Or is it, as has been suggested, that a bass is just plain dumb?

Bass strike a lure for all these reasons and then some. Primarily, however, bass strike a lure or attack prey fish because they are hungry or because they possess an almost killer instinct that is vital to their opportunistic nature. A bass will lie in ambush, waiting for the right kind of meal to come by, whereupon it will pounce on it and retreat to the protection of its ambush point. Reflexive attacks are part of the scheme of underwater life. Remember, there is a lot of competition in every body of water, and the motto is either Eat or Be Eaten, or Eat Now Before Another Fish Beats You to It. Bass are also protective; they take up residence in a particular area and guard their domain against intrusion.

Occasionally bass can be goaded into striking by repeated presentations of a lure or bait. More often than not, the fish will move off and then return in a short while, but sometimes they strike out, as if in anger. And some fish seem to check out a fish or bait as it goes by, perhaps even following it, as if curious. However, I don't believe that bass actually have these emotions. They can be impulsive, domineering, reflexive bullies, if you will, and their apparent displays of anger or curiosity are more likely protective behavior.

There are dumb bass too, but in these days of intense fishing activity, in all but the most remote or private waters, the dumb fish have been caught, leaving their warier progeny behind.

Hunger, reflex, protection, and competitiveness are the main reasons for a bass to feed and to strike lures or bait.

Bass are not high-class jewel thieves. They are thugs, the street toughs of the underwater world. Their nature is to be compulsively aggressive. They are repeat offenders, unreformable. And it is this aspect of their feeding behavior that so endears them to anglers.

RODS

Baitcasting tackle is preferred by many bass fishermen because of its casting accuracy and its ability to handle big fish in sometimes tough circumstances. Long-handle rods are in vogue today, as are narrow-spool reels with sturdy dual-grip handles.

AND REELS

The first step in selecting tackle is to assess your needs, likes, and abilities. What types of bass fishing do you do? What kind and size of lures do you use, and does a particular type of retrieve require a particular style of tackle? What is the nature of the cover you fish? Is it thick and tough on tackle, or is it sparse, offering lots of open-water angling? How much of your time is devoted to bass, and how much to other species with the same tackle? What is your level of skill at fishing various lures and in playing fish? What is your personal attitude about what constitutes "sport" in sportfishing? Are you mainly interested in big bass or in fish of all sizes?

The idea of one outfit for bass fishing is dead today for all but the one-lure, one-technique fisherman. Serious bass angling involves a range of fishing conditions, lure styles and sizes, and fishing methods. Adaptability, versatility, and preparedness are keys to success, and your fishing tackle must meet those demands.

Tackle Weight Classifications

Bass-fishing tackle runs the gamut from ultralight spinning to heavy baitcasting and fly-fishing. Fly-fishing is probably the least practiced method of bass fishing, although it's challenging and a lot of fun. In my opinion, fishermen would be better off to master bass-fishing techniques with other forms of tackle, fully understand the habits of bass, and become knowledgeable about the variety of bass-fishing conditions before taking up the fly rod.

At one end of the baitcasting- and spinning-tackle spectrum there is heavy and medium-heavy equipment. This tackle borders on the unsporting side at times, considering that the majority of bass caught by all anglers weigh less than 2 pounds. In places where brush, timber, and grass are exceedingly thick, and big bass are reasonably numerous, strong equipment has merit, but within reason. Superheavy tackle does help anglers free lures from impenetrable tangles, and it does help them manipulate lunker bass in tight quarters. But when you honestly evaluate the situation, how fair is it to catch bass with a broomstick-type rod and 25- or 30-pound-test line? There is good medium-action equipment available that will handle big bass and bad conditions and still be sporting. With it, you can use medium-strength line, switching to heavy line in the worst conditions.

Light- and medium-duty tackle, packed with 4- to 14-pound-test line, can handle most bass-fishing circumstances (with a few notable exceptions, such as flipping and vegetation-fishing) and still retain an element of fun and good sport. The best advice I can give is to use equipment that does the job under existing circumstances without sacrificing the element of sport. For bass, that usually isn't ultralight gear but it often is light. Assuming you have a balanced fishing outfit, I would classify line strength as follows: ultralight, 2- and 4-pound-test line; light, 6- and 8-pound-test line; medium, 10- and 12-pound-test line; medium-heavy, 14- to 17-pound-test line; heavy, 20 pounds and over.

As I've classified it, ultralight tackle is impractical for standard largemouth fishing. And in many situations light tackle may be impractical as well. Both are acceptable and even desirable for smallmouths, however. For the most part, smallmouth bass reside in open water and, when hooked, do not have to be powered away from obstacles other than the bottom. Bronzebacks aren't caught in grass or lily-pad clusters or around stumps and logs. In many regions they inhabit relatively clear, deep lakes. Because they are an especially wary fish, delicate presentations involving light, thin line, small jigs and other diminutive lures, and corresponding rod-and-reel combinations make light and ultralight tackle a fundamental part of smallmouth fishing success.

A largemouth, by contrast, is a close- quarters, object-oriented scrapper. Largemouths found in or near weeds, stumps, bushes, fallen trees, rocky ledges, boulders, lily pads, and such—most of the areas where they live—have to be forced away from these objects after being hooked, or they may be lost. With light and ultralight tackle it is difficult, if not impossible at times, to properly work weeds and lily pads and to finesse a weedless spoon, plastic worm, surface lure, or even a spinnerbait through them.

Ultralight gear is incapable of properly handling crankbaits except for the small, shallow-running variety. Diving plugs put a hefty bow in a supple rod and cannot adequately be fished at the depths and on the bottom where they are meant to be used. For certain types of surface plugging, ultralight rods hinder the proper lure action, and they lack the muscle to set the hook adequately in plastic-worm fishing.

Setting the hook is the most common of all the troubles that beset light-tackle bass anglers. Many fish that are played momentarily on light or ultralight gear are lost because of inadequate hook-setting. That's not to say it can't be done. It can, but it's difficult. And that's true for most aspects of light-tackle bass fishing. It can be done. It can be fun. But it requires some finesse.

A would-be light-tackle bass angler must be able to handle the equipment well and must be sensible about using it. It is not sport to use willowy rods and hair-thin line, let a fish run until it's exhausted, and then release it to an uncertain fate. And it is not sport to toss a light-lined plug into a batch of timber where a big bass will wrap you up and break off, toting your terminal tackle in its teeth.

Rods

There are many fishing rods available that will provide good service as bass-fishing tackle. But many bass fishermen use rods that actually impede their efforts. They are too stiff or too soft or too heavy to allow adequate, comfortable fishing.

These are the principal artificial baits for bass fishing: spinnerbaits, crankbaits, worms and jigs, floating/diving plugs, and surface lures. With a good rod, one that has guts and sensitivity, you can effectively fish the first three. For the others you need a gutsy rod with a softer tip action to impart effective lure motion.

For crankbait-, worm-, and jig-fishing, the soft-tipped or limber-action rod is a severe handicap. It takes a rod with backbone to set the hook as well as to feel the action of the lure. One of the biggest problems beginning worm fishermen have is that their learning is hampered by the use of a rod that is too light and too limber for the subtleties of the task. The same is true of crankbait-fishing. With a limber, soft-tipped rod you can miss—not even detect—many strikes. If you switch to a stiffer-action rod, you'll notice the difference and begin to detect those soft

In bass fishing, spinning tackle is generally used with finer line than baitcasting tackle, and with light or small lures. The reels on the left and right, spooled with 6- or 8-pound-test nylon monofilament, are typical. The reel on the rod at left sits in an adjustable ring seat; the reel on the right is fixed to a bare cork handle with tightly wound electrical tape. The middle rod, which is medium-action and features a fixed screw-down seat, holds a reel spooled with fused super line and capable of demanding bass fishing.

strikes you were missing before. The rod needn't be as stiff as a baseball bat. A stiff-tipped rod is difficult to cast and not sensitive enough to lure action. A strong, slightly flexible butt section does provide needed strength for hook-setting and for playing a fish, particularly a big one or a good-size bass in thick cover.

These requirements apply equally to spinning and baitcasting rods. There is not much justification for advocating one system over another for bass fishing, as long as you understand the conditions in which you're fishing, realize the demands you'll have to make on your fishing

tackle, and utilize that tackle to its fullest capability. Spinning tackle is more functional on windy days than baitcasting, particularly if it is necessary to use small baits or cast into the wind. Spinning reels are easy to use and not as prone to line fouling or backlashing, though the latest baitcasting reels are also remarkably good in this regard. On the flip side, a fisherman with a good baitcaster can usually be more accurate than a fisherman with a good spinning rod, and baitcasting reel drags are generally of better quality.

Which gear to use is largely a matter of personal preference. I'm partial to baitcasting rods (see photo on page 18) for most bass fishing, particularly for crankbait- and worm-fishing and working in heavy cover. A baitcasting rod offers slightly better casting control and is much better with big lures (a spinnerbait is a big lure by virtue of its overall size) and baits weighing more than ¼ ounce.

My preference runs to 6- or 6½-foot baitcasting rods, which are advantageous for casting (as opposed to short, 5-foot models), though admittedly a little harder to use in close quarters, and I prefer straight, rather than pistol-grip or ergonomic handles. The long rod helps achieve distance, if that is necessary, affords more control for fish-playing, and helps get crankbaits deeper. I'm 6 feet tall, however, and a shorter fisherman might find a slightly shorter rod just as beneficial and more comfortable.

Spinning-tackle fishermen looking for medium-duty equipment will like 5½- to 6 ½-foot rods. My spinning tackle for bass consists of light-action rods equipped with 6- or 8-pound-test line, which I use for fishing floater/divers, some surface lures, small jigs, and light spoons and spinners. My choice for open-water surface-fishing is long spinning rods—6½ to 7 feet. I use the same rods for lake- and stream-trout fishing as well as for other open-water light-tackle angling, so they fill more than one equipment need. For ultralight-lure fishing and smallmouth jig-fishing, I prefer a 5- to 5½-footer.

With spinning tackle you may find that a top-and-bottom sliding-ring reel seat, rather than a fixed reel seat, provides best feel and best rod comfort. The majority of spinning reels available, particularly the medium and heavy-duty models, feature fixed reel seats. The adjustable seats allow you to position the reel foot where the combination of rod and reel feels most comfortable to you. These also enhance the sensitivity of a rod and help transmit feel from the tip portion down through the butt into the seat.

For cold-weather fishing, I suggest wrapping the reel seat with electrical tape. This somewhat insulates the handle and keeps your hand from touching cold metal; some anglers with adjustable seats take the sliding rings off the rod and keep their reel permanently affixed to the rod with tape.

Trying to determine the action of a rod is tough to do by mere feel, but it is even tougher to do when buying, sight unseen, from a catalog. Although it may cost you more to go to a tackle dealer, he may be knowledgeable enough to

assist in the selection of tackle (mass merchandisers and discount-store sporting goods section clerks are woefully deficient in this regard). There, you can not only handle and flex the prospective purchase, you can actually put your own reel on the rod and maybe tie on a few lures or cast a dummy plug. This is the best way to determine if a rod suits your needs and anticipated fishing applications.

An alternative is to find other anglers who are satisfied with the rods they use for various bass-fishing conditions and try their equipment yourself. That way you can judge the performance of a rod you may then wish to buy from a mail-order supplier, tackle dealer, or sporting-goods store.

The best combination of characteristics in any good bass-fishing rod is strength, sensitivity, and lightness. If you'll be doing a lot of fishing for many hours at a time, the weight factor will become significant. Reels today have been

Almost any tackle can catch the average bass in open water, but sometimes fishermen find themselves in such heavy bass cover as this, and if your skills and your tackle aren't up to snuff, you'll land precious few fish.

downsized and streamlined; they have minimal line capacity and essentially fit in the palm of your hand. New materials and manufacturing processes have made rods lighter yet stronger, too.

The best graphite rods are strong, sensitive, and light. They are also fragile, in the sense that they will not stand up to continued abuse. Knocking them against the boat, dropping other rods and reels on them, and even minor mishandling can do more harm to them than to fiberglass rods. I've broken a lot of graphite and boron rods over the years, but not one has been broken in playing a fish. Some have broken during casting, some during lure retrieval, and some during freeing a snagged lure—probably as result of a crack in the sidewall of the rod. This means you can confidently apply maximum pressure to a fish with a graphite rod, but you can't repeatedly bang it against the gunwale of your boat or jab it into a corner.

Deciding which grade of graphite rod to buy is difficult for the budget-conscious angler and for the beginner unsure of his needs. The decision is further complicated by the fact that many rods are composites of graphite and fiberglass (or other materials). Rods that are all or mostly graphite are lighter than composites or those that are mostly fiberglass, although in some cases the difference is so slight, it's barely noticeable. Though lighter than fiberglass, graphite rods tend to be stiffer. And they are more expensive. For sensitivity in detecting a strike or feeling the movement of your lure, graphite rods are a definite asset in worm- and jig-fishing; they are of marginal value in surface-fishing and of some value in crankbait- and spinnerbait-fishing. In all cases, they are beneficial for hook-setting.

I use graphite rods for all types of bass fishing, and they excel for me in all areas. I especially like the more advanced grades of graphite available now, but I did just as well with earlier models. Experienced anglers and those who do a lot of fishing will appreciate the lightness, strength, and sensitivity of this equipment. A beginning angler should consider starting with a top-quality fiberglass rod, however, or a graphite-fiberglass composite. He can learn with it, hone his angling abilities, and work up to the next level as he becomes more familiar with his needs and skills and can appreciate the benefits of a graphite rod. Just as the best camera won't make you a good photographer, the best tackle won't make you a successful angler. It's how you use it that counts.

Reels

Reels have become significant in bass fishing since the early 70s. The technological innovations and advances of the 80s gave us extremely sophisticated, functional, high-quality bass-fishing reels, particularly baitcasters. And many manufacturers currently offer spinning, spincasting (also called *closed-face spinning*), and baitcasting reels well suited to bass fishing.

In the purest sense, a reel is nothing more than a device to hold your fishing line. In practicality, a reel aids casting, lure retrieval, fish-playing, hook-setting, and more, and should be evaluated from many fronts. The quality of construction and materials is one factor by which to judge a reel, but other important features are weight, line capacity, cast control, drag, retrieve ratio, and freespool.

Light weight is desirable in a reel, particularly if you expect to use it continuously for long hours of fishing. The larger reels of the past usually produced wrist fatigue by the end of the day. But some reels today are made partly or entirely of graphite or of graphite and titanium. These lighter materials greatly reduce the need for wrist strength, so that the reels are easier to use, especially for all-day casting. Petite baitcasting reels, which hold no more than 100 yards of 12-pound line, are popular, and if that line capacity meets your requirements, then small reels are a good choice.

And line capacity is not much of a factor in bass fishing. If you use the reel only for bass fishing, you rarely need more than 100 feet of line, and then only because you've made an extremely long cast to a distant school of feeding fish. The normal casting range in largemouth fishing is 30 to 60 feet. Furthermore, bass don't run away when hooked. They bulldog it, look for cover, and try to throw the hook or break off on an object. But if you'll also be using a baitcasting outfit for fishing that requires greater line capacity (such as striped-bass fishing), go for a wider spool that will hold 200 yards of 12-pound line or approximately 150 yards of 17-pound line. If not, a narrow-spool reel is just right.

With spinning reels, consider the size of line you'll be using. Light- to medium-action spinning and spincast reels are more than adequate for bass angling. Check the manufacturer's chart for line capacity, and note that smaller reels are not meant for use with heavy, large-diameter lines and that big reels shouldn't be used with light, small-diameter lines.

Cast control, an important feature on baitcasting reels, prevents backlashes caused by spool overruns. It is basically a spool-braking device. Most baitcasting reels augment or override their standard cast-control operation with magnetic spool braking. Magnets on the sideplate of the reel are adjustable and allow you to place a precise range of pressure on a reel. Gradients from zero (no magnetism) to 10 (the most) allow you to adjust spool-braking pressure according to the situation and your skills.

Under general fishing conditions, most good casters keep the magnetic cast-control knob set at a low level. You might increase spool-braking tension when you're casting light lures or casting into the wind. You can decrease it when you're casting heavy lures and aiming for long distances.

In theory you can cast without applying thumb pressure to a revolving spool and not have a backlash. That's why these modern reels are said to be backlash-free. However, it is possible to have spool overruns with these reels, so the smart angler will use an educated thumb while he casts with the magnetic spool-braking device at the preferred setting. Using these reels, a good caster can go all day without a significant backlash.

Magnetic spool-braking reels are excellent for fishermen who are new to baitcasting. A beginning baitcaster can set the magnetic control high (say 7 or 8) and make short- to medium-length casts until he's reasonably com-

Magnetic spool braking, shown on the top reel, is one feature of modern baitcasting reels that has improved casting. Single-handed operation through thumb releases, shown on the lower reels, is another benefit.

fortable with the equipment. In doing so, he will avoid the problem that his predecessors faced: untangling horrendous spool-overrun bird's nests, the inevitable result of learning to thumb conventional baitcasting reels. As he develops confidence, he can relax the magnetic tension until he's casting at all distances with accuracy and without backlashes, or remove all magnetic tension and simply use his thumb.

For years, fishing with baitcasting reels was such a chore that few people wanted anything to do with them. And when spinning reels, with their ease of castability, became available after World War II, baitcasting tackle took a back seat as functional angling gear. Today, the situation is markedly changed. Not only is baitcasting tackle functional, it is probably more functional for many largemouth-bass fishing situations than other types of gear and is unquestionably preferred by avid bass anglers. This shift has occurred as such functions as levelwind, cast control, and drag systems evolved from technological manufacturing advances.

In my thinking, a smooth drag system is essential for any high-quality reel, whether you expect to use that feature or not. Light-line and light-tackle users, particularly spinning-rod fishermen, call upon their drag more often than other bass anglers, due to the nature of the fish and the equipment; but in any case, if the drag is inadequate, it overshadows the other features of the reel. How to use and set your drag is discussed later.

Fast retrieve ratios are another aspect of modern reels, and they have mixed value for bass anglers. They can be beneficial when you need to reel in a lure quickly to make another cast, such as in reaching a moving school of bass busting shad on the surface. High-speed retrieves really shine when you're playing fish, especially big bass and fish in heavy cover; or when fish must be hauled out of or steered around bad objects; or when a bass rushes the boat, as it often will after it strikes your lure. To set the hook or control the fish, you need to catch up with it quickly.

Occasionally a fast retrieval ratio can aid in working a lure—speeding up a crankbait or spinnerbait, or recovering slack line. It does require less handle-cranking effort. However, a fast-retrieve reel can lull anglers into retrieving their lures faster than the fish like. Many an angler who uses a high-speed-retrieve reel has found that his mind wandered while he was fishing crankbaits for bass in cold water, and he was inadvertently bringing his bait through the water faster than the somewhat lethargic fish were willing to take it. Beware of high-speed retrieves when fishing hard-pulling, deep-diving crankbaits. The gears on some reels aren't strong enough to be subjected to repeated hard-and-fast cranking.

Most baitcasting reels sport a right-handed retrieve, so that if you cast right-handed you must switch the rod from your dominant hand to your left hand after casting, holding the rod and reel (and retrieving lures and playing fish) with your left hand while reeling with your right. This is contrary to how right-handed anglers use

spinning and spincasting tackle and requires some adjustment.

There are some good-quality left-hand-crank baitcasting reels, however. I've recommended them to many anglers who are just beginning to use baitcasting tackle but are already familiar with spinning gear. And most of them, with no preconceived notions about or bad habits with such tackle, adapt to it well. The standard right-retrieve baitcasters, of course, are fine for left-handed fishermen. Right-handed anglers who have been using a right-crank baitcaster for years are so used to the traditional way that they will find it difficult to make the switch. Also, to make the switch you need to replace all your current right-retrieve-model baitcasters with left-retrieve models, as having both in your boat causes confusion when you change from one type of reel to another.

Incidentally, baitcasting reels today are equipped with dual-grip handles, referred to as "power" handles by some. These grips are easier to latch onto and you don't have to see them to locate them readily. Not everyone appreciates them, however; fishermen with large hands and big fingers find it awkward to use dual-grip handles, which seem to have been designed for small hands. But they can be replaced with better, larger handles.

For more than a decade now, baitcasting reels have sported a so-called "flipping" feature; when the flipping button is depressed, line can be stripped off the reel, which is good for making a short flip or pitch, without putting the reel into freespool. Direct drive is a dubious feature for anglers who don't want to use their drag at all but who wind in reverse, or backpedal, the handle. If you do this while fighting a good fish, however, and you lose your grip on the handle (maybe it's wet), you'll have a wildly careening spool, an inevitable overrun, and bruised knuckles. A high-quality drag, set properly, should suffice for most anglers.

One-handed casting is now commonplace on all better reels and many lesser-priced ones as well. Most freespool releases are a recessed push-button on the sideplate; they enable you to

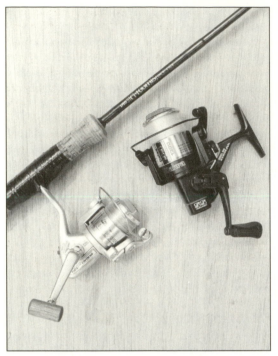

Wider spools for longer casting, convertible left or right retrieves, skirted spools, and lighter weight are key features of modern spinning reels.

improved dramatically, too. The popularity of light monofilament line made it necessary for reels to be forgiving, to yield line when strong fish applied extreme pressure. Multiple-disc, spring-loaded systems with a variety of settings evolved to fill that need. Rear, or stern- mounted, drag-adjustment knobs have also become popular, though many fishermen still prefer the older, top-mounted adjustment.

Spinning reels have gotten lighter, too. Some models now feature complete or partial graphite-composite construction. Previously, they were made from zinc alloys or die-cast aluminum. In addition to convenience, such reels provide greater resistance to corrosion. Ultra-light spinning is growing in popularity, and many ultralight spinning reels are useful for some types of bass fishing.

You'll notice that I haven't discussed spincasting tackle here, not because it isn't functional in its own right, but because I don't think it can compare with baitcasting or spinning tackle in many critical areas of bass fishing, including drag performance, casting accuracy, fish-fighting, and control.

Fly Tackle

Fly tackle is another matter. Fly-casting—casting a nearly weightless object with a weighted line—is the opposite of baitcasting or spinning. In most fly-fishing, small flies are used; in bass fishing, larger flies are necessary. In fact, often they are not flies at all, but cork-bodied poppers, big deer-hair bugs, streamers, and other large-bodied concoctions. To cast them and to muscle bass away from cover takes a long rod (9 feet is good) capable of handling an 8- or 9-weight fly line. The reel is basically just for fly-line storage, as there's seldom a call for backing. In stream-fishing for smallmouths, anglers can use lighter gear. Five- to 7-weight outfits are appropriate, and smaller flies are used. Fly-fishing, though fun, constitutes just a small portion of the effort that is expended by anglers in pursuit of bass. For a detailed review of this subject, I refer you

release the spool for casting by using the thumb on the hand that holds the reel. With older reels you had to reach over with your noncasting hand and depress the spool-release button before casting. The one-handed operation does simplify casting and saves a fraction of a second.

One-handed casting with spinning reels is accomplished simply by touching the bail or with a lever that enables you to lift up the line and open the bail with one finger. Previously, you had to open the bail with the hand that wasn't holding the rod.

Of the other significant changes in spinning reels in recent years, spool design is the most obvious. Spinning-reel spools used to fit inside the bail housing; that often led to line tangling around the shaft under the spool. Today skirted spools shroud the shaft and successfully curb tangling.

The drag systems on spinning reels have

to A. D. Livingston's *Bass on the Fly* (Ragged Mountain Press, 1994).

When you do select a rod or reel for bass fishing, be mindful of the equipment you expect to use with it. Most anglers apply the concept of balanced tackle when matching rod to reel. This basically means that the two products should complement each other. You can't use a medium-duty spinning reel with an ultra-light-action rod, or a miniature reel with a heavy-duty rod. The combined outfit should be neither too heavy in the tip section nor too heavy in the handle.

Most of the rods and reels appropriate for general bass fishing are top of the line. They cost more than the bottom- and midseries equipment, but they're made of better material and with better components. Price is not always an indicator of quality, so you should shop wisely and be aware that the bass-tackle market is competitive and trendy and a that a higher premium is sought for tackle that is, for whatever reason, currently in vogue.

If you buy good equipment and take care of it, it should last. Many anglers fish successfully with good rods and reels acquired years ago. Of course, you will wear out tackle if you fish hard every day, but few anglers do. Quality tackle is no substitute for angling savvy, but it will help your fishing by brightening your outlook and bolstering your confidence.

4

LINE

Bass anglers really test their line, especially its breaking strength,
when they fight a strong fish close to the boat.

Line is to fishing tackle as sewing thread is to a dress shirt. Remove all the sewing thread from a dress shirt and what happens? The collar detaches. The cuffs fall off. The sleeves come off. The buttons drop off. What remains is the makings of a shirt without the vital ingredient. What's lost is the essential connection that brings it all together and allows it to function as a shirt.

Now think about your fishing tackle. Remove the line and what happens? There is nothing to run through the guides. The spool of the reel is empty. The hook or lure is unattached. You have the makings of a fishing outfit without the vital connection that makes it function.

When most people look at a shirt, do they see the sewing thread? No. They see fabric, color, design, and buttons. When most fishermen contemplate fishing tackle, what comes to mind? The first thing is the lure or bait. Then the type of rod and reel. Often overlooked and usually unappreciated is the line. You don't have to be aware of the importance of your thread in order to wear shirts, but you must recognize the role of your fishing line in order to catch fish.

Line not only makes all of your other tackle function, it plays *the* prominent role in the three most important aspects of angling: presenting the lure or bait, hooking the fish, and landing it. In all aspects of fishing technique and tackle use, line is the single most important piece of equipment.

It is essential that anglers understand how to use their line to its utmost capability. The more you know about the fundamentals of line use and performance—for other fish as well as for bass—the better angler you will be.

Most fishermen know little more about line than what they've read in advertisements and on product labels—meager information. Worse yet, they do not exercise sufficient care in the handling and treatment of the one piece of equipment that is the most vital link between them and the fish.

Modern line is so far superior to what was available to fishermen earlier in this century that many fishermen have been lulled into thinking that their line needs no more attention than a simple fishing rod. Then, too, the average bass fisherman seldom catches fish large enough to really test even the poorest line and his own abilities, which only sustains his complacency. This is a mistake. Proper care and use of your line pays dividends over and over again in everyday fishing situations.

Understanding Fishing Line

In today's marketplace we essentially have nylon monofilament, braided super line, and fused super line. There is also fly line, but since this is a minor element of bass fishing, we'll devote this chapter to the three categories that presently garner virtually all of the attention of bass fishermen.

Monofilament means a single strand of line, but it has become synonymous with nylon line. Sales of nylon monofilament line accounted for 94 percent of all line sold in the United States until a few years ago; the remainder was braided Dacron (now virtually obsolete except as backing), wire or lead-core line (used for trolling and almost never by bass anglers), and fly line. Nylon monofilament has become extraordinarily popular with anglers since its premium introductions in the 1950s and with refinements in top-quality spinning and baitcasting tackle. As of this writing it still accounts for about two-thirds of the fishing-line market.

Nylon monofilament line, as the name suggests, is a single-component product. It is formed through an extrusion process (forcing molten plastic through a die). Nylon monofilament lines are polymeric byproducts of crude oil processing. Nylon alloys, a mixture of various types of nylon, are used to form fishing line also. Although various brands of nylon monofilament lines possess the same derivatives, the way they are processed and extruded and the way their molecules are compounded determine the characteristics and properties of a particular line. Additionally, premium-grade lines receive more quality control, more additives, and more attention in the finishing processes than non-premium line. As a result, they cost more.

Braided super lines are a dynamic and relatively new introduction to the fishing market. They did not exist until a few years ago. Called *performance lines* by some, they are braided from gel-spun polyethylene fiber (different grades or generations of Spectra, Dyneema, or Tekmillon) or from aramid fiber (Kevlar). The synthetic fiber itself, which is 10 times stronger than steel, has been used in industrial, aerospace, and military applications and is incredibly strong yet thin. Individual strands of fiber are married through an intricate, time-consuming, and costly braiding process. The result is an ultrathin, superstrong, and very sensitive line.

Fused super line is a completely new high-performance fishing line. As of this writing just three manufacturers have such a product, and in limited strengths. Multiple microfilaments of gel-spun polyethylene fibers are fused (not braided) to produce what appears to be a single-strand line that is also ultrathin, superstrong, and very sensitive, yet highly castable and cheaper than braided super line.

The Properties of Line

The characteristics of any fishing line include breaking strength, stretch, abrasion resistance, memory, knot strength, and uniformity. Color is an additional feature, but it does not affect the basic performance aspects of the line.

Breaking Strength

The most prominent feature of any line is its strength, that is, how many pounds of pressure must be applied before the molecules in the line part and the line is broken. (Perhaps the foremost desired feature is durability, but this is a function of all the properties of line.) All spools of line are labeled to indicate their breaking strength, but this can be misleading; the actual breaking strength of line may vary from that stated on the label, depending on the type of line.

There are two classifications of line: "test" and "class." A line labeled as 12-pound-test is so designated to assure that it breaks *at or above* 12 pounds when *wet*. Most break above their labeled rating, though a few regularly break below it. One frequently run advertisement by a line manufacturer compared its 10-pound-test line with others and claimed theirs was stronger, but the figures showed that their line really had a 17-pound strength. That's deliberate mislabeling, not greater strength.

The primary reason for this discrepancy is the fact—known to few fishermen—that there is a significant difference between how nylon monofilament line breaks when it is dry and when it is wet. Nylon monofilament line absorbs water, and its wet breaking strength is always less than its dry breaking strength. My tests in this regard have shown a range from 9 to 23 percent less, but 15 percent is about average.

It is meaningless to take a piece of nylon monofilament, wrap it around your hand, tug on it, and proclaim it has great strength. This is dry strength, and since your line is wet when you fish, dry strength is irrelevant. For many lines, including some of the supposedly better and so-called "premium" nylon monofilaments, the wet breaking strength is greater than the labeled strength of the line.

Class lines are predominantly used by saltwater big-game tournament fishermen and by any anglers specifically interested in establishing line-class world records (world records are kept for all species based on strength of line used as well as in all-tackle designations). Class lines are guaranteed to break at or under the labeled strength when wet, in order to conform to the world-record specifications of the International Game Fish Association (IGFA), which is the repository for world records in fishing. Class line is more expensive than test line and differs from test line only in wet breaking strength; its other properties should be similar to those of test lines. To illustrate the breaking-strength difference, "class" 12-pound line breaks at slightly less than 12 pounds when wet, and a good-quality "test" 12-pound line will probably break between 13 and 14 pounds when wet. That may not sound like much, but in some situations it's a considerable difference. Anglers who are seeking to establish records or who want to be absolutely sure of the wet breaking strength of their line will find class lines worthwhile, although they only account for a small part of the fishing-line market and an even smaller percentage of the bass-fishing-line market. Unless you buy a "class" or "IGFA-rated" line, you won't know exactly what you've got because the manufacturers aren't explicit enough with production information.

Super lines technically do not absorb water and therefore have the same strength wet as dry. However, tests indicate that their breaking strength varies a good deal from that labeled.

It used to be that the basic strength of a line was directly related to its diameter. The greater the breaking strength, the larger the diameter. However, in recent years manufacturers of nylon monofilament line have found a way to produce lines with the same performance characteristics as conventional mono, but which are ultrathin. The newer super lines are thinner still; a super line with 24-pound breaking strength may have the same diameter as a conventional 10- or 12-pound-strength line.

Right now this is all confusing. Most fly fishermen, basically because of their use of fine leaders and tippets, have some understanding of numerically based line diameter. But it is becoming evident that to compare line in the future, you'll have to know the diameter as well as the actual breaking strength. Some manufacturers are providing diameter information on their nylon monofilaments, but not on braided or fused super lines.

Abrasion Resistance

Abrasion resistance is one of the most difficult qualities of line to measure, because no laboratory test has yet been devised to accurately duplicate the abrasive contact that line is subjected to under fishing conditions. Some lines are more abrasion resistant than others, either due to greater diameter or to the composition of the line. And some brands seem to be considerably more abrasion resistant than others, but those are subjective judgments based on personal experience. Lack of abrasion resistance was braided Dacron's biggest drawback back when it was a commonly used line, and super lines are only somewhat better. Manufacturers claim that the new fused super lines have better abrasion resistance than nylon monofilament, but this remains to be proven on the water. They claim that the high number of filaments used in the manufacturing process allows for some abrasion without sacrificing the integrity of the line. There are some premium nylon monofilaments, incidentally, that have excellent abrasion resistance.

Sometimes a bass fisherman has to cut off nicked line every half hour or so because the terrain he's fishing is so tough on line. The thinner your line, the more damaging abrasion can be. Contact with rocks, trees, stumps, and emergent grasses can wear heavily on your line, so selecting one with satisfactory abrasion resistance is important. No line completely withstands abrasion, however.

Stretch

Most lines stretch. The issue is how much they stretch and how this impacts your fishing. Stretch is both good and bad. It allows for mistakes in fighting a fish, inadequate drag setting, or countering sudden close-to-the-angler surges by strong fish; but it hampers the inattentive angler who forgets to keep slack out of the line when setting the hook or who is inexperienced at detecting strikes, especially at long distances.

The average stretch in wet nylon monofilaments, according to tests I've conducted in the past, is around 30 percent. Wet line has more stretch than dry line. Lines with high stretch (I've seen more than 45 percent) are great for casting, but terrible for hook-setting and playing fish because they have the elasticity of a rubber band. The cushioning effect provided by lines with a controlled-stretch feature has been important to many anglers, and they are accustomed to it.

On the other hand, low stretch should increase your ability to detect strikes, aid hook-setting, provide more control in playing a fish, increase your sensitivity to what a lure or bait is doing, and theoretically help you catch more fish. Those are the most important attributes of super lines, which have virtually no stretch.

A simple way to detect the difference in stretch between wet super line and wet nylon monofilament as it relates to a typical angling situation is to take a 40-foot length of each and attach one end to a firm object and the other to identical fishing rods. Set the hook on each. The lack of stretch and the greater hook-setting ability of the fiber line will be immediately apparent.

A similar test is to apply an equal amount of tension to each line. If you attach a 40-foot length of wet super line to a good scale and pull on it until only 1 pound of pressure is exerted, you'll see it doesn't stretch. Attach a wet 40-foot length of good-quality nylon monofilament, do the same thing, and it will stretch a long way.

You may have seen film of fish sucking in a lure and then spitting it out, without the fisherman's knowing he'd had a strike. This illustrates the direct relationship between stretch and sensitivity. The less stretch, the more sensitivity; the more sensitivity, the better you should detect fish.

My final point on this subject is about *ultimate elongation*—the amount of stretch a line will take before breaking. Good-quality nylon monofilament lines have the ability to return to their normal state after severe pressure and stretching, maintaining their basic strength. Stretch is not a permanent condition under average fishing conditions. However, ultimate elongation varies among lines, and poorer quality lines usually do not recover as well as premium lines. Lines that have seen the severest stress warrant close examination because they might not return to their normal state. If in doubt about the continued serviceability of your line, replace it.

Memory

The molecular structure of nylon is such that nylon monofilament line has a memory. When placed in a certain position (such as on a spool) for an extended period, it remembers and returns to that position. Lines with less memory are said to be limp and are more castable than stiff lines. This property is important in light-line angling. Some lesser-quality nylon fishing lines tend to be stiff, contributing to spooling and twist problems and making casting difficult. Castability is related to limpness (which engineers refer to as *bending modulus*). The most

When bass fishermen try to free their lures, they put a lot of pressure on their line. Premium nylon monofilaments will stretch, but they return to their original state after tension is released. However, there is a point of no return, and lines that have been repeatedly stretched to the max might need replacing. By snapping the line as shown, you may be able to free a snagged lure without having to pull too hard.

castable line would be limp as a noodle.

Castability is affected not only by limpness but also by water absorption (wet lines cast better than dry lines) and line diameter. The greater the diameter and strength of the line, the harder it is to cast. With nylon monofilaments, the stiffer the line, the less stretch it has but the more difficult it is to cast. Thus, there is a dramatic tradeoff between castability and stretch in nylon monofilaments. It's a good idea to wet nylon monofilament line (place the spool in the water) before you start using it on a given day.

Super lines are different in this respect. They have low stretch, good limpness, and high castability, wet or dry. If fishermen can adapt to them and accept their other characteristics, they'll be buying a lot of it for bass fishing.

Knot Strength

Generally speaking, once you tie a knot in a fishing line, it becomes weaker. Furthermore, knots are weaker in wet nylon monofilament than in dry. Manufacturers of nylon monofilament line claim that their technological processes produce molecular formations that result in specific knot-strength abilities for their line. Since the same knots are tied with various levels of expertise by different anglers, this is hard to verify. Nonetheless, if you are tying knots carefully and uniformly, and they're not holding, it could be because the knot strength of the line is deficient.

Conventional knots do not hold well in super lines, and accommodations must be made to achieve optimum strength. We'll discuss that later.

Uniformity

It is reasonable to expect that what you get at one end of a line spool you should get at every point along that spool to the end. With premium lines you generally do. Sometimes, however, the manufacturing processes may alter the diameter of the line in certain spots or in some way alter the characteristics in unidentified areas. You may find a spot that is thicker than the rest of the line. Here, the molecules have not been well oriented, and this part of the line will be weaker than the rest. Conversely, a thin spot will be stronger. With the premium lines on the market today, you should encounter none of this. With bargain-basement specials—those lines selling for $2.99 for a 2,000-yard spool—you get what you pay for: junk.

Line Use

Line Twist

Twisting is probably the greatest problem most fishermen experience with their line. And many anglers incorrectly blame their line. If your line twists and you think it's because the line is no good, take a brand-new consumer spool of that line, lay out some of it, and wait for it to twist. You'll be waiting forever. The point is that you have to do something to make line twist; it doesn't twist by itself. Line twist can occur as a result of too loose a drag, improper spooling, improperly playing a fish, using certain lures without a swivel, fishing in swift current, and using a lure that isn't running properly.

If the problem is a faulty lure, you'll need to adjust the lure so it runs without spinning, or try using a split-ring, snap, or snap swivel (see also Chapter 8, page 119), all of which help to prevent spinning and twisting. Certain lures, such as most spinners used in flowing water, require the use of a snap swivel to prevent twisting.

If your drag is too loose when you're fighting a fish, it will slip while you're reeling in and cause line twist. Similarly, if you crank a fish by forcefully reeling it in with spinning gear,

instead of pumping and retrieving line, you will put a bad twist in the line.

You'll know whether your line is twisted when you retrieve a lure by watching how it dangles from the tip of your rod. If it begins to rotate, the line is twisted. Another way to tell is if coils develop in the line when you give it slack. Often an angler will be retrieving a lure, let it momentarily rest, and not notice that a coil develops near the reel. He continues retrieving, only to pile line up on the reel arbor on top of the loose coil. During a subsequent cast he is likely to get a bird's nest, the severity of which will depend on how twisted his line became.

Twisted line is not difficult to cure if you're in a boat or near running water. Line will untwist itself if you let out a long length of it behind your boat, with nothing attached to the end (no snap, swivel, split shot, hook, lure), and drag it along for a few minutes. The faster your boat travels, the quicker the line unravels. Reel the line back in and you're ready to attach terminal gear. You can achieve the same effect on moderate- to fast-flowing water by letting the unweighted line float downstream and then holding it in the current for several minutes.

Line twist can be impossible to cure if the problem has not been recognized until the line is a mass of twists and curls. When line twist is this serious, cut off the problem section and start anew, being careful to remedy the cause of the twist before fishing again.

Filling Your Reels

Many problems associated with line actually begin at the first step of line use, in putting new line on a reel spool. Knowing how to put on line and how much of it to put on are the keys to minimizing difficulty.

The best performance of your line and reel is achieved when the reel has been spooled properly. This means filling it to within $1/8$ to $3/16$ inch of the edge. This allows you to achieve good casting distance and accuracy, and permits better drag functioning. (A full spool also provides more line for playing a large fish,

Fill your reels properly for the best performance. Baitcasting and spinning reels should be filled to within 1/8 to 3/16 inch of the edge. Line twist will develop if spinning reels, in particular, are not filled correctly.

though this is not relevant to bass fishing.)

If you overfill a spinning reel, line will fall off loosely when it's given slack, causing snafus to develop; several loops of line will pile up and jam in the spool or in a rod guide. Also, line can become pinched in the side flanges of the spool of an overfilled baitcasting reel.

A properly filled reel allows you to achieve good distance in your casts, particularly with light lures. An underfilled reel hampers your casting range, since more coils of line (causing more friction) must come off the spool. Eventually, after you've cut through some frayed line, tied some knots, and experienced some breakoffs, your line will become too low on the reel. In addition to hampering casting in some fishing situations, this creates the danger that a big hooked fish will take all the remaining line off the reel (depending on the capacity of the reel and which species of fish you encounter besides bass; as mentioned in the previous chapter, bass are not likely to run all the line off your reel unless you have hardly any on to begin with). Additionally, drag pressure increases as line on the reel arbor decreases, creating a sometimes difficult situation for the angler when fighting a strong, surging fish.

You can put twist in the line by improperly spooling it, which happens often to unknowing or inexperienced anglers. Because nylon monofilament, unlike super lines, has a memory, and returns to its remembered state after use, it develops a set in a position it has been in for a long time, such as wound on its plastic packaging spool.

Line on a consumer spool not only has taken a set, it was already slightly coiled as part of the manufacturer's spooling process. The manufacturer has huge bulk spools of line in its plant from which it fills the smaller retail spools. Line that comes off the outside of a full bulk spool is less coiled than that which comes off the core.

You and a friend could conceivably possess the same brand of line in the same strength, and one would be noticeably more coiled than the other. The reason is probably that they came from different locations on the bulk spool, or that they were produced at different times (in which one batch of line was more coiled than the other). In any event, the longer that line stays on the retail spool, the more its coils conform to the diameter of the spool.

Many anglers have told me that they were dissatisfied with a certain brand of nylon monofilament line because it was "too coily" or twisted "too easily." That complaint has been made about all the major brands, but you'll find that coiling is less pronounced in the top-grade lines.

Line on baitcasting reels, which are aptly called levelwind reels, is fairly free of the twisting problems caused by spooling because the line is wound straight onto the reel arbor in a direct, level, overlapping manner. The spooling suggestions that follow can also be applied to baitcasting reels, with respect to uniform winding, proper tension, and so forth.

Open-faced spinning reels and spincasting (closed-face) reels pose many problems in line spooling for beginning fishermen because these systems actually put a slight twist in the line as it rotates off the bail arm and onto the arbor. If the line is of poor quality or if it already has a fair degree of manufacturer-instilled coiling and the angler improperly spools it onto his spinning reel, the result can be twisting, curling, coiling line—endless trouble unless it is run out behind the boat and rewound.

The first secret to successful spooling is watching how the line comes off both sides of the manufacturer's spool. Take line off the side with the least apparent coiling. Then apply moderate pressure on the line before it reaches the reel.

Here's a good technique for proper spooling: Place the supply spool on the floor or any flat surface. The line should balloon or spiral off the spool as you pull it up. After you've threaded line through your rod guides and attached it to your reel, hold the rod tip 3 to 4 feet above the supply spool. Make 15 to 20 turns on the reel handle and stop. Now check for line twist by reducing tension on the line.

Lower the rod tip to 1 foot from the supply spool and check to see if the slack line twists or coils. If it does, just turn the supply spool upside down. This will eliminate most of the twist as you wind the rest of the line onto the reel. If the other side has more of a natural coil or twist, go back to the first side and take off line while it is face up. The trick here is to take line from the side with the least amount of coiling. In effect, this method counterspools the line on your spinning reel and counteracts its curling tendencies.

I do not recommend using a pencil or other object inside a spool to let the spool run freely while you put line on your reel. This seems to compound the spooling problem.

Keeping moderate tension on the line with one hand as you reel with the other is also impor-tant. Do this by holding the line between your thumb and forefinger with your free hand. Lack of spooling tension causes a loosely wound reel and loops of line on the reel spool. Excessive tension, however, can bind up the line and allow more line to be spooled than necessary, as you will later discover when the line bunches up after being used and spooled naturally by reeling.

Changing Line

In a sense, new fishing line is like a new auto-mobile. When you drive it off the dealer's lot, it becomes a used car. When you put new line on your reel and fish with it, it's used. A new auto-mobile that is driven frequently, but stays in the garage and is taken on only the best roads, is likely to stay in top condition longer than one that is used daily, constantly exposed to the ele-ments, and driven on bad roads. Line is much the same. The age of the line is much less impor-tant than how much and under what conditions it has been used.

The primary reasons for changing line are that it is too low on the spool, it's old, or it has had such extensive, stressful use that a caution-ary replacement seems warranted.

When line becomes too low, it hampers cast-ing and reduces effective drag settings, so the reel needs to be refilled. Many reels with large line capacities have half their capacity left, even when there's not enough line left on them for good casting. If the line has not been on the reel too long, it is still worth using. You should con-sider taking it off by tying the end to a tree or post in an open area (or on the water) and back-ing away so the line does not bunch up or become tangled. Remove it from the reel, and put on a suitable amount of backing of stronger line (this varies with the size of the spool, capac-ity of the reel, and the length of line being reused). Then take the end of the monofilament that you tied to the post and tie it to the backing. When your spool is full, you have the fresh, unused back section of old line for fishing.

If you have a large-capacity reel, but will only need a third or half of it for bass fishing and will not need it for other kinds of fishing, attach a backing to the spool before putting on new line.

If you wish to replace the full capacity of line on a reel, simply strip it all off and discard it (in the garbage) or put it in a recycling bin at a tackle shop. You can do this fairly quickly by giving it the old clothesline palm-to-elbow wrap. Another method is to use an electric drill. Affix an old consumer spool or some other large-capacity object in the drill bit head, set the reel on freespool or reduce the drag setting to the least amount of tension (this is also a way to break in a drag), and run the drill until the line is off. A third method is to use a battery-operated line stripper.

Old nylon monofilament line needs to be replaced completely, as does line that has been used often in punishing fishing conditions. Some anglers have had nylon monofilament line on their reels for years—so long that they have no idea how old the line may be. They'll be sorry when a big fish comes along or when there is a lot of action, and the line won't hold up.

How long can you use line before replacing it? The answer depends on the original quality of the line, the strength of the line, how much fishing you do, the size and aggressiveness of the bass you regularly catch, and how much care or abuse your tackle receives. An angler who fishes only a few times a year would be well advised to change his line at least once a year, preferably before the start of each season. A slightly more frequent angler should change it at least twice a year. And anglers who fish regularly should change their line every few weeks. I use a lot of reels in a wide range of fishing conditions and for many species of fish in the course of a season. Some of my reels may go all year without being changed (but will be changed before the next season), while others—the most heavily used—may be changed half a dozen times or more. Super line may need to be changed much less frequently than conventional line because it is more resistant to light and extremely durable.

Fishing circumstances can also serve as a guide. Fishing in unobstructed water puts fewer demands on a line than does fishing around

rocks, logs, timber, docks, and the like. In a week of fishing in heavy cover, I have changed line (actually stripped off the top layer and replaced it with fresh line) two or three times. Light line, because of its thin diameter, requires more frequent changing than heavy line.

Inspecting Your Line

You can't tell much about the thickness of line by feeling it, since variations are generally in thousandths of an inch. You could use a micrometer to measure the diameter, but few anglers have reason to own or regularly use this costly piece of equipment.

You can detect abrasion by feel, and this is quite important. A nick, cut, or fray in nylon line can weaken it, sometimes by 50 percent or more. A 10-pound-test line, which ordinarily wouldn't break under less than 10 pounds of pressure, may break under as few as 5 pounds if it is abraded. Super lines are said to be weakened less by cuts and frays, but it's not worth taking a chance. The only way to assure 100 percent strength is to cut off abraded sections.

Line breakage due to undetected abrasion leads many an angler to question the quality of his line, when in fact he, himself, is to blame for not checking the line. It's a good idea to periodically run your fingers over the first few feet (more if necessary) of line to detect nicks or frayed areas. When you do find such spots, cut off the damaged section. If, for some reason, you find it difficult to detect abrasion manually, try running the line through your lips.

Abrasion usually results from underwater contact with objects and fish, though it can occur when a lure hangs up and a portion of your line contacts tree limbs or stumps. Occasionally, however, imperfections in your rod or reel cause abrasion. A nick or burr on a rod guide, reel pickup arm or levelwind guide, or spool edge can be the culprit. If line abrasion occurs regularly throughout the line or when you're fishing in unobstructed water, you should check the tackle and correct the problem.

Another sign of old line, and possibly

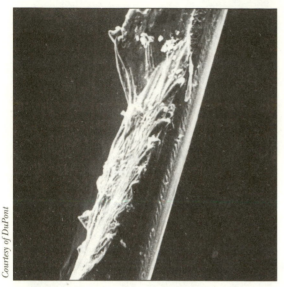

Courtesy of DuPont

Inspect your line frequently. A nick or cut can weaken it dramatically. Here, 20-pound-test nylon monofilament has been magnified 35 times with an electron scanning microscope to illustrate that line abrasion, which you can barely detect, can be damaging.

well-worn line, is the visibly faded look, which may be the result of age or extensive exposure to sun. With nylon monofilament, it's due to the evaporation of the fluorescence from exposure to ultraviolet light. Sometimes anglers find that line on their reel suddenly seems to have lost its strength. The reason usually remains a mystery. Old nylon line does, however, become stiff as the result of the seepage of its plasticizing agent (monomer, which is the white chalky buildup you sometimes get when spooling line on a reel) and thus becomes brittle and weaker. The condition is evidenced in lighter lines by failure to hold knots well or by the easy breaking of unknotted sections.

In some cases, this old line will be serviceable again if it's soaked in water, but it's good to regard fading as a wear indicator and replace the line.

Line Care

In my mind the jury is still out on the factors that may affect the performance of super lines, but it

pays to be careful nonetheless. Nylon monofilament, however, has a longer track record, and we know that it is not ageless. Its effective life depends on how it's treated and what it's subjected to. Long exposure to sunlight can affect nylon, so don't store it, either on a consumer spool or a fishing reel, where sunlight falls on it daily. The ultraviolet elements of the sun's rays are strong, and to diminish their effect, premium lines feature an ultraviolet-retardation element, which prolongs the life of the line. Fluorescence is especially vulnerable to ultraviolet light and will fade in time. The best storage for line is a cool, dry environment sheltered from sunlight, perhaps in a garage, closet, or basement. Don't leave a spool on the dashboard of your automobile or a reel by a sunlit window.

Many anglers lose track of the strength of the line on a particular reel or can't recall when they put on the line. In some cases they are mistaken as to which brand they are using. All this can be avoided by marking the reel. Some line manufacturers supply gummed labels with each spool, so an angler can jot pertinent information on it and affix it to his reel. I use some form of gummed labels to put data on all my reels, using a number-letter code. For example, the markings 12/3/96 ST would signify 12-pound-test Stren line put on the reel in March 1996. The marking 12-17/3/96 XL would signify 12-pound-test Trilene XL over a 17-pound-test backing, spooled in March 1996.

You should also be careful about what substances come into contact with your line. Some of these can alter its characteristics in unsuspected ways. WD-40, for instance, which is commonly used on reels to inhibit rust, may leach out some of the plasticizers of nylon monofilament, resulting in somewhat stiffer line. If the line was in contact with water soon after contact with the WD-40, there would be no effect. If the reel were sprayed with WD-40 and then stored, damage to the sprayed line would occur.

Suntan oil can pose a problem, too. A spokesman for one line manufacturer informed me that suntan oils "generally contain certain active ingredients which can serve to plasticize the nylon monofilament and actually make it softer. There are some constituents in suntan oil that can have a beneficial effect and for a short time, at least, raise the knot strength of the product. Ironically, most of the ingredients in suntan oil tend to have a negative effect when it comes to actual fishing qualities because their plasticizing action causes an increase in elongation and the lines become excessively stretchy." The spokesman also said that there is an active ingredient in some insect repellents that, for a short time, creates dramatic improvements in knot strength. As a precaution, it's a good idea to clean the palms of your hands before touching your line (and lures).

Protracted contact with gas and motor oil can also cause damage. If a line is soaked with gasoline, a 50-percent reduction in strength can occur. Motor oil is not as potent as gasoline.

The most harmful substance to line, even for short contact, is battery acid. This sulfuric acid attacks nylon line almost immediately and advances oxidization. Light lines in particular are vulnerable.

Perhaps more serious is the possibility that these substances may impart an odor to the line that is not noticeable to humans but is detectable by fish. What effect this may have on fish behavior is unclear. It surely cannot be positive.

This information is not meant to alarm you or to complicate your angling. It is not farfetched to imagine that you might spray yourself liberally with bug repellent and then touch your line while tying a knot, or that coils of line might fall on an uncovered battery when you lay down your rod, or that gasoline or oil might be inadvertently spilled on your reel. Just take care to keep such substances off your line for extended periods.

Knots

Your line will normally be strongest when it's unknotted and dry. But it is fished wet and with a knot in it, and this can weaken the line. There are knots, and then there are fishing knots. Your objective is to tie the strongest, most reliable fishing knots you can, to achieve maximum strength from your fishing line. If you regularly use a knot that has only 75 percent of the strength of your line, the knot will break before the unknotted line does, under maximum stress. If, however, you tie a knot that has 100 percent of your line's breaking strength, the unknotted line will usually break before the knot. Of course, you want neither to break, but perhaps the line was too light for the conditions, the fish was too big, the drag was too loose, or the rod was too soft. The important point here is that under extreme circumstances your line did as much as it was capable of doing.

Knot performance varies from one angler to the next. Even with the most detailed and uniform instruction, people vary in the way they form their knots, how many wraps they make, how fastidious they are in tying, and so forth. A knot is only as good as the angler's skill in tying it. Practice to achieve uniform knot-tying, so that once you have mastered a knot and use it for bass fishing, you can expect it to perform reliably time after time.

Here are some fundamental pointers for effective knot-tying:

- Use plenty of line so that you can complete your tying steps without having to compensate for insufficiency.
- Be neat. Keep your twists, spirals, and other steps uniform so that when you draw your knot closed, it is neat and precise.
- Snug up all knots tightly with even, steady pressure. Knot slippage under pressure can cut the line, so watch the knot for evidence of slippage and redo it if necessary. Don't pop the knot to tighten it.
- If your knot breaks repeatedly when you tighten it, check your hook eye or lure connection for rough spots that are cutting the line.
- Wet the line to help you draw it up smoothly. If your hands are wet and will wet the line, fine; if not, place the knot and line in your mouth momentarily.
- Be careful not to nick the knot with your clippers when you cut off the protruding tag end. This can cause serious weakening.

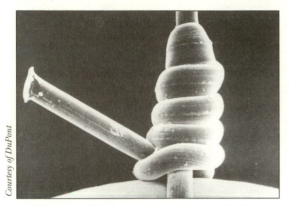

Courtesy of DuPont

This magnified photograph of an Improved Clinch Knot demonstrates the perfection necessary to achieve full knot strength. Good knot-tying is the result of precise, even-handed procedures.

- When using double lines, keep them as parallel as possible and avoid twisting them as the knot is being tied.
- Test your knots occasionally with a scale to see if you're getting the performance you need. Tie the line to the hook of a reliable spring scale. Have someone wrap the unknotted line around his hand several times, using a towel or cloth to keep from getting cut. While he pulls on the line, you hold and watch the scale, noting at what poundage the line or knot breaks. If the line broke, your knot held; if not, check your knot-tying.

Using this scale is a good way to monitor the basic strength of your unknotted line as well, although the test should be conducted when the line and knot are wet. Don't be too alarmed if your knot breaks before the line, as long as the breaking point is quite high. A typical top-quality nylon monofilament 12-pound-test line that's wet and unknotted will break when roughly 12.8 pounds of pressure is applied. A wet knot delivering 95-percent strength will break when 12.2 pounds of pressure is applied, while one delivering just 90-percent will break at 11.5 pounds. If you have a knot that delivers consistent breakage at or near the labeled strength of your line (which in this example is 12 pounds), then you

should be satisfied with it unless you can do better or can find a better knot.

Certain lines seem to accommodate particular knots better than others, perhaps because of differences in the molecular structure of the fiber or material. Nylon-monofilament manufacturers say that knot strength is built into fishing line and massaged in the finishing process, so it would seem that this quality may be stronger in some brands than in others. With nylon, knot failures are usually due to improper tying rather than to the properties of the line itself. With braided super lines and fused super lines, a failed knot is usually the wrong knot.

Improved Clinch Knot

The Improved Clinch is the knot I use in most of my freshwater fishing for making terminal-tackle connections with nylon monofilament line. It is best used for lines under 20-pound-test. Tied properly, this knot can give 90- to 100-percent strength; poorly tied, it may yield only 75 to 85 percent, which is not enough, especially for a light line. It is not a good knot to use with super lines.

To tie the Improved Clinch (not cinch) Knot, pass the line through the eye of the hook; then make five turns around the standing part of the line. Thread the end through the loop ahead of the eye and then bring it back through the newly created large loop. Moisten the knot with saliva and check that the coils are spiraled properly and not overlapping. Pull firmly to tighten. Test the knot with moderate tension and clip off the loose end.

Personal testing of this knot has shown me that six spirals are best for line through 12-pound-test, and five spirals for 14- to 17-pound-test. For 20-pound-test and over, I make four spirals and often use a pair of pliers to pull on the loose end and snug up the knot.

If you experience slippage with this knot, you may try running the line through the hook eye twice before completing the other steps. This is called a Double Improved Clinch Knot. A variation on this is the Trilene Knot, which also features two turns around the hook eye but in which the tag end comes back through both turns and is then snipped off.

Palomar Knot

Line manufacturers say this knot is easier to tie than the Improved Clinch and more consistent. And because it's easier to tie, fewer anglers experience difficulty with it. Tied properly, it yields 90- to 100-percent strength and is meant for terminal connections. I use it mainly for tying leader tippets to flies, since it is a smaller-profile knot than the Improved Clinch. It's especially valuable with braided super lines and fused super lines, provided that two or three turns are made around the eye, because it doesn't slip.

To tie the Palomar Knot, double about 6 inches of line and pass the loop through the eye of the hook. Tie an overhand knot in the doubled line and pass the loop over the entire hook. Moisten the knot, pull on both ends, tighten, and clip the tag end. Take care not to twist the doubled sections of line.

This knot presents a problem only when it is used for large, multihook plugs. In that case, a longer loop must be created for the big lure to pass through.

Uni Knot

This knot is a versatile creation with applicability to most bass-fishing situations. It can give 90- to 100-percent strength as a terminal-tackle connector. I use it primarily to tie two lines together or to tie a leader to fly line. Some people double it when tying super lines.

To join two lines of fairly similar diameter, overlap them about 6 inches. Hold them in the middle of the overlap with your left hand and make a circle with the line extended to the right. Bring the tag end around the double length six times, pulling snugly after the last turn. Repeat the process in reverse direction on the other side. Pull the two sections away from each other to draw the knot up; moisten it; then pull it firmly and clip both loose ends. Quicker and

easier to tie than the time-honored Blood Knot, the Uni Knot is equally reliable.

Loop Knots

There are several good specialty loop knots, including the Surgeon's End Loop and the King Sling. I use a Uni Knot or an Improved Clinch to form an end loop. With the Improved Clinch, I merely place my finger between the hook eye and the first spiral to form a large loop. I then tie the knot as usual, pulling it snugly to my finger at the end. I then pull firmly on the tag end to cinch down the knot. This holds fairly well for most fish, but under severe stress the knot will slide toward the eye and hold fast, becoming a complete Improved Clinch again. Afterward, I cut out this section and retie the knot. A loop knot is valuable in fishing crankbaits, some surface lures, and some shallow-running plugs.

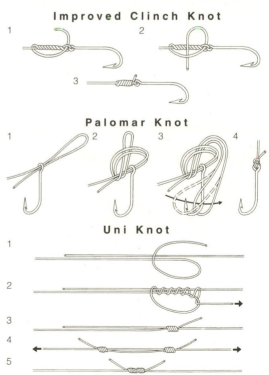

Tying the Improved Clinch Knot, the Palomar Knot, and the Uni Knot, which connects two lines.

LURES

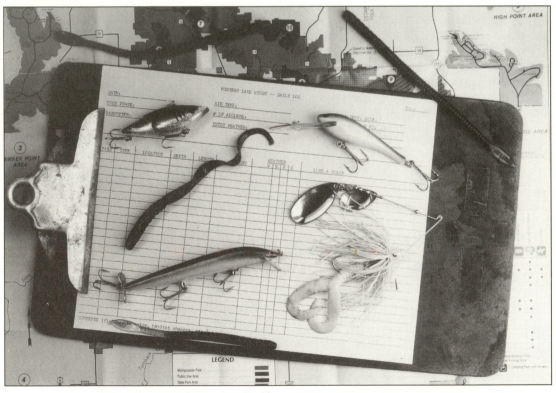

Choosing the appropriate lure for the conditions and being able to retrieve it skillfully are keys to bass-fishing success.

All lures are designed to perform a specific function. In most cases, their success or failure is primarily due to the way the angler uses them. The more you know about your lures and the fish you seek and the better you understand the conditions in which you seek them, the better prepared you'll be to make a knowledgeable lure selection. The fisherman who knows his quarry and matches his lure selection to the habits of bass and the prevailing conditions is the one who is most consistently productive. The angler who is completely familiar with the characteristics of each lure and can make the lure work to its maximum designed ability is the angler who will score when the chips are down.

There is a host of available lure types. Many of them overlap in application and technique, but others are suitable only to particular conditions and require specialized usage. In general terms, lure choices shape up for bass fishing as follows.

In shallow water, where everybody most likes to chase bass, floating/diving plugs and spinnerbaits get the call. In the plug category, minnow-imitating wood or plastic lures that float at rest and dive only a foot or two on retrieve are traditional, proven baits. Spinnerbaits are excellent lures, particularly in the spring when fish are shallow and also in vegetation. They can also be used quite effectively in deeper water,

crawled slowly across the bottom, or jigged.

For medium-depth angling (4 to 12 feet) you'll generally want to fish with a straight-running dive-to-the-bottom-on-retrieve lure. Bottom-hugging bass plugs such as these are called *crankbaits,* and they are manufactured in shallow-, medium-, and deep-diving versions, all of which are determined by the size and shape of their lip. Medium and deep divers are usually the most useful to bass fishermen, and they are fished in spring, parts of summer, and fall, in many locales. Worms and jigs are also highly effective bass baits in this depth range.

For deep-water fishing (10 feet or more, though often in shallower water as well), the bass angler without a plastic worm or who doesn't know how to use it, is in for a rough time. Bass seek the comfort of cooler, deep water in late spring, summer, and early fall; and at these times plastic worms are probably more effective than all other lures combined. Another bottom scrounger, particularly effective on small-mouths, is the jig. It can be fished at any depth but is extremely effective in very deep water as well as along rocky bluffs and sharp-sloping shorelines, and on underwater mounds.

Surface-fishing, a favorite technique of bass anglers, is generally less productive than below-surface methods at most times, because of the habits and habitat of the quarry. Surface lures run the gamut from soft-plastic floating baits to wooden or plastic plugs that twitch, wobble, chug, and sputter.

There is a *time and a place* for all lures. Remember above all else that *each lure is designed to perform a certain function in certain fishing conditions.* A lure won't catch fish merely because it is supposed to. There are good lures and bad lures, good times to use them and poor ones, good usage of lures and bad usage. A lure also won't catch bass merely because it looks good. The bottom line in the lure business is that the product must catch *fishermen.* Most anglers, in turn, expect the lure to catch fish. But these expectations are misguided. Cars don't drive; they are driven. Guns don't shoot; they are shot. And lures don't catch fish; fishermen do. Lures are just a means by which an angler can accomplish his goal.

Not that the lure isn't important to his success. But there's a lot more to productive bass fishing than possessing a well-stocked tackle box. Recognizing the abilities of a lure, using it to its full potential, and injecting a dose of angling savvy are all vital factors in the game.

Crankbaits

"Crankbait," a term that became popular in modern times, has come to be associated with various treble-hook diving and sinking plugs with a built-in vibrating, wiggling, swimming action. The term derives from the fact that the simplest and most practiced way to fish such a lure is to chuck it out and crank the reel handle steadily to bring it in on a nonstop retrieve. That's not the only way to use this lure, however, nor is it necessarily the best.

For any bass fisherman, even one with the most meager selection of lures, several crankbaits ought to be mandatory tackle-box fare. Although crankbaits have limited versatility, they have several notable characteristics. First, they are easy to cast. A novice fisherman who has mastered basic casting motions will have no difficulty tossing out a crankbait, even under windy conditions, provided that the lure is not too

light or too heavy for the rod, reel, and line he is using. Nor will he find his line fouling around the hooks or the hooks becoming entangled (they are usually well spaced). Because of their streamlined shape, crankbaits do not meet the air resistance that some lures do, so they do not have a tendency to tumble in the air but will fly well even if the cast is poorly executed.

Crankbaits are also relatively easy to fish with. While it seems that bass blast these lures with profound determination most of the time, it is a fact that the combination of a basically quick retrieve, the swift attack of a bass on what it thinks is a rapidly departing prey, and the usual two sets of treble hooks, all lead to slam-bang action at the moment of impact. A bass will often hook itself on this lure (nonetheless it is important for the angler to set the hook). These facts add up to excellent hooking potential and consequently more fish caught per strike than with many other lures.

Crankbaits can also catch bass 12 inches or better. Although I have caught very small bass on very large crankbaits, it is the nature of these

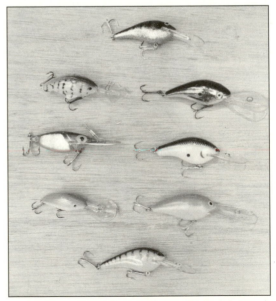

A selection of deep-diving crankbaits for bass fishing. The design of their large and near-horizontal lip has a lot to do with their ability to get deep.

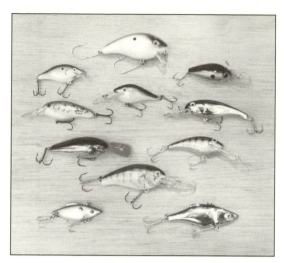

A representative sample of shallow- and medium-running crankbaits. The two lures at the bottom are lipless crankbaits.

plugs to catch more than their share of keepers. Despite all the attention given to lunker bass, I think most fishermen are satisfied with an abundant number of keeper-size fish, even if they aren't keeping them.

Crankbaits also fit well into the most common bass-fishing method: plugging the shorelines. There are advantages and disadvantages to constant shoreline cruising, but it is popular with fishermen. If you spend the whole time plunking the shore, you'll probably catch stray bass, and the crankbait is a good lure on strays.

Most crankbaits have clear plastic lips, which are presumably less visible to fish than metal or colored plastic ones. I have found little difference in effectiveness between these lipped baits, although the action of rectangularly fronted lures differs from that of ovally fronted lures.

It is the lip, of course, that generally controls the standard running depth of the lure and contributes greatly to its action. The larger the lip, the greater the running depth. Lures that are not designed to float but sink immediately to the bottom may have smallish lips but their working depth is determined by their weight, the amount of line you have out, and

your method and speed of retrieve.

Crankbaits cover a range of depths. Depending on lip size, they can be classified as shallow, medium, or deep diving. It is clear that certain baits have applications for working specific bottom depths. But on the whole, bass-fishing crankbaits are most appropriate in waters to 15 feet deep. There are crankbaits that will dive deeper, but it is my general experience that greater depths are better scoured with jigs and plastic worms.

The standard fishing technique with crankbaits is the cast-and-crank method. It is probably used most of the time by crankbait fishermen, and it works. But it is not enough to plop down on the lake and whiz this lure along any old place. Keeping in mind the depth of water you want to work, it is generally a good idea to retrieve fast in warm water and slow in cold water, and fast in clear water and slow in muddy water. Regardless of water color, however, I have found it a good technique to work sharp shoreline drop-offs and, particularly, rocky shorelines by casting in close to shore and retrieving a deep-diving crankbait fast. Largemouth and smallmouth bass alike respond to this tactic, and often the strike will come after a few feet of retrieve. If you fish like this for most of the day, you'll have a noodle arm that night, but that may be what it takes to catch fish. If the bass aren't responding to this technique, try other lures or other crankbait-fishing methods.

If you are working the shoreline without results, you may be scratching only a short section of the bottom. Depending upon how sharp the drop-off is and if you're casting into shore from your boat, the lure may not be reaching all of the bottom that it should and therefore isn't getting to the depth where the fish are holding. Try casting parallel instead of perpendicular to the shore, and make sure that your plug is working the right depths.

Bottom-scratching is critical in most bass-fishing situations with crankbaits. Try to keep your plug rooting along the bottom, over objects, and along impediments. This isn't a problem with the right floating/diving crankbait. With the sink-

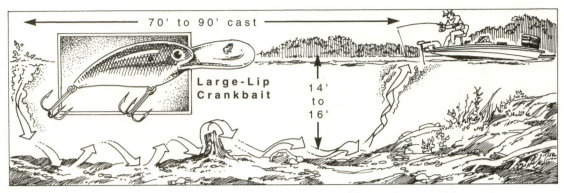

Not all crankbaits are fished strictly along the shoreline; most of the time they are used for scouring the bottom. A deep-diving crankbait that is fished slowly along the bottom in a stop-and-go fashion enables the plug to periodically rise slightly.

ing version, let the lure settle to the bottom (or count it down to a particular level) and make your retrieve at a rate slow enough to keep the plug on the bottom or as close to it as possible.

Floating/diving crankbaits are exceedingly buoyant, adding another dimension to their fishability. If you stop your retrieve, these plugs will bob toward the surface like a cork, and you can take advantage of this feature. A pull-pause action is easily accomplished by retrieving in the standard fashion and stopping momentarily, then repeating the procedure. In its most exaggerated form, this can be extended to stopping the retrieve long enough for the lure to float to the surface, and then resuming the retrieve. Try making the lure hesitate by stumps, brush, and other objects. This technique can be used repeatedly throughout the retrieve and might be the tactic to stir up otherwise unexcited bass.

The buoyancy of crankbaits varies from lure to lure. Floaters rise and divers sink. How fast they rise or fall depends on their density in relation to the density of the water. Sometimes a slow rise is preferable to a quick rise. I have seen bass strike a crankbait when its steady retrieve was interrupted by the angler, momentarily stopping the lure so that it rose only slightly.

A few lures have little or neutral buoyancy. They remain stationary in the water when stopped. Suspension has a lot of validity in fishing crankbaits, which essentially represent small baitfish. I've noticed that baitfish rarely rise or sink significantly in their natural environment. When they stop, they stay at the same level, using their fins as stabilizers and relying on their internal organs to maintain their level. Stopping and suspending a lure at its running level is the most useful when you are fishing over some type of cover that's likely to hold bass. A good example would be working a crankbait over a submerged grass bed, which likely holds bass buried in the holes in the vegetation. These bass might hit a crankbait swimming briskly by. They probably won't be induced to strike a bait that stops and floats quickly to the surface. But a bait that stops and hovers over the grass could be the most attractive offering of all. The same can be true for fishing over treetops or drop-offs. You can suspend crankbaits and other plugs or make them rise slowly by adding strips or dots of lead tape to them. Storm Lures offers SuspenDots for this purpose.

Rock walls and roadways, underwater islands, and other irregular features that lures can reach are particularly well worked with a crankbait. Sunken or exposed bridge abutments are worth working and so is flooded timber. In all cases fish to, from, over, and around these objects, and don't be concerned about bumping the lures against them.

The best way to fish an object—a stump, for example—with a crankbait is to cast beyond it so that when you retrieve, the lure will be able to get down to its running depth before it reaches the object. This is possible, of course, only when the area behind the object is open enough to permit it. When casting to a long-fallen log, for instance, cast beyond the target but position yourself to be able to retrieve your crankbait down the length of the log as closely as possible.

It is possible to work crankbaits around heavy cover, a tactic that can be successful if you can keep from getting hung up in weeds. Six wiggling, vibrating, exposed hook points is not my idea of a weedless bait, though; for fallen trees, heavy weed growth, thick lily pads, and so on, a specifically weedless lure can be used with more effect and less chance of alarming the natives. (A modification that will make crankbaits a little more weedless is to cut off the front hook of the treble or replace both trebles with a single Siwash-style hook.) Occasionally you can free a hung-up crankbait by giving slack to the line, allowing the lure to float free. If near-shore weed growth is not too great, crankbaits will work well for the shore-based fisherman, too.

One critically important aspect of crankbait-fishing overlooked by many anglers, particularly beginners, is the diving ability of the lure. If bass are holding at 12 feet on a rocky bank and you are using a plug that you think dives that deep but that in reality reaches only 8 feet, you can cast till your arms fall off and you won't be successful. To be effective with it, you must know how deep any diving plug runs. Diving abilities depend on the lure, the size of your line, and the speed of retrieve. Use the information supplied by the lure manufacturer as a guideline, but don't rely on it. Find out for yourself how deep your lures run.

When retrieving, it is not necessary to crank the handles as fast as possible to achieve maximum depth. In fact, some lures lose depth when worked too fast. Crank the lure fast for a moment to get the bait down; then retrieve at a moderate pace; this will keep the lure as deep as it will go, depending on your line. Large-diameter lines offer more resistance and inhibit lure diving. The thinner the line, the deeper a diving plug will go.

If you are flinging long casts, a thin-diameter line will make a difference in achieving depth. If you are trolling, with relatively long lines out, it's especially significant. Also, remember that current, if it is present, will affect diving ability. Lures retrieved with the current, or sideways to it, do not run as deep as those worked into it.

Determining the diving depth of a plug can be simple if you fish it over known bottom terrain or around objects of a known depth. For example, find a flat that is 7 feet deep. Try a medium- or deep-diving plug; if it touches bottom you know it will go 7 feet deep. Move out a little deeper until you lose contact with the bottom to determine running depth at its maximum. If you're not hitting bottom, go shallower until you make contact.

There are, incidentally, lipless crankbait —for example the Rat-L-Trap—that are used more as swimming plugs than as divers. Many of them sink, some float. Lipless crankbaits are excellent lures for catching schooling fish, for casting over submerged vegetation, and even for deep-running using a countdown method to get sinkers near the bottom. In the early part of the year, they are often fished in a stop-and-go manner, retrieved a few feet and then paused momentarily before being retrieved again.

One trick to fishing any kind of crankbait is to keep your rod down at all times. This not only assists in hook-setting and reacting to a strike, but it also allows your plug to run deeper. If your rod tip is close to the water, you'll gain an extra foot or two of depth over someone in the same boat with the same lure, whose rod is angled toward the sky. Those extra few feet could make the difference in getting down where the bass are holding, which is especially relevant in dingy water. To attain the greatest possible depth, you can kneel or sit down in the boat, lean over, and stick the rod tip into the water. The longer your rod and the farther into the water you place the tip, the deeper the lure will go. It makes no sense to do this, however, if you can achieve the same thing by using a similar crankbait that dives deeper. On the other hand, you may find yourself in a situation where you have just one crankbait of the particular size and color that's

When fishing a crankbait, especially if you're trying to get it to run as deep as possible, stand up and lower the rod tip as this angler is doing.

working; then you may need to do whatever you can to get the lure down to the proper level.

When you're working the shoreline or a weed line with crankbaits, how you present your lure and position your boat are keys to your success. The best way to cast a crankbait to such areas is by working parallel, rather than perpendicular, to it. When two anglers are in the boat, it is a good tactic for both of them to fish from the front (as when casting from a bass boat), with each one's cast overlapping the other's as the boat is maneuvered close and parallel to the area.

The vibration and noise of some crankbaits are other aspects worth mentioning. The best crankbaits have an enticing side-to-side action that does more than look good. The vibrations it produces may simulate those produced by the erratic movement of wounded prey. Bass strike some crankbaits they cannot see (in murky water or at night) because they have detected the change in water pressure and the vibrations produced by the lure. The better the lure, the better its action and vibration.

Some crankbaits also contain rattle chambers. These lures feature one or more BB-like spheres of varying size, which move around in the chamber, creating a rattling sound. I discovered just how pronounced this sound is while testing a plug in an above-ground pool with a vinyl liner, supported by a circular aluminum wall and aluminum framing. I heard a distinct clicking sound. At first I thought it was my reel. But when I stopped turning the reel handle, the noise stopped. I moved away from the pool and didn't hear the noise. I returned and stood next to the pool and plainly heard the noise. It was produced by the rattling lure and was resonating off the aluminum walls of the pool. If you think of this in terms of an angling situation like a riprap bank or a rocky cliff shore, you can imagine that a rattling crankbait could be highly detectable to a bass.

Of course, the food eaten by bass doesn't rattle. But in addition to the vibrations produced by all fish, some prey, such as crayfish, may well produce audible noise as they crawl over rocks. What's most important is that the rattle can make the lure more detectable in low light and turbid water conditions and draw the attention of a bass. Although many times rattling crankbaits are no more effective than nonrattlers, sometimes they are. So, it pays to know when rattling plugs can be useful and what their advantages are.

The last major factor in success with crankbaits is color. The color you choose should relate to the color and visibility of the water you're fishing and to the primary forage of bass. Crankbaits are available in many colors, but the best-sellers for most manufacturers year-in and year-out are the silver, shad, and crayfish versions, which best resemble the primary forage of bass. If you know what that forage is, you have a head start on color selection.

Unfortunately, there are no strict guidelines on the influence of water color. In blue-green water, chartreuse seems to stand out especially well, and crankbaits in this color, or with some chartreuse undercoating, are quite effective. In sand-colored or muddy water, I like light baits with flash. In water darkened by tannic acid, a gold or chrome color in a plug has merit. In very clear water darker colors seem to be less alarm-

ing to bass than light, flashy ones. Depending on water color, a more subtle tone to a plug may be all that is needed, for instance, a lightly colored crayfish pattern rather than a dark one.

The popularity of the "natural finish"—painting or photofinishing that reproduces a bait right down to its scale patterns and gill structure—crankbait comes and goes over the years. As I mentioned earlier, lures must first catch fishermen. Natural finishes are certainly eye-appealing. Because they look good to you, the angler, you may have more confidence in them and fish them more often and more intensively. This can result in greater productivity; if so, terrific. The best application for a natural-finish plug is in water of high clarity. There, light line use, fine presentation, precise lure action, and lure color and detail can make the difference between catching bass and being frustrated. In water of limited visibility, however, your lure's looks are less important than its action and vibration.

At times, a touch of red or orange on the belly of a lure makes a difference. At times, a green-and-white crankbait, which resembles nothing, is more successful than one with conventional colors. There aren't always explanations for fish behavior, which is the way it should be and one of the reasons people like to fish. It pays to have a selection of crankbaits in your tackle box that's varied both in terms of colors and diving abilities so you can handle whatever conditions you may encounter.

Two remaining aspects of using crankbaits should be mentioned here. The first is that crankbaits must run true to be effective. They must run straight on the retrieve, not lie on their side or run off at an angle. Some lures do this fresh out of the box and some do not. There are ways to "tune" your crankbaits to make them run true. The fine-tuning of these and other lures is covered later in this book.

And the second, sometimes overlooked, is that crankbaits can do double-duty as trolling lures. I have, at times, caught big bass while trolling deep-diving crankbaits and feel confident using them in this manner, either on a flatline or aided by a bottom-hugging sinker.

The author caught this Alabama largemouth on a deep-diving photofinish crankbait in about 16 feet of water. Long casts and slow retrieval help get crankbaits to maximum depths.

Crankbaits are the best lures for trolling; and though many anglers pass up this technique for bass, there's something to be said for it.

Although I would like to recommend crankbaits in particular to beginning fishermen, it's hard to do so fairly, since crankbaits come and go over the years. I use whatever seems appropriate for the time and circumstance, regardless of brand name. Mann's, Rebel, Normark (Rapala), Bagley, Luhr Jensen, Storm, Bomber, Bill Lewis, and Norman are all represented in my tackle box.

Spinnerbaits

A spinnerbait is one of my favorite lures and my principal springtime bass catcher. I have introduced many friends to spinnerbaits, and I recommend them highly for fishermen of all skill levels, but most especially for newcomers to bass angling. Spinnerbaits are more-than-able fish catchers, relatively easy to use and remarkably weed- and tangle-free. More importantly, it's exciting to fish these lures.

A spinnerbait is not a spinner. Looking at it sideways, you see a V-type configuration. The bottom of the V features a leadhead hook with a skirt or soft-plastic grub attached. The upper part of the V features one or two spinner blades that revolve around the shaft. The entire ensemble resembles an open safety pin, which prompted some early users to dub it a *safety-pin spinner*. When the lure is retrieved steadily, the blades and upper arm should run vertically above the bottom part of the lure.

What a spinnerbait is supposed to look like is uncertain. It is not meant to look like any particular bass food, but it possesses certain qualities that attract bass, especially in the spring and fall. Through blade color and movement, a spinnerbait offers visual flash and auditory vibration. Fish can both see and hear it well. With a good skirt on the lower half, a spinnerbait also offers pulsating movement and the impression of having enough substance to be worthwhile chow. Add to this the fact that it can be effectively fished in all but the thickest cover, and you have the elements of a lure that really catches bass.

A spinnerbait may also appeal to the predatory, reflexive instincts of a bass. A bass must strike it because he is hungry or because it grabs his eye and looks like something vulnerable that another fish will snatch if he doesn't. A spinnerbait is a good lure for fishing in and around cover, and because bass are often concealed when this flashy morsel comes by, its appearance must trigger a reflexive strike.

Cover is the key word for anyone wondering what places are best to fish a spinnerbait. Lily pads, grass, stumps, brush, treetops, boat docks, rock piles, logs, and similar fish-holding places can all be effectively worked with a spinnerbait. Though they may be fished at any depth, these lures are most productive in shallow water.

The most common technique of fishing a spinnerbait is to retrieve it close enough to the surface that you can see the lure through the water on the retrieve. Fish the lure a few inches to several feet below the surface, depending on the clarity of the water and the structure.

It is not only beneficial but highly enjoyable to watch a spinnerbait when it is being retrieved this shallow. If you can see the lure, you will see the fish strike it nearly every time. Sometimes a bass seems to dart out of nowhere. Other times it comes from right where expected. This is much like surface-fishing; the excitement of anticipating and seeing the strike is always present. Spinnerbaits are usually struck from the side, suddenly forcing the lure sideways as if it were hit by a gust of wind. When this happens, jam the hook home fast. Another distinct advantage of this technique is that you can see the fish that attempt to strike the bait, as well as those that do. You can often see if a bass misses the lure, hits short, or is merely taking a close look. Sometimes these fish can be caught with another cast in the same area.

It is also interesting to watch the lure as it is retrieved right to the boat. Sometimes, particularly on shallow, stumpy flats, a fish may come from almost under the boat to chase the lure, yet turn away at the last second as the lure nears the boat. Chain pickerel and northern pike are two species of fish that especially love spinner-baits and characteristically follow them right up to the boat.

For maximum effectiveness when working the shallows, it's important to begin retrieving a spinnerbait the moment it hits the water. With spinning tackle, this is no problem, but right-handed baitcasters will have to switch the rod to their left hand during the cast so they can engage the reel as the lure hits the water, or their lure may get fouled initially or fall too deep to fish the nearby cover.

Sometimes bass are holding by objects at a level deeper than your lure is being retrieved, and they will not come up for it. If you're fishing a spinnerbait shallow with no results, let the lure sink out of sight to a depth between 4 and 8 feet, and retrieve it steadily at that depth. Occasionally, you'll have to fish a spinnerbait out of sight along the bottom like this. Some anglers are even more versatile with a spinnerbait and fish it very deep by fluttering it down sharply sloping shorelines, drop-offs, rocky ledges, and the like, using a short-armed spinnerbait (make sure the blade turns freely and regularly when the lure is dropping) and working it in a series of short hops or in a jigginglike motion.

The places where I have most successfully used a spinnerbait are grass, lily pads, stumps and logs, stickups, and bushes. In all cases, get as close to the object as possible. Do this by casting the lure beyond the target, bringing it back into contact with the target, then continuing on. I usually make several casts to each object, from every angle, paying particular attention to the deep and shady sides of it as well.

An effective method for working weed beds and weed lines is to crawl a spinnerbait slowly over the tops of the grass, when it is submerged a few feet. For grass beds with definable weed lines, however, I may cast parallel to the edge or bring the lure over the top and let it flutter down the edge. For lily pads, it is best to work the channel-like openings, but don't be afraid to throw into thick clusters, work the bait in a pocket, ease it over the pads, and drop it in another pocket.

Perhaps the most reliable pattern for spinner-bait-fishing, especially in the spring, is working the wood. This includes stumps, logs, and stick-ups. Make sure your spinnerbait is close to these objects; in fact, bump them with the lure at times. The momentary fluttering of the bait's blades and the object contact seem to produce strikes. Stickup trees, bushes, and floating logjams (as often found in coves) are also productive. You should get your bait as far back in them as possible before commencing the retrieve. Boat

This flooded brush is great spinnerbait water, and a hot spot for aggressive shallow largemouths in the spring.

Stickups, stumps, blowdowns, and similar woody cover are good spinnerbait country.

docks and boathouses, too, fit in this category.

Spinnerbaits come in single- and tandem-blade versions. Single-blade spinnerbaits are effective when fished shallow as the season progresses, and they're better bait for deeper retrieves. Tandem blades on the overhead arm of the spinnerbait usually feature a small spinner followed by a larger one. Tandem-blade spinnerbaits are mainly for shallow fishing and are best in the spring.

Most spinnerbaits feature Colorado- or Indiana-style spinner blades. The Colorado is pear-shaped and produces more vibration than the Indiana. The common size is No. 4, which is roughly the size of a quarter. Colorado blades are often found on single-blade spinnerbaits. Indiana blades are teardrop- shaped and work well on tandem-blade lures. They produce good vibration, too, though they spin faster.

A third style of blade, the willowleaf, was less commonly used until recent years. These long blades are used on a tandem rig with a big No. 4 or 5 willowleaf in silver or copper behind a smaller Indiana blade. The willowleaf doesn't vibrate as much as the other blades, but it revolves freely and produces a lot of flash. Baits with big blades are generally reserved for waters with distinct big-fish potential. This is not to say

you won't catch big bass on smaller lures—I've caught big bass on small and large spinnerbaits —but the probability is that you'll catch fewer smaller bass with an oversize bait.

Something to note on all spinnerbaits is the thickness of the wire in the shaft arms. Thin wire gives you good feel and good lure action but can snap under the strain of a big fish, and, in general, will not withstand as much use as thicker wire. Some of my light-wire spinnerbait arms have snapped after a lot of use. Wire arms that are too thick, however, detract substantially from lure action and feel.

Formerly, many spinnerbaits featured overhead blade arms that extended well beyond the hook on the bottom arm. This was of some help in preventing hangups, but it hampered hook-setting. Now many spinnerbaits have a shorter shaft, in which the blade assembly is located directly above the hook, which is thus unobstructed. The downside is that short-arm spinnerbaits hang up frequently in thick brush, stumps, and timber. If you need to roll such a lure over a log it often won't make it, because the overhead shaft is too short to afford any protection. If you take a short-arm spinnerbait attached to fishing line and gently try to pull it over your arm, you'll see what I mean; if the hook pricks your arm, it will stick in a log. For such cover, a long-arm spinnerbait is best.

Spinnerbaits have to be periodically tuned to be kept running properly. A good spinnerbait runs straight, without twisting 360 degrees or leaning off to the side. You can adjust a spinnerbait so that the blades and hook run vertically in the water by bending the entire overhead shaft arm in the opposite direction from which it is running astray.

The spinner blades on these arms come in different colors and impressions. Silver and copper are most popular, followed by gold and painted white, chartreuse, and orange. Most are hammered or otherwise indented to reflect light rays and create flash. Copper, generally the favorite of most anglers, is good for slightly turbid and off-color water. Silver works well for me most of the year, especially in the spring and in clear water. Painted blades, most notably chartreuse, have worked well in murky green water. Many newer blades are painted with various patterns and with sparkling, flashy designs. They look great but don't seem to be more effective.

As for spinnerbait bodies, color is sometimes unimportant and sometimes crucial. White is

Spinnerbaits can sport long or short arms, single or tandem blades, various blade styles, trailer hooks, and plastic curl-tail bodies.

good for the early season and in murky water. Then all-chartreuse and chartreuse-and-blue (or black) combinations take over. On many occasions, the skirt color makes no difference in the number or size of fish caught.

The material of the skirt and how it is applied are important, however. Most spinnerbaits today are supplied with rubber-tentacled or "living-rubber" skirts, but they used to be primarily dressed with vinyl skirts. Rubber holds up well in cold water and offers good body-swimming action. The disadvantage in rubber is that the tentacle arms have a tendency to stick together in the tackle box; you can avoid this by sprinkling some talcum powder in the compartments that house your spinnerbaits and by using trays that allow you to store spinnerbaits with the skirts hanging loosely rather than bunched up. If the legs get molded together, pull the skirt off and replace it with a fresh one. Synthetic Lumaflex skirts, some with elaborate colors and designs, have appeared in recent years, as have skirts made from processed fish.

The best way to apply a rubber skirt is as follows: Hold it up so that the tentacles hang straight down; then turn it upside down so that the tentacles come out and over the stem of the skirt, resembling small streams of water being shot out of a fountain. Now thread the stem over the hook point and the shank until it fits snugly on the base of the leadhead. This backward skirt produces far more pulsating action than a straight-back skirt would.

It's a good idea to dress up spinnerbaits, especially large ones, still further by adding a curl-tail worm, grub, or pork chunk to the main hook. I'm partial to 3-inch twin-tail soft-plastic trailers, which swim feverishly just behind the skirt, and give a valuable extra dimension to the look of the lure.

An important modification on a spinnerbait is a trailer hook. Trailer hooks account for many bass that would otherwise have been lost. It is not necessary to use them all the time, but it doesn't hurt, especially if the fish are visibly striking short or hitting merely to stun. The trailer hook should ride up like the spinnerbait hook.

To keep the trailer hook from sliding off, block it with a small piece of surgical tubing. Place a small ring of this material over the eye of the trailer hook; then bring the point of the spinnerbait hook through the eye and tubing, and secure it.

Most spinnerbait-fishing is directed at, thus much of this information applies to, largemouth bass. But in the spring, smallmouths can be caught on spinnerbaits. Spinnerbaits are effective lures at that time, particularly when the fish are shallow, spawning in shoreline areas.

My experience has been that spring and early summer are the best times for spinnerbaits. At those times they enable you to cover a lot of ground quickly and effectively, while you watch your lure work and the fish strike. Midsummer is generally not good for spinnerbaits, although in some well-timbered lakes where bass remain relatively shallow, spinnerbaits are effective. As the

This largemouth took a white spinnerbait on the edge of brush and pads. In such thick cover, a trailer hook gets snagged too often and impedes lure action.

water cools in early fall, spinnerbaits again become reasonably productive lures.

There are a lot of good spinnerbaits on the market, including many made and sold within the same regions, so you shouldn't have to look far to find something suitable. If you keep a supply of extra blades, barrel swivels, trailer hooks, and skirts so you can modify your spinnerbaits as necessary, you'll be able to enhance the lure's effectiveness and increase your angling success.

Surface Lures

Surface-fishing for bass is exciting no matter what time of year you choose to do it. Summertime is probably when bass fishermen give the surface the most pounding, mainly early in the morning and late in the day. Bass, however, are bottom- and cover-oriented fish, and you usually have to get down to the level at which they are holding if you expect to catch them regularly. Nonetheless, at certain times surface-fishing does have much merit, if you understand when and where to be working the top.

Surface-fishing is generally restricted to relatively shallow water—12 to 14 feet—and to areas with cover. It is important to work a surface lure where there's bass cover; unless you're casting to bass feeding on schools of baitfish in open water or trying to call bass out of the tops of submerged trees, it is usually unproductive to fish most surface lures in open, deep-water areas. Also, accurate casting and full mastery over the workings of your lures are important in surface-fishing.

These, then, are the keys to successful surface-fishing for bass: knowing when, and when not, to use them; knowing what type to use and how; knowing where to use them; knowing when to quit fishing on the surface (a common mistake is to stick with surface-fishing long after the surface activity has petered out); and being able to put those lures in the most productive position.

Essentially, I classify as a surface lure any lure that is worked as a topwater plug or used within 3 feet of the surface. There are four types of

Surface-fishing is the most exciting way to catch bass, though it isn't always the most productive. Overcast skies early and late in the day, lightly rippled water, and shallow cover usually produce surface-fishing success.

surface lures: popping and wobbling plugs, floating/diving plugs and darters, propellered lures, and stickbaits.

Poppers and Wobblers

There are two distinct lures in this category: those that pop or chug and those that wobble. Poppers include such plugs as the Arbogast Hula Popper, Cordell Near Nuthin', Storm Chug Bug, Rebel PopR, and Lewis' SpitFire. Wobblers principally comprise lures like the Heddon Crazy Crawler and Arbogast's Jitterbug. All these plugs are strictly for use on top of the water.

Poppers. A popper, to my way of thinking, doesn't resemble the actions of any popular form of bass bait. Nothing that I've seen in the water deliberately calls attention to itself or makes pop-pop-popping or chug-chug-chug-

ging sounds. A remote possibility is that this noise is construed by bass as the surface-feeding activity of other fish. More likely, the vibrations simply attract feeding fish or call curious ones out of hiding.

All poppers (also called *chuggers*) have a concave, soup-bowl–type mouth. They function mainly noisemakers and attractors. They may be worked in a continuous-retrieve manner in locations where bass feed on schooling shad, but otherwise they should be fished with pauses of varying duration during the retrieve. You achieve the actual popping or forward chugging motion by jerking your rod up or back, not by reeling in line. It is best to keep your rod low and pointed toward the lure to prevent slack so that you can work the lure well and be in the best possible position to react to a strike.

This plug can be popped with varying degrees of emphasis. Seldom is it worthwhile to jerk the rod hard to create a loud commotion. That can be an effective technique for schooling striped bass, but only occasionally is it warranted for black bass, and that would likely be when they too are schooling and chasing baitfish pods near the surface. When the surface is calm, you need effect only a mild popping noise; a loud noise under this condition would probably be alarming. When the surface is disturbed by a mild chop, a slightly noisier retrieve is warranted, so you'll have to make your plug pop louder.

If it appears that bass are feeding fairly actively, you can shorten the time between pops, but it is usually best to maintain long pauses, several seconds in duration, between them. Poppers are obviously time-consuming lures to use, and do not cover a lot of area well. On the other hand, when worked slowly and enticingly in places with good concentrations of bass, they can be dynamically effective. A good tactic with poppers is to let them lie motionless a while after splashdown, then take up all your slack line and gently jiggle the rod just enough to impart the slightest sign of life to the lure. This tactic works well for just about all surface lures and sometimes makes a striker out of a bass that has been attracted to the landing of the plug in the water but might be spooked by the first quick pop.

Poppers work best near cover and in water that is not too deep, roughly to 12 feet. The best fishing times for this lure are early and late in the day (particularly in the summer), at night, and on cloudy days. I've seldom had success with poppers until late spring or after midfall; the combination of bright light and noisy lures does not seem to be one that bass favor. I don't recommend continuously using poppers unless you're having exceptional success with them. Poppers are good for spot-fishing, that is, making a few casts in selected areas and then switching to another, different type of lure. They are also favored more by largemouth than smallmouth bass, which you might expect owing to the habitat differences of these fish.

Wobblers. Wobbling plugs are used much in the manner of poppers. Wobblers, too, are more effective for largemouths, but I've caught some dandy smallmouths on them at night. Wobblers, in fact, are probably more effective in the dark than at dusk, daylight, or dawn.

Wobblers are characterized by their to-and-fro undulating action. The Jitterbug has a wide, double, spoon-filled metal lip that causes this motion, while the Crazy Crawler has two metal "wings" that rock the bait from side to side. The common retrieval method is a straight, continuous motion. At times, though, a worthwhile technique is to make the lure stop and go, or to give it a pull-pause motion, particularly as it swims next to an object like a stump or dock support. As long as there is some cover present or the water is not excessively deep under the boat, it's wise to work this lure all the way back to the boat. These plugs may be hit at any point along the retrieve, especially at night.

Keep your rod tip low and resist the urge to reel too fast. The action of these lures isn't as good when they're retrieved quickly as when they're worked slowly. Moreover, a fast retrieve is more conducive to missed strikes. Many bass strike and miss wobbling surface lures, perhaps because they have difficulty pinpointing the lure's location or more probably because they are

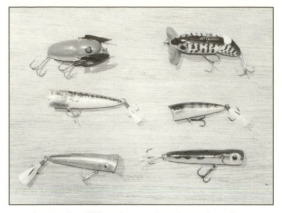

Assorted wobbling (top row) and popping plugs.

intending to stun this surface-swimming creature. You may find it advantageous when experiencing a lot of short strikes to fashion a trailer hook behind the lure (if this doesn't hamper the action) or to resort to a more frequent stop-and-go retrieval cadence. For some reason, many fish that strike and miss fail to hit the lure when you toss it out a second time. Try to resist the urge to set the hook the instant a fish slashes at the bait and momentarily wait to feel the fish take your plug before setting the hook sharply. This hard-to-master delay is effective in fishing weedless spoons in grass and works well on wobbling surface plugs as well. If the fish misses altogether, try stopping the lure in its tracks and twitching it a little, then moving it a few inches and stopping it. Repeat this procedure again before resuming the retrieve.

I recommend very light or very dark colors in these lures. My greatest success overall has been with black wobblers and poppers, but chrome, clear, and frog-patterned models are also effective. The size of the lure can vary with the conditions and expected catch. In waters with large bass, or when specifically looking for big fish, I'll use ⅜- or ½-ounce plugs. In northern waters, where bass usually run smaller, I seldom use the largest plugs, preferring a ¼-ounce popper most of the time, a ¼-ounce wobbler in the daytime, and a ⅜-ounce wobbler at dusk and at night.

Floating/Diving Lures

Probably the most universally applied method of surface or near-surface fishing involves the use of floating/diving plugs. These lures are made either of plastic or wood, are generally minnow-shaped, and sport a small lip that serves to bring the lure beneath the surface at a maximum of about 3 feet on a conventional cast-and-retrieve. (These same minnow plugs, incidentally, will get down to a depth of 6 or 7 feet when trolled slowly on at least 150 feet of light line.) Though this type of lure is manufactured in sizes from 2 inches on up to 8 inches, the most practical size for bass fishing is the 4- to 6-inch model, since this is usually large enough to interest a bass but still representative of baitfish. Although both the larger and smaller models will be effective occasionally, you'll generally catch more small bass (and panfish, too) on the smaller ones, but they are more difficult to cast.

Floating/diving minnow plugs are highly effective for both largemouth and smallmouth bass. They'll catch largemouths all season long in the right locations, but are more of an early- and late-season bait for smallmouths except in the most northerly waters, where some smallmouths can be found shallow even in the summer.

These lures are most effectively worked in a

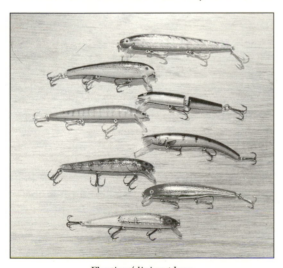

Floating/diving plugs.

deliberately erratic fashion to imitate a crippled baitfish. If you've ever seen a dying shad, alewife, sunfish, perch, or shiner, you may have noticed how it lies on its side, wiggles its tail fin occasionally, goes around in circles, and sometimes gets up enough energy to swim a few inches underwater before bobbing to the surface. This is the activity you want to mimic in the retrieval of a floating/diving lure. Being an opportunist, a hungry bass is likely to charge such a defenseless morsel with gusto, creating an electrifying strike.

To get the most out of this lure you have to fish it convincingly. The results you get are a direct consequence of the action you put into it. The first thing I do when fishing a floater/diver, as I do with just about all lures, is to reel up all the slack line. I also make sure that my rod is not pointed skyward. The reason for both is that a bass often strikes a well-cast surface lure shortly after it hits the water or has been retrieved only a few feet. If a fish hits that lure while it's first sitting still in the water and you have either slack line or a sky-busting rod, it's hard to set the hook. You probably won't get another chance at that fish, so no opportunity should be squandered.

How you fish most topwater lures in the first few feet of retrieve is critical to your success. This is especially true of floating/diving lures. It seems to me that the vast majority of bass caught in the daytime on surface lures are taken within half of the total retrieving distance. Buzzbaits are the exception.

Thus, your objective with a floater/diver is to make it gyrate as enticingly as possible in a stationary position. Keep the rod tip pointed low toward the water and use your wrist to move the rod. Jiggle the rod tip in a controlled, not frantic, fashion. Then jerk the lure back toward you a few inches. Then gyrate it some more, all the time reeling in an appropriate amount of line to keep the slack to a minimum. This is not difficult to accomplish, particularly if you have a rod with a fairly limber tip. Stiff-tipped rods don't allow for soft lure movement, and I have found that long, light-action spinning rods generally work well with these lures. The 4-inch size, being light, is easiest to cast with spinning tackle and 6-

to 12-pound-test line anyway, especially under windy conditions.

Another way to use this lure type is on a straight retrieve, allowing it to run a foot or two beneath the surface. This is like using it as a crankbait, and sometimes bass strike it that way. But a better technique, especially when bass won't hit this bait on top of the water, is to make it run just below the surface in a series of short jerk-pause movements, running it forward half a foot with each motion. This retrieve is more in the style of darters, those plugs that float but have no significant surface action and are used, solely, just below the surface. L&S MirroLures and Creek Chub Darters are characteristic of this lure type, as is Bomber's Suspending Long A Minnow and Mann's Loudmouth Jerkbait. All are fished with the jerk-pause retrieval technique employed for floating/diving plugs. Some lures fished this way, incidentally, are called *jerkbaits* by bass anglers, and some manufacturers use the words *jerking* or *ripping* in labeling such lures made for stop-and-go retrieves.

Some good floating/diving plugs for bass that I could recommend for all-around use are the floating Rapala, Rebel Minnow, Bagley Bang-O-Lure, Smithwick Rogue, and Cordell Redfin. The Rapala and Bagley lures, which are made of balsa wood, don't seem to rise as quickly to the surface after being pulled under as do the plastic lures, and best represent the behavior of small fish. The silver version probably outcatches all the others combined. Gold is good under certain water-color conditions, and sometimes, in clear lakes, perch, smelt, and bass patterns may be productive.

Perhaps the best place to use floating/diving plugs is over submerged grass that grows to within a few feet of the surface. This lure is good not only for catching bass there but also for locating possible concentrations of fish, which may then be tapped with a plastic worm. Any type of relatively shallow cover can be a target for floating/diving lures. And they can also be effective in locations with less cover, like long, shallow points; the backs of bays; and rocky shorelines. Smallmouth bass are particularly receptive to these lures in late spring and early summer, when they're in shallow water. Look for every sizable rock or boulder and toss a floating/diving minnow plug to it.

In the early part of the season and again in the fall, there is no preferred time of the day to use this type of lure. In shallow lakes in the early spring, I've had most success from midmorning to midafternoon, after the sun has warmed the water; however, this lure is good for spring mornings when bass are shaking off the effects of a cool night. Later in the spring you may be able to catch fish on these lures throughout the day. In the summer, early morning is the best time, and just before dark can be fairly good. At night, though, these lures don't produce as well as others.

Propellered Plugs

Propellered surface plugs have provided me with exceptionally good fishing at times for both largemouth and smallmouth bass in all areas of the country. These lures, in 2- to 6-inch sizes, are basically shaped like small cigars or torpedoes; they may feature propellerlike blades both fore and aft, or they may have only one blade at the rear. The 3½-inch bait seems best for smallmouths. More wary than their brethren, these fish are less likely to hit very large plugs. Small and large sizes are productive for largemouth bass, and it is likely that the larger plugs account for the larger fish.

The basic technique for retrieving this lure is similar to the surface retrieve of floating/diving minnow plugs, discussed earlier. The retrieve constitutes an erratic jiggling-jerking-pausing motion that represents a struggling or crippled baitfish. As in fishing with floating/diving lures, you need to keep the rod down, utilize the rod tip to effectively impart action, and make your wrists do the work.

You can retrieve a propellered plug either quickly or slowly. I lean to the slow retrieve when prospecting for unseen fish, using a deliberate, convincing action. The propellers will make a loud churning noise with some bubbly effect, and this may aid in attracting the attention of bass in the vicinity. A rapid, ripping retrieve is warranted for schooling largemouths, and the noise thereby created seems to imitate the slashing, surface-breaking feeding activity common to this situation. At this time, if you can keep with the school and if they stay near the surface, you may get a lot of action on a propellered plug. Northern anglers may not witness this type of fish behavior, as it generally occurs (with varying degrees of frequency) in southern impoundments with abundant concentrations of threadfin shad, where bass have gathered to chase and feed on these baitfish. Even in northern reservoirs with a good population of alewives (shad can't tolerate the cold winters in this region), bass seldom exhibit this surface schooling behavior.

Propellered surface plugs can be fished in the spring, summer, and fall, though summer is the most productive period. At that time it's best to fish them for the first few hours of daylight and occasionally in the evening. I've caught most largemouths and smallmouths on these baits in 3 to 10 feet of water. Areas with heavy cover are prime; in northern waters especially, shore-hugging weed lines before a gradual drop-off are quite productive. These lures do not work well in deeper water, other than for school situations. I have occasionally had a stray strike from a largemouth or spotted bass in the open, in water 15 to 18 feet deep, but don't count on these lures to call bass up from unobstructed depths.

You won't find an abundance of these propellered surface plugs in most stores, particularly in northern areas, but that's not because they don't catch bass there. They do—as well as pickerel, pike, inland stripers, and saltwater fish. In fact, one of the two times that I caught two bass at once on the same lure, it was on one of these baits. One fish weighed 2 pounds; the other, 5; and I saw several others come up with those! The top lures in this category—I've used them with excellent results—are the Smithwick Devil's Horse, Heddon's Tiny Torpedo, Luhr Jensen's Woodchopper and Nip-I-Diddee, and Bagley's Bang-O-Lure Spinner.

Buzzbaits

One type of lure that especially appeals to a bass's aggressive nature is a buzzbait. Some form of buzzbait has been around for a long time. The Harrison-Hoge Weedwing has been a popular lure with some fishermen and is foremost among old-time buzzers. But a new variation of it evolved with the modern-day popularity of the spinnerbait.

Two types of buzzbaits are available: those with overhead configuration and those with in-line configuration. The overhead model resembles a spinnerbait in its construction, while the in-line version features a weedless spoon or bucktail behind the blade. The revolving buzz blade itself is of unique design, vaguely resembling an airplane propeller, and having cupped ends that give the lure a clicking, chop-chop-chop sound that accounts for the name of the lure.

The noise of a buzzbait is attractive not only to feeding bass but also to shallow nonfeeding bass. Its effectiveness is not limited to one time of the day, to one season, or to a specific geographic location. It is generally not productive in bright sunlight, but good for warm water and hot weather. Moreover, in my experience, this lure is an excellent producer of big fish, and certainly of larger-than-average bass. They are much more productive for largemouths than smallmouths, but will occasionally catch a pike or a muskie.

A buzzbait is at its very best in areas with thick cover. It is deadly in emergent vegetation that is not too thick to prevent free lure passage and over submerged vegetation that comes fairly close to the surface. It is also highly effective around brush, in timber, and around any fallen wood that might conceal a bass. The closer you can work a buzzbait to such cover, the better.

A well-designed buzzbait is reasonably weed-free and can be fished effectively in all but dense concentrations of matted vegetation. Even in fairly thick areas, with accurate casting and a little side-to-side rod manipulation, you can pick your spots and work a buzzer. In light vegetation, I have little trouble fishing some models of buzzbaits with attached trailer hooks. Mid- to late spring, of course, when lily pads and grass have not fully grown up, is an excellent buzzbait season, provided the water is warm enough.

Bass will hit a buzzer in warm water—and they don't seem to care how warm—but they won't come up for it if the water is too cold. The upper 60s is the lower end of the temperature range for buzzbait action. The summer and early fall are consistently productive buzzbait times, usually in the first few hours of the morning, in late evening, and at night. I often fish a buzzbait in the evening and at night, and it is twice as exciting then as in daytime.

A particularly good feature of buzzbaits is that they are basically shallow-water products. I rarely catch bass on buzzbaits in water more than 12 feet deep, even if the vegetation comes to the surface. Furthermore, if you want to cover a lot of water for feeding fish and all other factors are right, a fast-working buzzbait will allow you to do just that.

When bass strike a buzzer, they usually crush it. There are times, however, when they either miss (this happens a lot at night) or strike short. I think this occurs when the bass are not necessarily feeding, but looking to worry or

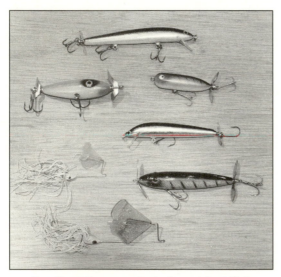

Propellered plugs come in single- and dual-blade versions. At lower left are small and large buzzbaits, each with a plastic triple-wing blade.

stun the intruding creature. A lot of short strikers can be caught if you use a trailer hook. It's rigged the same as a spinnerbait trailer.

There are many buzzbaits now on the market. In selecting, I look for these characteristics: the ability to be worked effectively at a slow retrieval speed, a bullet-shaped leadhead that can cut through the water and ride over the vegetation neatly, heavy-gauge shaft arms, an overall slim profile for lightweight lures to permit easy casting with baitcasting tackle, and large hooks, generally in the 4/0 or 5/0 sizes. Buzzbaits made by Norman Lures, Blue Fox, and Jim Rogers have been good for me. I favor a plastic triple blade for its subtlety rather than a clanking metal blade.

I basically use black, white, and chartreuse, depending on the color and clarity of the water, and the relative brightness of the day. Sometimes color makes no difference. Whatever a buzzbait represents and for whatever reason bass strike it, it certainly brings out the fighting side of the fish.

Stickbaits

Excitement and anticipation are the norms for stickbait-fishing, a form of surface angling that I prefer above all else. When I fish with stickbaits, I don't merely think or hope a fish will strike my stickbait, I fully expect it.

That expectation isn't based on a stickbait's appearance. Resembling a cigar or tapered broom handle, this lure is the antithesis of the natural shape and imitative design of many lures. An artsy paint job may dress up this lure, but essentially it's still a torpedo in costume. Most of the baits in this category are similar in size and conformation to propellered plugs, except that they don't have propellers or a lip. They are retrieved much like, and are fished in the same areas as, propellered plugs and to a lesser extent floating/diving lures. Stickbaits do not have a lip or concave popping mouth, and they are weighted in the tail so the head sits off the water and the tail rests slightly under the surface. Stickbaits are also known as splash baits or jumpers because of their darting activity on the surface and the way they splash and seem to lurch in and out of the water.

Although appearance has little to do with a stickbait's appeal, its activity when retrieved has everything to do with it. A stickbait can't be tossed out with abandon and then cranked back in. The secret of its effectiveness lies in a masterful retrieval technique. Because all of the action must be supplied by the angler, retrieval skill is more important with a stickbait than with any other lure.

Many anglers find stickbait retrieval difficult to master. And maybe that's why stickbaits haven't been more popular. They are effective for largemouth, smallmouth, and spotted bass, and also productive at times for stripers, muskies, pike, pickerel, snook, tarpon, and an assortment of other saltwater fish.

Stickbaits come and go among manufacturers, but the one standard is Heddon's Zara Spook. Cordell's Boy Howdy, Jim Rogers' Walker (formerly known as the Jim Dandy), and the Luhr Jensen Woodwalker are some others of note. The Boy Howdy is fairly popular in southern bass circles; and though it doesn't swim or walk as well as the others, it is a good splash or jumping bait in the hands of an artistic retriever. The Zara Spook, the grandfather of the stickbait family, is widely known and even revered in some circles. The largest and most productive of the Spooks are the ¾- and ⅞-ounce versions, which are 4½ inches long.

Learning to retrieve these lures may come fairly easy to those who are familiar with techniques for fishing floating minnow plugs. The principal stickbait retrieve causes the lure to step from side to side. This side-stepping technique for stickbaits is called *walking the dog*, a term that originated with the Zara Spook.

To retrieve a stickbait, you must begin with the rod tip at a low angle, preferably pointing toward the water. This permits a desirable angle of pull and allows the head of the lure to lurch in and out of the water most effectively. The all-important lure action is achieved through an adroit combination of rod-tip twitching and reel-handle turning. You make a continuous series of short jerks—never long sweeps—that cover roughly a

6- to 10-inch distance, while at the same time advancing your reel handle perhaps half a turn with each rod-tip twitch to take up slack. By slowing the pace, you widen the lure's path of travel; by speeding it up, you narrow it. (*Slow-walking* and *fast-walking* are the terms occasionally applied to these respective speeds of retrieval.) A skilled stickbait angler can just about keep the lure in the same place, making it nod from side to side while barely moving forward.

If you have a long length of line out, you can effectively walk the dog while keeping your rod tip high. But eventually, as you reel in line, the angle of pull will become too great, and if you keep the rod tip up, you'll jump the bait out of the water and reduce its designed action. So as the length of line decreases, lower the rod tip, a move that also puts you in a better position to respond to a strike.

An advanced technique for retrieving stickbaits is *half-stepping*. The peak of stickbait retrieval skill, this technique can drive a fish wild. In the half-step, a stickbait moves repeatedly to one side instead of from side to side. Imagine that you're in a position to work your lure past the entire length of a log. If you walk the plug, it will dart in toward the log, out away from it, back toward it, out again, and so forth. When you half-step it, however, the plug darts away from

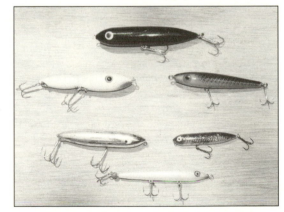

Stickbaits don't have a particularly impressive appearance, yet they can be extremely effective at catching bass, particularly large ones. These lures require a skillful retrieve.

Walking the Dog with a Zara Spook

To be effective, stickbaits must be skillfully retrieved in a side-to-side walking manner. For tantalizing results, try slow-walking a lure from side to side while barely moving it forward. It is especially productive to walk a stickbait along a fallen log and through the lanes in vegetation.

the log at first, then comes in, then comes in again, then in again, and so forth, repeatedly butting its nose up against the object as if it meant to climb it or hide by it.

To half-step a stickbait, first jerk the rod tip to bring the lure in the desired direction. Then barely nudge the rod tip, a maneuver that doesn't advance the bait, but causes it to turn its head just slightly outward. Now jerk the rod tip as before, and the lure will dart back in the same direction it last headed. Nudge the rod once again, then jerk it. Again the plug will head inward. If you use the half-step to work the lure around a bush, along a log, or into a big stump, it can be nearly irresistible to a big bass.

A propensity for attracting big fish, incidentally, is one of the prime virtues of stickbaits. On the average these lures produce bigger fish than most other types, and it seems that the larger the plug, the larger the fish.

One difficulty with these lures is that they are hard to fish from a sitting position, especially from a low seat. Sitting on a pedestal seat or, preferably, standing improves your performance. Also, a relatively limber-tipped rod is better than a stiff-tipped one. I use a 6-foot, fast-taper graphite baitcaster for fishing a Zara Spook, and it's just barely limber enough to work the lure.

Using a snap or a loop knot with a stickbait is especially important. A No. 3 snap (not snap

swivel) works well for many anglers, though I prefer a loop knot to allow the line to go back and forth quickly and unimpeded. Tying a conventional knot snug to the eye of the lure definitely hinders the action. I've found that my baits work best on medium- strength line; stickbaits don't seem to perform as well on 8- or 20-pound line as they do on 12.

Stickbaits can be productive in all cover where you'd expect to find bass. Working specific objects is usually the best bet, but I've had success fishing blindly over thick, submerged grass beds and on weedy points. Stickbaits may be most effective, however, around wood, particularly stumps, logs, and fallen trees, and for calling up bass from submerged timber. They should be worked along the full length of logs and as close as possible to stumps and bushes. When casting to a specific object, land the lure well past your target. Slow-walk the lure up to the object, then fast-walk it past. Vary your retrieval speeds. A moderate retrieve is often best, though there are times and lakes in which bass will not respond to these lures unless you work them slowly and seductively. A quick, constant retrieval speed is generally least effective.

At times, stickbaits will catch fish throughout the day. But when it's windy, you'd be well advised to abandon stickbaits or at least fish with the wind if you must fish them. A light wind that ripples the surface is sometimes desirable, and cloudy, overcast, drizzly conditions are good. Bright sun can be inhibiting. When the angle of the sun is low, retrieve the bait toward the sun, rather than away from it.

As for colors, my greatest success is with clear (transparent) Walkers and frog-, perch-, and shad-colored Zara Spooks. Charlie Campbell of Missouri, perhaps the dean of stickbait practitioners, once offered me this wisdom regarding color selection: "The darker it is, the darker the color of Zara Spook I go to. The biggest fish seem to come on frog or black, and on cloudy days I go to these colors. In clear water I go to a light color. In the early morning I'll use a dark color until the sun comes up, and go dark again in the evening. For suspended bass and in mid-day use, I prefer a light color, and the chrome version has proven to be a good daytime color."

A lot of fish strike or boil after a stickbait and miss it. Many of these fish can be enticed to strike again if you control your reflexes. When

A frog-pattern Zara Spook caught this bass around thick grass and pads. Though stickbaits can call bass up from the depths, they are most effective at coaxing bass out of cover.

fish strike a stickbait, the overanxious angler often rears back to set the hook and jerks the lure away from the fish. Try to hold back your reactions until the fish has clearly taken the lure. If he misses the bait and you don't jerk it away but keep it walking along, there's a good chance he'll hit again. If you jerk the lure clear away from the fish, you probably won't get a second hit. Then it pays to toss out another lure to the same spot immediately. A spinnerbait, floating minnow plug, or worm are good choices.

It's important to cast a stickbait accurately. In thick cover, you'll need to lay the line in such a way that you help direct a clear, desirable path of travel for the lure. If you've been fishing another type of lure for some time and then switch to a stickbait, you'll find it hard to cast precisely in close quarters until you get accustomed to the larger, heavier lure.

Pay close attention to the working action of every stickbait you fish. These are critically balanced lures, and though they may come from the same manufacturer, they are not identical. Some lures may need smaller treble hooks to perform well; with others you may have to fiddle with the line-tie screw to lower the angle. It's not uncommon to find one stickbait that works better than an identical one from the same manufacturer. Out of a dozen, it's a fair bet that one or two will have superior action. They're the ones you don't want to lose, lend to another angler, or leave in an open tackle box until they're warped by the sun. Treasure and protect them.

Specialty Surface Lures

The soft-plastic frog and soft- and hard-plastic lures that are meant to swim through and over heavy cover don't quite fit into any of the previous categories. Examples include Heddon's Moss Boss, Mann's Super Rat, the Harrison-Hoge Super Frog, Renosky's Natural Frog, and Mister Twister's Jerk Rat.

I like these lures most in their natural colors, with white or yellow bellies, and in all-green and all-black versions. These baits are strictly for fishing the vegetation—the thicker the better. Some

Weedless lures are used for fishing the surface in the midst of nearly impenetrable cover. With these lures, it's important to delay setting the hook until you feel the fish has the lure.

of these lures you can swim steadily along, while others, like frogs, you must fish extremely slowly and deliberately, and delay in setting the hook. The delay requires a lot of patience on the angler's part, and in fact with soft-plastic frogs it's best to work two such lures on separate rods at the same time, in different locations, alternating retrieval between them. When a fish hits, you have to delay your hook-setting momentarily until you actually feel the fish with the lure. That's less of a problem with this type of lure than with others because of its soft consistency; since it feels more natural, the bass holds it a bit longer than he might otherwise. When you do set the hook, it must be done hard.

Jigs

As one of many dedicated jig fishermen, I feel compelled to endorse jigs as one type of lure I'd like to have on hand if fishing were my only hope of survival. Jigs have the simplest appearance of all artificial lures, the longest history, and an unparalleled advantage over other lures in their ability to appeal to nearly all species of gamefish. Jigs are particularly good in several

forms and manners of presentation for largemouth and smallmouth bass.

Jigs are an anomaly in that, at rest, they don't particularly resemble fish, insects, or other aquatic forage. Also unusual for a lure type that attracts such a wide range of species, a jig is not the throw-it-out-and-reel-it-back-in-and-watch-the-fish-go-crazy kind of lure. Because they find working these lures hard to master, many anglers do not use jigs, despite their productive potential. Success with jigs is directly proportional to your ability to impart action to the lure, effect a proper style of retrieval, and detect strikes.

Although jigs can be fished in all types of situations and at all depth levels, for bass they are primarily fished on or close to the bottom. Failure to reach and keep these lures on the bottom is the bane of many jiggers.

The simplest way to get a jig to reach the bottom is to open the bail of your spinning reel or depress the freespool mechanism on a baitcasting or spincasting reel and let the lure fall freely until the line goes slack on the surface of the water and no more comes off the spool. If the water is calm and the boat still, you can readily detect when you're on the bottom. If it is somewhat windy or if current is present, you have to watch the departing line carefully to detect the telltale slack and to differentiate between line that is leaving the spool because the lure has not reached bottom and line that is being pulled off by a drifting lure or boat. If you're fishing from a boat, a depthfinder can help you determine when your lure has reached the bottom because you will have some idea of the local depth.

The lighter and thinner the line and the heavier the lure, the easier it is to reach the bottom. The stronger the line, the greater its diameter and the more resistance it offers in the water. A ¼-ounce jig will fall quicker on 8-pound line than it will on 14-pound line, for example. The advantage here (the magnitude of which depends on fishing conditions), is that it is easier to get your lure to the bottom and keep it on the bottom with 8-pound line than it is with 14-pound line.

Once you are on the bottom, of course, you

need to maintain contact with it. Assuming that you have cast your jig out, let it settle to the bottom, and are now retrieving it, you should keep it working in short hops along the bottom as long as the sloping bottom and length of line out enable you to do so. If you're in a boat and drifting, the jig will eventually start sweeping upward and away from you and the bottom as you drift, unless it is very heavy, so you occasionally need to pay out more line until the angle of your line has changed significantly; then reel in and drop the jig back down again. When drifting, face the wind or current, and drop your jig out on the windward side of the boat. If you drop it on the lee side, the boat will soon drift over your line and you'll be in an awkward position for fishing.

Choosing the right weight in a lure is critical to most types of jigging. The ideal is to use a lure large enough to get to the bottom and stay there under normal conditions, but not so large as to put off the bass. Most anglers who fail to reach bottom not only don't use the right retrieval technique or compensate for wind or current, but also use a jig too light to get to the bottom under the conditions they face.

I once sat in an underwater observatory in

An assortment of jigs for largemouth and smallmouth bass.

Silver Springs, Florida, and watched a plastic worm being worked by a renowned tournament bass fisherman. This man was no stranger to jigs and worms, yet in the moderately flowing Silver Springs current, his plastic worm was being worked nearly 5 feet off a sandy bottom in 15 feet of water. Later he was surprised to find that his lure was nowhere near where he thought it was; he was sure that he was working the worm off the bottom. That can happen to anyone, particularly someone not accustomed to fishing in moving water. Whether fishing a worm or jig, you have to take into account the effect of the current. This particular angler needed a much heavier weight to accomplish his normal retrieval under those conditions.

When fishing a jig in current, you should cast upstream or up and across stream. Engage the line pickup system as soon as the lure splashes down, reel up slack, and try to keep the line taut by letting the jig drift or by reeling in slack (whichever is appropriate). You want to achieve a natural drift, not swim the jig up or toward you, and to maintain contact with the lure to feel a strike. Don't cast downstream; there'll be too much slack in the line as the jig sinks and the line is swept away. Fishing directly downstream won't allow you to work the jig naturally or for any distance, and makes it difficult to detect strikes.

At times you won't want to fish a jig on the bottom. When bass are schooling and chasing baitfish, a jig is often a great lure to toss into the fracas. Then you just need to effect a twitch-reel-twitch action, swimming the lure just under the surface. In vertical jigging, however, you may be prospecting for fish at any level between the bottom and the surface, or suspended at a specific level well off the bottom.

If you know what depth to fish, you can let out the desired length of line and commence jigging, never reeling in any line and paying out line only if you begin to drift. Here's one way to know how much line you're letting out: reel the jig up to the rod tip, place the rod tip on the surface, let go of the jig, and raise your rod tip to eye level; then stop the fall of the jig. If eye level is 6 feet above the surface, your jig will now be 6 feet deep. Lower

Jigging a Ledge

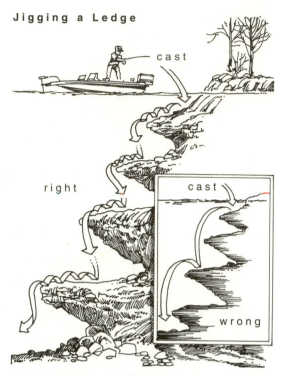

Bass rarely hit a jig when it jumps up, but usually take it on the fall. When fishing a ledge, try making short, slow hops to crawl the jig along; then let it flutter down off the edge. Long sweeps bring the jig out and away, missing most of the best cover.

your rod tip to the surface and repeat the procedure. Now you've let out 12 feet of line. Continue until the desired length is out. With a levelwind reel with a freely revolving line guide, you can measure the amount of line that is let out with each side-to-side movement of the line guide; then multiply that amount by the number of times the guide travels back and forth. If you use a reel that doesn't have such a guide, you can strip line off the spool in 1-foot (or 18-inch) increments until the desired length is out. Another method is to time the lure's descent. A falling rate of 1 foot per second is considered standard and may be accurate for medium-weight jigs, but you should check the lure's rate of fall in a controlled situation first, to ensure accuracy.

For some vertical jigging you may need to let

your lure fall to the bottom and then jig it up toward the surface a foot or two at a time. Bring the lure off the bottom and reel in the slack; then jig it there three or four times before retrieving another few feet of line and jigging the lure again. Repeat that until the lure is near the surface. The only problem here is that you don't usually know exactly how deep a fish is when you do catch one, and you can't just strip out the appropriate length of line and be at the proper level.

Once you learn how to present a jig properly and can fish it where it will be doing the most good, you're two-thirds of the way toward success. The final step is detecting strikes, and here experience has to be your teacher. Describing what a strike on a jig feels like is difficult. To say that there is an almost imperceptible tap or light tick is to be vague yet accurate.

Fish rarely hit a jig lying still, but grab it as it moves upward or falls downward, mostly the latter. As a result, it takes a knack for discerning the irregularity in the lure's movement that indicates a pickup. A sensitive rod with a fast-action tip is a plus for most forms of jigging, particularly when light line is used. Graphite and boron rods are particularly good for jigging. In jigging, unlike other forms of fishing, it is often necessary to keep your rod tip pointed upward to help detect strikes. (In other types of fishing it is best to keep your rod tip low to aid in hook-setting.) Because of that, a few fish will be lost, though well-sharpened hook points can be helpful in this regard. It is also advisable to fish a jig relatively slowly. Beginning jig fishermen in particular have a tendency to rush the retrieval of a jig, swimming the lure too far from the bottom, a method that seldom attracts fish.

The two basic categories of bass jigs are the jig-and-pork combinations, and jigs with either bucktail or soft-plastic bodies. They are fished differently and have distinct characteristics and applications.

Jig-and-Pork

The jig-and-eel, which is basically a jig with a strip of pork rind, is an old-time bait. In recent times, however, jigs with pork have gotten a facelift and are being noticed for their versatility as well as their effectiveness. The new genre of jig-and-pork now includes the venerable and multidimensional jig-and-eel, plug jigs adorned with pork chunks (alias jig-and-chunk, jig-and-pig, jig-and-frog, and so on). Pork strips used with a jig-and-eel are made of pork rind that has been stripped of fat. Chunks have a layer of fat on them, giving them bulk and weight in addition to extra action. These baits are available from several manufacturers and in a variety of forms: with worm trailers, with twin-tail plastic or pork trailers, with pork frog chunks, with pork rind strips, with plastic lizards, with rubber skirts, with bucktails, with or without weedguards, and probably more.

Whereas the jig-and-pork combination of yesteryear was thought of principally as a cold-weather, semideep bait, today it's a hallmark of versatility. Where do you fish the born-again jig-and-pork? Just about anywhere you want. With a weedguard it penetrates the most imposing tan-gles. Without it, try the open-water sanctums. Fish it deep, shallow, or in between.

The most successful application of this jig is probably in bushes, brush, and submerged tree-tops. In the springtime, bass often hold deep in the middle of the shallow bushes along the banks, which may be in 5 to 10 feet of water. Few anglers toss a lure into the heart of these tangles; after all, a plastic worm, tossed from a good distance away, often only scours the periphery of the bush and may not be effective unless bass come out after it. By getting close to the object, you can flip or pitch a jig right into it, work it through and out of the entanglement, and snake out a hooked bass with less difficulty than would otherwise be possible. The same is true for logjams, the roots of stumps or trees, and other thick, hard-to-fish spots. That's why the technique of flipping (discussed later) is so effective, and why these lures are part of that bass-fishing method.

Rocky banks can be another strong jig-and-pork locale, particularly if they have steep drop-

The jig-and-pork combination, used to catch the potbellied largemouth at left, is one of the most effective heavy-cover bass lures. Flooded timber, treetops, and brush are good places to flip or pitch a weedless jig-and-pork.

offs and a lot of craggy, ledgelike formations. Bass seek refuge in the crags and under the ledges but aren't usually susceptible to diving plugs or falling-away plastic worms. Here these jigs can be flipped or cast. In both cases, present the jig close to the edge of the rock and allow it to fall vertically close to the bank. Crawl it off each ledge, over each rock, swimming it along as unobtrusively as possible, and working it under the boat or as deep as your cast will permit. Always work the lure slowly, keeping light tension on the line, and be prepared to set the hook the instant a strike is detected.

Yet another prime application for these jigs is when bass are holding tightly in dense cover, such as milfoil, hyacinths, floating mats of hydrilla and debris, grassy shoals, or bridge pilings and boat docks. The latter can be difficult to fish with conventional casting techniques, but by getting close and quietly (and accurately) flipping a jig around them, you can achieve excellent results. In the thickly matted clusters, you should drop your jig into any visible hole and jig it up and down repeatedly. In some cases you may even have to make your own holes.

The weight of the jig depends primarily on the depth of the water but also wind and current conditions. For deep-bank work, a ¼-ounce jig on light line might do the trick, but it is more likely you'll need a ⁵⁄₁₆-ounce jig, and you may even have to go up to ½ ounce. For flipping the bushes and such, the jig size may vary from ³⁄₁₆ ounce to as much as ¾ ounce. Use a dark color; black, brown, or purple are your best bets. You'll need a weed-guarded bait (the forked style seems best) in the worst areas, so it's a good idea to have some jigs with and some without this feature. For pork chunks, a No. 11 Uncle Josh Pork Rind (which weighs ¼ ounce and measures 1 inch wide x 2½ inches long) is favored, in black or brown. The chunk, incidentally, can be trimmed with a knife to make it fall faster, if that seems desirable. Two-tone pork chunks are also available now. Although I haven't used them, I suspect that in some places, such as murky lakes, a black-and-orange or black- and-chartreuse combo might be the ticket.

To care for your pork baits, keep them in the container and brine they came in. Keep the pork wet while you're fishing or it will dry and shrivel up, becoming useless. One way to keep it wet when it's not being used is to toss the jig-and-pork into your livewell. After you're finished with a pork chunk, put it back in the manufacturer's jar or some other fluid-filled container.

To attach pork to a lure, locate the slit at the head of the bait and insert the hook point through it. To remove the pork, turn it sideways at a right angle to the hook point, grab the hook with one hand and the pork with the other, and carefully exert pressure to pull the pork down while pulling the barb out.

These are, obviously, big baits. Even a ¼-ounce jig with a twin-tail trailer or pork frog chunk weighs close to ½ ounce. What they represent specifically is a bit of a mystery, though crayfish and salamanders seem plausible. Unquestionably, these unobtrusive baits ring the chow bell in both cold and warm water for largemouth and smallmouth bass, and constitute one of the better big-bass baits in use today.

Soft-Plastic and Hair Jigs

Common bass jigs come in various head styles, featuring either bucktail or synthetic-hair bodies, or soft-plastic bodies. Soft-plastic bodies come in many styles. Some are hellgrammite, crayfish, or shad imitations, while others are spider legged or have a grub or tube body. Grubs and tubes are probably the top soft-plastic body forms. Grub bodies are solid and either flat tailed or curl tailed; they are threaded onto the hook from the head and have a tight, well-defined action if rigged properly. Tube jigs are hollow with many squidlike legs in place of a tail; a tube-jig head is worked through the body from back to front with only the line-tie hook exposed, and the jig has an erratic action when fished on a drop-and-fall.

The weight of the jig is the most consequential aspect of fishing it, and the weight may vary from ⅛ ounce to ½ ounce. Your choice should be determined by water depth and clarity, wind con-

Bruce Holt

*Rock shorelines are good places for working light
hair- or grub-style jigs on spinning tackle.*

ing. Casts are easier with spinning tackle because the bail remains open and the lure falls relatively straight. With baitcasting gear, it's usually necessary to pay out line by hand after the cast to get the jig to fall straight.

A flat-tail grub should be placed on the shank of the jig in such a way that its tail rides flat, or horizontal, to achieve a good side-to-side falling action. For rigging a curl tail, use the side seam as a guideline and rig the bait so that the curl tail rides up vertically in the same direction as the hook. The length of these flat-tail or curl-tail soft plastics varies from $1\frac{1}{2}$ to 3 inches. There are many successful colors for soft-plastic bodies. Gray (or smoke), green, black, purple, white, and chartreuse are traditional; but pumpkinseed, june bug, and assorted combinations are popular now. For hair bodies, the best colors are black, brown, yellow, and white.

These jigs are good for all bass, but they are particularly successful on smallmouths, which generally prefer a more diminutive meal. These lures vaguely resemble crayfish and are most effectively fished in rocky areas, along rocky bluffs and drop-offs, ledges, sunken islands, shoals, points, and the like—typical smallmouth habitat.

To work hair-bodied and grub jigs, you must first let them settle to the bottom wherever you've cast. When fishing a moderately sloping shoreline or point, you should slowly pull the lure a little bit off the bottom, let it settle down while you maintain contact with it, take up the slack, and then repeat the procedure. When working a ledge or a sharply sloping shoreline, slowly pull the lure over the structure until it begins to fall; let it settle, and then repeat. Don't hop the jig up quickly here, as it will fall out and away from the bottom, most likely missing a good deal of the important terrain. A good technique with grubs is to make them jump quickly off the bottom rather than take short hops. You can also swim a grub on the edges of cover by reeling it slowly across the bottom and giving it occasional darting movements with manipulation of your rod tip. Most of your jigging strikes will come as the bait falls back down, so be alert for a strike then, and keep both a good feel and

ditions, and your lure. This may sound complicated, but it really isn't.

Use the lightest jig that you can under the circumstances. You don't want a jig to sink too fast, which would appear unnatural, yet you need the appropriate size to attain necessary depth. When fishing in a lake with current or in flowing water like a stream or river, you'll need to use a heavier jig than you would in still water. Another influential factor is wind. The harder the wind blows, the more difficult it is for the unanchored fisherman to hold bottom with a light jig. Jigging depth is also influenced by the size of your line. The heavier the line, the greater its diameter and the more drag it has in the water; to achieve depth, it therefore requires a heavier jig, which will fall too fast. Then, too, the clearer and shallower the water, the more important it is to use light jigs for less obtrusive presentations. This all adds up to interpreting the effects of the elements and selecting the best lure size for the conditions.

Light hair jigs, grubs, and tube jigs are usually better fished with spinning tackle than baitcast-

an eye on your line to detect it. Tube jigs are better fished in a hopping motion than a crawling one. Hop a tube jig off the bottom and let it flutter back. These lures spiral downward rather than dive, and they're often used on lighter jig heads (like ¹⁄₁₆ ounce) than other lures, as well as on light or ultralight spinning gear, which has led some to refer to their use as "finesse" fishing.

Spoons

Jigging Spoons

There are a number of spoons that can be used in open, deep-water fishing situations for large-mouth bass. Usually metal or lead, and slab sided, they are white, yellow, silver, or gold in color. Some newer ones, made by Tom Mann's Fish World, sport photofinishes. Jigging spoons vary from ¼ ounce to ½ ounce in weight and are basically used only for vertical jigging in situations where bass may be schooled or suspended. One of the best examples of this type of lure is the Hopkins Spoon, which was originally a salt-water-striped-bass and bluefish catcher before being used inland in smaller sizes for black bass and now freshwater stripers.

In vertical jigging you may look for suspended bass near specific submerged structures, such as rock walls, roadbeds, islands or humps, and even timber. To use these jigs, lower them either to the bottom or a specific depth, jerk your rod up, and let the lure flutter down. Repeat this procedure for a while at the same depth. The lure should rise a foot to a foot-and-a-half with each upward motion, then be allowed to sink back slowly as you keep gentle contact with it. Most strikes come on the fall back. Super lines are especially good for this fishing because of their high sensitivity.

Weedless Spoons

These lures are quite unlike jigging spoons and are used in a totally different manner. Weedless spoons are used for fishing in and around thick vegetation, such as lily pads, bulrushes, saw grass, and milfoil. They are generally not 100-percent

A weedless spoon (top) and a weedless spoon with spinner (bottom) are good for working thick vegetation.

snag-free, but they will usually get through most vegetation with the aid of a wire hook guard. Examples of good lures in this category are the perennially favorite Johnson Silver Minnow and the weedless Dardevle. These lures are best used with ripple pork rind, soft-plastic curl tail, or rubber-skirt trailer to spice up their swimming action, and some anglers like to garnish them with a pork chunk. Good colors are silver, gold, black, chartreuse, and frog green; the best sizes are ¼ ounce and ½ ounce, although in some cases you might try the ¾-ounce model.

The basic technique for fishing a weedless spoon is to cast it far back into the vegetation and work the lure over and through it, allowing it to ease into and flutter down every little opening possible. In working thick lily pads, for example, you would cast back into the pads and slowly reel the lure up to an opening, let it slither off a pad into a pocket, and ever so slowly bring it through that pocket and then over or through more pads to the next pocket. Fishing grass and pads is discussed later, but the important point to realize about weedless spoons is that you must fish them slowly and pick your way through the vegetation. Also, as with some other lures already described, you have to delay a moment in setting the hook when a fish strikes. Numerous missed strikes or "boils" by bass on these lures are due to the nature of the cover, so you must be sure your lure's been taken before you try to hook a fish.

A sometimes useful modification of this type of lure is the placement of a spinner blade in front, so that a small silver or gold blade revolves around a short wire shaft ahead of the basic lure. This lure is typified by a longtime successful bass catcher, Hildebrandt's Snagless Sally. This combination gives an added flash and attraction to the bait that will bring it to the attention of reluctant bass when the lure appears in holes or openings of thick grass or lily-pad clusters.

Spinners

Spinners were more prominent on the bass scene many decades ago and are not usually thought of as a bass lure by many anglers these days, particularly those who chase largemouths exclusively or who never fish streams. Spinners as a whole, however, are one of the most popular lures in the world and in North America. Anglers currently use spinners to catch stream trout, pickerel, trout in lakes and ponds, panfish, muskies, walleyes, and smallmouth and largemouth bass. Plenty of other species also succumb to spinners every year under all kinds of circumstances. In this era of imitating prey, spinners

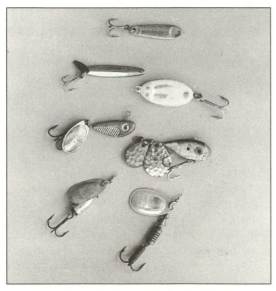

Jigging spoons (top three), tailspinners (middle two), and spinners (bottom two).

continue to be effective even though they do not look anything like a fish. But in action, their wobbly flashy motion strongly suggests bait movement and offers an irresistible temptation to many fish. Though spinners are generally of minor value in largemouth-bass fishing, they are quite valuable as stream-smallmouth lures and are frequently successful for shallow-water, early-season smallmouth fishing in lakes.

Spinners come in many sizes and colors, and with various blade configurations. They feature a freely rotating blade (or blades), mounted on a single, in-line shaft. Behind the blades are beads or bodies of lead or metal. Feather or hair skirts or plastic tubing may be added to increase their appeal. They are available in weights from $\frac{1}{32}$ ounce to several ounces; with single, double, and treble hooks; with blade lengths from $\frac{1}{2}$ inch to several inches; and with assorted tail material. The $\frac{1}{16}$-, $\frac{3}{8}$-, and $\frac{1}{4}$-ounce sizes are best for bass fishing.

The blade design controls the action and the angle of blade revolution. The lighter the blade, the faster the spin, which is why round, Colorado-blade spinners are so popular. They are light, spin slowly, and work far from the shaft. The actual spinner blade is available in many colors, but the blade's color is not nearly as important as its visibility under fishing conditions. A good reflective quality is desired. Spinners also give some vibration when retrieved, a fact that is important to the fish and that probably accounts for the success of spinners when used at night and in turbid water.

Factors like blade design, weight, and surface area are related to how the lure is retrieved and how it casts. Like spoons, spinners are most commonly used with treble hooks, though single hooks are favored by many and are more desirable in some situations, particularly when a single-hook-only lure is required. A favorite single-blade spinner for bait fishermen is the so-called *june bug spinner*, which features a long-shank hook and a single rotating blade, with beads along the shaft. Variations of it, also known as *weight-forward spinners*, are popular for smallmouth-bass (and walleye) fishing on northern lakes. A Mepps Lusox, Earie Dearie, or similar spinner is garnished with a live worm and drifted across rocky reefs.

In moving water, you generally don't fish a spinner downstream, but cast it upstream at a quartering angle (ten o'clock viewed from right, two o'clock viewed from left). The lure is tumbled by the swift water and also reeled forward at the same time. Fish it as slowly as you can under the circumstances; you should be able to feel the blade revolve with a sensitive rod. The depth of retrieve can be altered by raising or lowering the rod or by changing the speed of retrieval. Improper use may be the reason that spinners often hang up. In streams it's important to get the lure working the moment it hits the water. Hesitation often means hung spinners, particularly when casting across stream in a fast flow.

One of the best times to fish spinners for smallmouths in lakes is just before spawning (provided the season is open, which it is not in some northern waters) and in the fall, when bass are just off rocky shorelines in 5 to 8 feet of water. You can cast parallel to the bank and allow the lure to sink to the bottom; then reel it in very slowly, just enough to rotate the blade and keep the lure swimming over the bottom. You also might be able to catch these bass at the same times by using jigs or crankbaits, but spinners may be as or more effective, owing to their slow retrieval rate and small, flashy appearance.

Spinners are best used with spinning tackle, though the larger sizes can be cast and fished adequately with baitcasting gear. For stream-smallmouth fishing, though, light tackle, light line, and small spinners are the rule. Good spinners for bass include Sheldon's Mepps, the Blue Fox Vibrax, the Harrison-Hoge Panther Martin, the Abu Reflex, and the C. P. Swing.

Tailspinners

This type of lure is totally different from a spinner and perhaps doesn't even belong in this category. Nonetheless, I mention it here because the lure is known to all bass fishermen by the designation "tailspinner." A tailspinner is nothing more than a small lead-bodied lure with a treble hook under its belly and a revolving spinner blade at its tail. Typical of these lures are Mann's Little George, Cordell's Gay Blade, and Gapen's Slip (which performs the same functions but does not feature a spinner blade).

Tailspinners are at their best in schooling situations, when largemouths are near the surface and feeding frenziedly. These lures are aerodynamically shaped and can be cast a country mile, particularly with spinning gear and light to medium line. They are then worked in a quick pump-and-go style, just under the surface. Tailspinners can also be fished deep, in vertical jigging style, for suspended bass in deep water near some particular structure, or they can be hopped off the bottom in fishing submerged islands, rocky points, and such. Effective colors are white, silver, and gray.

Plastic Worms

Plastic worms are unquestionably the most productive bass lure. My guess is that more worms are sold each year than all other bass lures combined. What a worm represents is more of a mystery than why it is successful. Earthworms are not common to lakes and ponds, certainly not in significant numbers nor at other times than after heavy rains or flooding. They could represent leeches, which are present in many bass waters. Snakes do populate many areas, but I have worm-caught loads of bass in lakes where I've never seen a water snake. And though eels can be found seasonally in some lakes, that does not explain the appeal of worms at other times and in locations devoid of eels.

Not questionable, though, is why a worm catches bass. It looks like a fairly substantial morsel; it must have a realistic feel to a bass when inhaled; it has good action and moves enticingly and relatively naturally through cover; and can be worked effectively down at the bottom and in protected hideaways. Moreover, one of the pleasant effects of successful worm-fishing is a sense of accomplishment.

Some lures require little more than accurate casting and routine retrieval to be effective, particularly when bass are active. But a worm must be worked with your brain as well as your wrists; how you give it action, detect strikes, and react reflexively are major factors in its effectiveness.

Although it seems intricate, worm-fishing is really not too difficult. It does take time, practice, and patience, however, to become successful. Beginning worm fishermen often become discouraged by failure to get strikes, by missing a fish, or by setting the hook into objects that they thought were fish but weren't. Don't be discouraged. Even experienced worm anglers miss strikes or set the hook falsely. Beginners also have a tendency to give up on the worm and fall back on previously successful techniques without using the worm enough. I suggest that learners go out bass fishing a few times with nothing but worms. Don't bring any other lures or bait, just a supply of different-color worms, hooks, and sinkers. By forcing yourself to stick with it, you'll get the experience—and the fish.

Sizes, Colors, Shapes, and Styles

There are hard worms and soft worms, floaters and sinkers, straight tails and curl tails. They come in a whole spectrum of colors and may sport light tails, light heads, light bellies, stripes, and polka dots. They are made in small, medium, large, and huge sizes. Some are scented, some are oiled, some come prerigged. In short, there is a veritable smorgasbord of plastic worms.

The most important features of a worm, in descending order, are: softness, buoyancy, size, color, shape and tail design, and scent.

Softness. Softness is vital. A soft worm feels lifelike to a fish when he grabs it, and it aids the angler in setting the hook. Until the early 70s, before worm-fishing became as entrenched as it now is, most worms were tough. In fact, they were rubber, not plastic. Today, all worms are plastic,

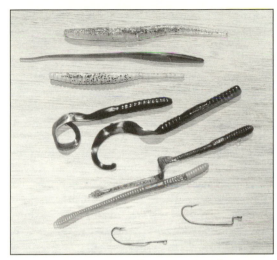

Plastic worms come in all sizes, shapes, and colors. The top three lures are jerk worms, followed by curl-tail worms and a conventional straight plastic worm.

and advances in the chemical composition of certain plasticizing agents allow for manufacturing control over the toughness of a worm.

A worm that is too soft is also fragile; it will tear when it comes into contact with objects and will barely hold a hook. A worm that is too hard feels unnatural and offers more resistance to hook-point penetration, which can be crucial in the timing of hook-setting. Most manufacturers try to make worms tough enough to withstand reasonable use but soft enough to aid fish catching, although for Carolina rigging, which will be discussed shortly, worms should be a little tougher than usual.

Buoyancy. Worms should have a high degree of buoyancy. The better worms are light enough to float on the surface of the water without a hook. Some will even float with a 1/0 or 2/0 hook in them, which is useful for fishing a completely unweighted worm on the surface over thick cover.

When a worm that floats rests on the bottom, its tail section rides up, accentuating both the behavior of the worm when it is moved and its appearance when stationary. Some specialty worms, such as the very large and prerigged versions, are not meant to float and understandably do not.

Size. The size of worm to use varies with the fishing conditions and the size of the bass you expect to take in any particular water. Small bass generally disdain the largest worms. However, I've caught big bass on small worms and small bass (including some that were shorter than the length of the worm) on big worms.

But if you are expressly interested in a trophy-size lunker, then you should fish with nothing less than a 7-inch worm. In Florida, where 10-pound bass lurk in many bodies of water, an 8- to 12-inch worm is your best bet. In northern states, where bass weighing more than 6 pounds are caught infrequently, a 7- to 8-inch worm is as large as you need.

Most bass fishing is done with 6-inch worms. All but the largest bass are good candidates for this bait, and in waters that are heavily fished, this size worm is relatively unobtrusive and unalarming to fish that are probably well conditioned to the presence of artificial baits.

In some locations, such as heavily fished, clear-water lakes, it's necessary to use 4- and 5-inch worms. On the other hand, if you have been catching small bass at a particular lake with a small worm, you might increase the size of your worm to appeal to larger fish.

Color. I'm not inclined to recommend one color strongly over another, though I will note that dark-colored worms are far more popular and successful than light ones. I've been partial to black and purple worms, though I carry and use red, blue, grape, and motor oil as well, plus the two-tone shad colors and metal-flecked varieties. Many newer combination colors, like fire and ice, june bug, tequila, electric blue, and red shad are also good.

Water color and visibility play a part in the selection of worm color. At times one color outperforms another because it stands out better in a certain type of water; at other times, several colors are equally productive. More important

than color, perhaps, are having confidence in your lure, fishing in the right places, and utilizing proper technique.

I do a fair amount of fishing with fire-tail worms and recommend them, especially when it's slow going. Fire-tail worms are simply those with a light color blended into the tail section. I particularly like black, grape, blue, and purple worms with either a light pink or lime green tail. Unfortunately, fire-tail worms are even more attractive than one-color worms to other species, including pickerel, bluegill, and rock bass. And they can be a nuisance.

Shape and tail design. One feature of a plastic worm that has a debatable effect on success is its appearance in terms of shape and tail design. The basic body shape of most worms is round, with a moderate taper from head to tail. Some worms are flat on one side, which I do not find as appealing as fully round models and which do not seem to have as good an action or object resistance.

Most worms have circularly molded indentations along their length, much like an earthworm, but a few are completely smooth. I don't believe it makes much difference to a bass or to the action of the worm whether it is smooth or slightly rippled, though there are few of the former available any longer. Some years ago, however, a company marketed worms with raised rings that trapped air between them; air bubbles were released as the worm was worked. These worms did not appeal to bass any more than the standard versions and had a tendency to grab onto grass, pads, rocks, and limbs more so than other worms. This hampered their action and restricted their ability to move freely over objects. A fad for a while, that product eventually faded into oblivion, but variations of it reappear from time to time.

Many worms come with straight tails, and an equal or greater number sport some type of curl tail. A few have beaver or paddle tails. The beaver-tail models tend to be bulkier than other worms, and you have to get used to the different feel of fishing them. They produce more action and vibration than a straight-tail worm, but I haven't had comparable success with them. They make a nice trailer behind a jig, though, especially when you're flipping.

Curl-tail worms include those with a simple J-bend at the end as well as those with opposite-curl features either at the end or two-thirds of the way through the body. I'm not convinced that they are any more productive than straight-tail models, but the curls do produce a nice swimming action with only the slightest assistance from the angler. Straight-tail worms are good products, however, and I use them regularly.

It is worthwhile to experiment with different designs, just as it is to carry an assortment of different-size and -color worms in your tackle box. Eventually you'll place most of your confidence in one particular design and use it for almost all worm-fishing.

Scent and flavor. Scent and flavor are also a matter of personal preference. Some worms are scented; most are just oiled; some are made from processed natural materials. I have yet to notice a decidedly greater productivity with any worm that came from the manufacturer prescented or -lubricated, either with anise oil or some similar licoricelike essence, or with one of the supposedly fish-attracting potions. These substances may help mask human odors imparted to the soft-plastic worms through hand contact, but it's hard to say that they, themselves, contribute to attracting fish. I'm not convinced that they do. (They help keep the worms soft though.) Processed-bait worms may be held in the fish's mouth a little longer than other worms, giving you a little more time to detect a strike and set the hook. You'll have to be the judge of that.

Some worms are better known by flavors.

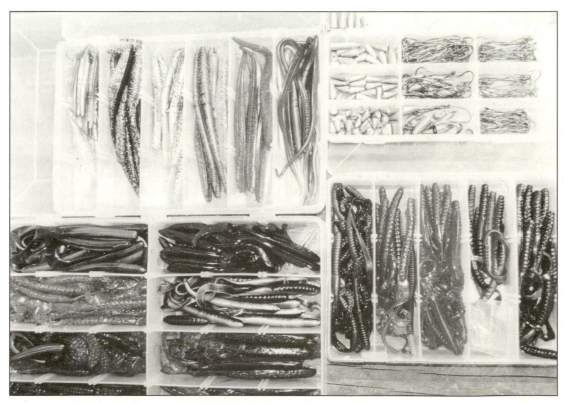

Bass fishermen have plenty to choose from in plastic-worm fishing.

Again, there is nothing to the flavor gimmick other than the fact that the impregnated flavor helps mask the human odors. Salt worms, which are impregnated with salt (put the worm in your mouth and you can taste it), are popular in some areas and are thought to induce bass to retain them longer than they might otherwise, but I think this advantage is merely psychological.

Use a soft, floating worm in the appropriate size and color and fish it well. That's what's most important for successful worm-fishing.

Rigging a Worm

The Texas rig has been the standard rigging method since suppliers stopped making worms out of hard rubber in favor of soft plastic. It can be used in almost any bass habitat, though it has limited value in really deep water and with heavy weights.

The Texas rig incorporates nothing more than a worm, slip sinker, and hook, with the hook point turned back and embedded in the neck area of the worm so that it is essentially snag-free. To accomplish this, put a cone-shaped slip sinker onto your line, narrow end first; then tie the line to your hook. Take the point of the hook and embed it into the center of the head of the worm up past the barb; then bring the point out the side of the worm. Pull the shank of the hook through this passage and rotate it 180 degrees. Bring the shank all the way out until the eye of the hook is secured in the worm head. Slide the point into the body of the worm so that it is firmly embedded and does not pierce the body. Do not curl or rotate the worm, but be sure that the hook and worm are aligned and that the worm is straight and at full length, not bunched up.

The slip sinker will slide freely on this rig, but there are times, such as when you are fishing in thick cover, when it is advantageous to prevent the sinker from sliding freely and getting hung up. To do that, jam one end of a toothpick in the head of a sinker as far as it will go, and then break it off. Jam the other end into the back of the cone, and break it off.

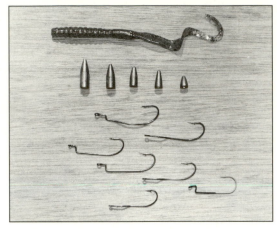

Ingredients for a Texas rig. The sinkers are all of the free-sliding slip variety. The hooks shown (top to bottom) are a single 5/0, a single 4/0, four different styles of 3/0, and a single 2/0.

The biggest problem with the Texas rig is that the worm tends to curl or bunch up. That causes the worm to spin when it is retrieved, producing an unnatural, unappealing action and contributing to line twist.

The theory behind the unpegged Texas rig is that when a bass grabs the worm, he does not feel the hook and does not detect the weight, which slides up the line. Theoretically this gives the angler an extra moment in which to react and set the hook. When he does set the hook, it should freely pierce the worm, one of the reasons why the worm should be relatively soft.

The size of slip sinker (which is also called a *worm weight*) used varies from $1/16$ ounce to $1/2$ ounce and depends on water depth, wind conditions, and the general activity of the fish. They are still primarily lead, but that could change in the future to brass or stainless steel alloys. Some anglers like painted sinkers, but unpainted weights are overwhelmingly popular.

A plastic worm is meant to be fished slowly and hopped or crawled along in a natural, unalarming fashion. The slip sinker plays a vital role in the worm's performance, depending on how the angler actually accomplishes his retrieve.

The lighter your sinker weight, the more likely

you are to have success. Sinker weight must be matched to the terrain and fishing conditions, but using the lightest sinker you can while still fishing correctly under those conditions, brings the best results.

The heavier the sinker, the larger it is and the more detectable it may be to a bass. This is particularly true when fishing pressure is intense or when the bass are sluggish. Also, the worm is moved more naturally with a light sinker than with a heavy one, which makes the worm's action more dramatic and pronounced. A worm with a light weight swims more convincingly than one with a heavy sinker. Light weights don't hang up as much as heavy ones, and they aid in detecting strikes. For these reasons, I prefer to use the lightest slip sinker possible for the conditions.

I use a 1/8-ounce slip sinker most often, with 3/16-ounce running a close second. I will go down or up in size if necessary, usually to no more than 5/16 ounce, unless flipping a worm, when I may go to a 1/2-ounce sinker. Sometimes, strong winds or current make worm-fishing difficult, and you have to use a larger-than-customary weight to gain casting accuracy and to maintain a feel for the bottom. In shallow water you can usually get away with a light sinker, but as you fish deep, you may need to increase the weight of the sinker. You can cast small worms and light weights more effectively with spinning tackle than you can with baitcasting equipment. Light line is conducive to light sinker use, since it does not offer as much resistance as the thicker, heavier line.

Hooks vary from 1/0 to 6/0, depending on the length of the worm. There's a general guideline for their use: 1/0 or 2/0 with 4- to 6-inch worms, 3/0 with 6-inchers, 4/0 with 7-inchers, 5/0 with 8-inchers, and 6/0 with larger worms.

If the size of the hook seems large to you, rest assured that it isn't. Big, strong hooks will stand up better under the force of hook-setting and the strain of very large bass. It doesn't require a big hook to land a bigmouth bass; after all, plenty of fish, including large trout and salmon, are routinely landed on extremely small hooks. But in worm-fishing, a large hook with a large bite is needed to keep the worm from balling up and impeding hooking. A bass usually has its mouth closed, with the worm inside, when you set the hook. The force of that setting brings the barb forward, pushing the head of the worm down the shank, where it balls up. If the hook is small, the worm balls up so much that it can misdirect the point, slowing hook penetration. As a result, the angler misses the fish and retrieves a fully balled-up worm, with a hook point that has barely pierced its body. Large hooks minimize this problem.

A number of worm hook styles are popular with fishermen, and there is a dizzying array to select from now. I particularly like a keel, or offset, hook shank with a wide, or so-called *southern,* sproat. The offset shank retains the worm pretty well, and the wide gap gives plenty of room for hooking. You might try experimenting with the various hooks that turn when you strike a fish, and see if you have a style preference. Hooks with outside edge barbs are showing up, and you should give those a try. Above all, make sure your hook point is as sharp as it possibly can be. That is the single most important factor in a plastic-worm hook.

The Texas rig may be the most popular plastic-worm rigging method, but it is not the only one. The Carolina rig, especially good for deep-water bottom-fishing, features a floating worm that rises up unweighted. This rig sports a medium-weight sinker, followed by a barrel swivel, an 18- to 36-inch leader, and a hooked worm. The hook is generally no larger than size 1/0 (a small hook gives greater buoyancy to the worm) and is usually exposed, though it can be embedded in the worm Texas-rig style when there are obstructions present. The sinker, which can be barrel-, egg-, or cone-shaped, weighs 3/4 ounce to 1 ounce and slides freely to the swivel, so a fish can take the worm and move off without feeling resistance. The length of line between barrel and worm is somewhat arbitrary; 18 to 24 inches is the norm, but some anglers like to go with as little as 8 inches for swimming the worm through weed beds.

Another variation on this rigging method

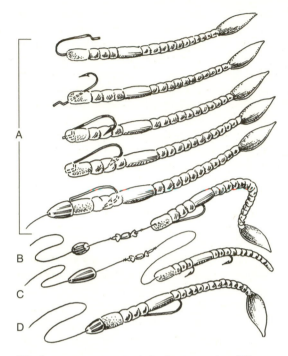

Plastic worms are easy to rig in the conventional Texas style (A), with the hook point buried in the body of the worm. With a Carolina rig (B) the hook may be buried if there are obstructions in the water, or slightly exposed if not, as in the do-nothing rig (C). With careful insertion, a hook can be threaded farther into the plastic worm (D) to bury the point in the middle.

that is useful for unobstructed open-water fishing is the so-called *do-nothing rig*. It features a heavy (½- to 1½-ounce) sliding slip sinker ahead of a barrel swivel, 3 to 5 feet of line between the swivel and worm, two panfish-size hooks, and a short, straight worm. The hooks are rigged in tandem and are exposed; the worm is roughly 4 inches long. Some anglers use a small plastic bead between the sinker and swivel to prevent knot abrasion. A little tough to cast, this rig is fished in a slow, reel-cranking manner without any special rod or retrieval action. Despite its name, it does enough to interest reluctant, bottom-dwelling bass.

The manner of hooking worms is frequently subject to experimentation. Setting the hook into the bony jaw of a bass is often hard, especially if the hook point must first pierce the worm body; that's one reason why supersoft worms are preferred by Texas-rig users. Hooking variations, therefore, are usually directed at improving hooking efficiency.

Some anglers put the hook through the head and leave the point exposed for fishing on the surface (without a weight), or they hook it in the collar or near the midsection for weightless, extremely slow, free-swimming simulation. A variation on the latter, with Texas-style hooking, is to thread the hook from the top of the worm to down near the midsection, then bring the point out and embed it in the worm. It's fished without a weight and has been called a spawning rig for bedding bass, which normally take a worm in the middle and swim off to remove it from the nest area.

Multiple hooking is another possibility, especially for short-striking fish. You can rig small worms with one hook toward the rear by using a long, thin sewing needle to bring the line through the body, then tying it to the hook and inserting the shank of the hook in the worm, and either leaving the hook exposed or embedding it to be weedless. A two-hook rig, in tandem with snelled hooks, is a little tougher to execute, but many anglers prefer it. Such a rig enables anglers to catch bass whether they strike the head or the tail of the worm.

Worms can also be attached to jig hooks; many anglers have summer-bass success with 4-inch worms behind small jigs, fished on light line.

Where and When to Fish a Plastic Worm

I generally don't use a worm much in the spring, when the water is cool and bass are energetic. In the spring, bass are usually responsive to spinnerbaits and crankbaits, which can be worked quite fast. When you want to cover a lot of territory fairly rapidly, a worm is not the best bait to use. If, however, in doing this, you catch a couple of fish in one area, it may pay to switch to a worm in order to work that area more thoroughly and more productively.

Summer is traditionally the best time to fish a worm. When the bass are well secured in or near some type of cover, you need a worm to work that cover extensively. This is one of the true benefits of worm-fishing: you cover the area well, and you fish the bottom, where the bass are. Though swimming a worm over cover may at times have merit, primarily you fish it on the bottom.

A plastic worm rigged in weedless fashion is at its best when used around typical bass-holding objects like stumps, fallen trees, grass, pads, hyacinths, hydrilla, docks, milfoil, and the like. When bass have left the shallows of the reservoirs for the *breaklines* (distinct drop-offs to deeper water), worms are effective.

When making a cast to a particular object, such as a stump, for example, cast beyond and to one side of that stump (such as the shaded side)

initially, working the worm slowly up alongside and then past the stump. Baitcasters should take care to cast beyond where they want to fish a worm, as the worm does not drop straight downward, but usually falls on an angle toward the caster due to tension on the line. With a spinning reel, keep the bail open to allow the worm to fall relatively straight down when it hits the water.

Sometimes a worm can be used to catch a bass that has missed another lure. For example, when a bass strikes but does not get hooked on a spinnerbait, surface lure, or shallow-running plug, he may not hit the same lure again if you throw it back. But there is a good chance that he'll hit the less obtrusive worm if you cast it out in that area quickly afterward.

Bass are receptive to worms in relatively warm water because the worms are soft and feel natural. In really cold water, I think plastic worms

Stumps, brush, and various forms of cover are good places for a plastic worm. This bass, which weighed nearly 12 pounds, was caught by the author on an 8-inch worm from one of the tree stumps in the background.

harden and thus are more quickly rejected by bass. In temperatures below 55 or so, worms don't seem to appeal to bass; from 55 to the mid 60s, they have some appeal; from the mid 60s on up, they are at their best. I have caught bass on worms in water temperature as low as 50 and as high as 92.

Worms work well at any time of the day, particularly during the summer, and at night. I don't often use a worm early in the morning even though it can be effective then. At that time bass are more likely to be on the move and feeding, and other lures can be as or more effective before the sun rises and bright light forces the bass to seek deep shelter or cover.

Retrieval Techniques

The two most difficult things for a beginning worm fisherman to master are how to retrieve the worm most effectively and how to detect strikes. Mastering hook-setting rates a distant third in difficulty. These are also the three most basic components of worm-fishing techniques.

The strike of a bass on a worm has often been said to feel like a double tapping at the end of the line. This is so, and I believe that the first tap is what you detect when the bass makes the motion to inhale it, and the second is what you detect as it enters the fish's mouth. If you feel a third tap, the bass is probably expelling it.

Differentiating a strike from contact with underwater objects is the most difficult aspect of worm-fishing, and there's no shortcut to learning it. An ability to detect strikes and learn the feel of a worm comes through experience. The more you fish with a worm, the quicker you'll develop this feel.

One trick I've suggested to beginning worm fishermen is to practice in their backyard or in shallow water where they can see the worm. Drag it over rocks and logs and tree limbs. Crawl it on gravel surfaces. Watch it work in a clear pool. Simulate fishing conditions.

Another key to detecting strikes is to watch your line. In the most radical instances, an eager bass may pick up a worm and immediately run

with it, in which case your line noticeably moves off to the side or away. Sometimes you'll see the line move like this before you feel the strike. Usually, however, there is a barely perceptible flickering of the line, particularly the section nearest to the water, which is a result of the bass inhaling the worm and drawing it (and the line) toward him. In time, you'll come to see and feel the strike at the same instant.

To retrieve a plastic worm, begin with your rod butt and arms close to your body, with the rod held perpendicular to you and parallel to the water. Raise the rod from this position (we'll call it 9 o'clock) upward, extending it between a 45- and 60-degree angle (moving it from 9 o'clock to 10:30 or 11). As you raise the rod, the worm is lifted up off the bottom and swims forward, falling to a new position. Make this motion slowly, so the worm does not hop too far off the bottom and swim too fast. When your rod reaches that upward position, drop it back to its original position while at the same time retrieving slack line. Keep your motions slow. When you encounter some resistance, as you would when crawling it over a log or through a bush, first gently try to work the worm along; if that fails, try to hop the worm along with short flicks of the rod tip.

Sometimes the slip sinker gets hung up under rocks, and if you jiggle your line, the sinker falls back and becomes free. Other times, the sinker will fall over a limb and slide down the line while the worm stays back behind the limb, making detection and retrieval difficult. You can avoid that by pegging the slip sinker with a toothpick and breaking it off, thus preventing the sinker from sliding up the line. The sinker remains directly in front of the worm.

Pegging a worm is useful for fishing brushy areas, lily pads, hyacinths, moss, and grass as well as amidst stumps and trees. I seldom fish an unpegged worm in such areas and find that this modification makes retrieval and strike detection easier. It goes against the theory of having a freely sliding slip sinker so a fish can pick up the lure and run off with it without detecting the weight, but any negative effect is minimized by a quick hook-setting reaction, a sensitive rod, and a sensitive line, all of which help you detect strikes more readily.

However you develop your style of retrieval, it is important to remember that the worm should be on the bottom, or right near it, at all times. Sometimes wind and current work to hamper bottom-scratching, and you should be aware of that.

The time to set the hook on a bass is usually as soon as you can after detecting a strike. Remember that since the worm is rigged weedless with the hook embedded in it, you can't simply rear back when you feel a strike, as you might when fishing a lure with exposed hooks.

Here's how to set the hook when using a plastic worm: as soon as you detect a strike, lower the rod tip, extend it out, and point it toward the fish. (This momentarily gives the bass slack line and helps keep it unsuspecting.) Quickly reel up the slack, and as the line draws tight, set the hook. Continue to reel in line to counteract the effect of stretch and to ensure that no slack is present. When I set the hook, I bring the rod butt up into my chest, not high over my head, and I constantly maintain pressure on the fish. The whole maneuver is accomplished in an instant and appears to be one fluid motion.

Remember that removing slack line is critical, since your hook must penetrate not only the balled-up worm, but the cartilaginous mouth of the fish as well. Take notice of where your worm-caught bass are hooked, and you'll find that many are hooked in the upper part of the inside of the mouth, near the lips, and that many are hooked on the sides of the mouth, again near the lips. In some cases, when an eager bass has quickly swallowed the worm, he will be stomach-hooked. But most times the fish is hooked near the edge of the mouth, ample evidence that you barely got him and that in another fraction of a second or with a little hesitation, tension on the line, or too much slack, you'd have missed the fish.

There are some useful variations to the standard worm-fishing technique I've detailed here, and you may want to try them if conditions warrant. It is difficult, for instance, to fish a worm properly in wind. If there's a specific place you want to fish and it's buffeted by wind, you may choose to anchor your boat in such a way that you can fish directly upwind or downwind of that spot. At other times you may elect to drift and fish, using an electric motor to either slow the drift speed or keep a desired position. If you have to drift, fishing in the direction the boat is headed is difficult but may work because it allows you to fish a spot before the boat drifts over it. On deep water, it only makes sense to drift behind the boat.

Fishing against the wind can be almost like trolling and can be effective, provided your boat is not moving too fast and your sinker is heavy enough to keep the worm down. One problem with trolling a sinker-rigged worm is that bass strike and reject it quickly; but if you slow-troll it without a weight, it can be a different story. You might try that on shallow, weedy lakes.

Occasionally, you may find it beneficial to swim the worm slowly just off the bottom. This works best in lily pads, areas with moderately thin grass, and similar spots. Though I am not much for fishing an unweighted worm, some anglers do so in thick vegetation. It's difficult to cast an unweighted worm with most baitcasting equipment, though not too difficult with spinning tackle.

One trick I use when I am doing a lot of worm-fishing is to cut down on the length of my retrieve. Many times I do not fish a worm all the way back to the boat. Rather, I work it through and along all the necessary cover, and if nothing is present between that cover and the boat, I'll reel the worm right up and make another cast, since I know there is little likelihood of a bass being away from the cover in open water.

Jerk Worms

These soft-plastic (although not as soft as conventional worms) have become a part of the worm angler's repertoire over the past decade and deserve separate mention. Some folks call them *jerk worms*, or *soft-plastic jerkbaits*. Many are vaguely wormlike in appearance but could imitate baitfish or other creatures in a general sort of way.

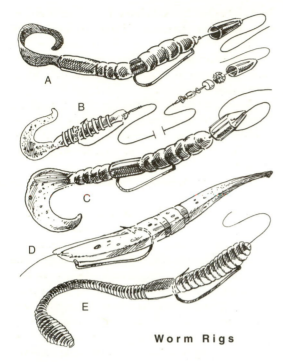

Worm Rigs

Plastic worms and rigging methods: conventional Texas rig (A), Carolina rig (B), Texas rig for flipping (C), sinkerless jerk-worm rig (D), and sinkerless floating-worm rig (E).

Jerk worms are usually fished suspended or just under the surface in a pull-pause, slow-jerking retrieve. This is unusual for soft-plastic lures. Most plastic worms are known for their slithering, shimmering, undulating action, and are generally worked on or close to the bottom.

I was at first underwhelmed by the Lunker City Slug-O (the original jerk worm) and then by many other soft-plastic jerkbaits when I fished them years ago, but I've since found them to be fish catchers. Perhaps they attract bass because they're different or because they have an atypical wounded action.

Getting confidence in using jerk worms, despite their lackluster appearance, is most important. Actually, when jerked, these soft plastics do look a lot like a wounded darting fish, and when paused, they descend slowly like a dying fish. Like conventional plastic worms, they

are rigged with a single hook embedded inside, which makes them reasonably snag resistant and capable of being fished amidst heavy cover, especially vegetation. Lily pads, with their frequent openings on the surface and ample clearance below it, are good locales for these lures. Sinkers are not ordinarily used with jerk worms. But you can make jerk worms sink deep to get down to the fish rather than make the fish come up; a split shot placed above the worm will do it, or you can try a weighted hook.

Some jerk worms dart well from side to side, and others have a more slightly canted, darting-rolling action. You should experiment a bit with hook size and placement to achieve the desired effect, and also be attentive to proper rerigging after a fish has been caught.

Generally you have to keep your rod tip down and pointed at the water. You can jerk these worms quite well on a raised rod (angled at an 11 to 12 o'clock position) but only when the lure is a long distance away. A low rod angle also aids hook-setting.

Tackle

My recommendation for worm-fishing is a good-quality rod with an even taper, a strong butt and backbone, and a "fast" or relatively limber tip. The disadvantage of a rod with a stiff tip is that it casts a worm poorly and is not sensitive enough to detect strikes. Having a special "worm" rod to fish plastic worms is not necessary. A graphite or good composite rod is strong and sensitive and is an advantage to a fisherman skilled at detecting pickups. I like to use a 6-foot baitcasting rod for worms, but the popular choice is a 5½-footer.

Spinning rods are not used as much for worm-fishing as are baitcasting and spincasting rods, but they are perfectly acceptable if you have a fast-action rod that allows you to detect even faint strikes and to set the hook. Most people who fish worms on spinning rods use a rod that is too limber, and they are unable to set the hook.

There are no special criteria for reels for worm-fishing. Line is a topic we've previously covered, although it is worth noting that worms are fished in all manner of cover, so the line you use should be high quality and particularly resistant to abrasion and able to withstand sudden shock-loading.

Flies

The lures used in fly-fishing for bass generically fall under the catchall term *flies,* but there's actually quite a variety here.

Surface fly-fishing is accomplished with an assortment of poppers, bugs, and floating flies. Poppers are usually made of cork, foam, and balsa wood but also from other nonhair materials. They sport a concave, bullet, or angled head, each of which produces a different noise and splash effect when jerked on the surface. All sport some type of leglike hackle at the rear, and are fairly large and cumbersome to cast.

Bug is a term that is used interchangeably by many anglers with *poppers* and with all floating bass lures for the fly rod, but I consider bugs to

Poppers, bugs, and some flies are used by flyrodders, especially in shallow areas.

be hair-bodied lures. Like poppers, they come in varying shapes and sizes, have leg hackle, are large and sometimes tough to cast, and are trimmed to resemble a frog, mouse, or other surface-swimming creature. Deer, caribou, or elk hair is used.

Other surface lures used by flyrodders include large versions of trout flies, as well as spiders and hoppers. These are especially effective on small largemouths, and on smallmouth bass in streams.

Surface-fishing is certainly the favorite flyrodding tactic, but, as in baitcasting or spinning, it is often necessary to fish mid-depth or deep to have success. Innovative fly-tyers have come up with a host of attractions for fishing deep. Essentially, in streams and rivers, wet flies and nymphs can be used to catch smallmouths just as they would be used for trout. Streamers and bucktails have merit for relatively shallow fishing in rivers and in lakes or ponds. Large streamers are usually necessary to catch bigger largemouth bass, however. Weighted flies that resemble baitfish, worms, or leeches are necessary for deeper scouring and, of course, are fished with sinking or sink-tip fly lines.

Many of these fly-rod lures for bass are made by individual tyers and some are available commercially, although not widely. Many of the flies used for bass do not hook fish as well as they should because the hooks they're tied on are too small. For bass, hooks with a long shank and wide gap help minimize the problem.

Natural colors and materials are popular in bass flies, but hair can be dyed to produce some brightly colored bugs. Yellow, lime green, black, brown, and purple are favored in poppers and in bugs.

Live Bait

Using live bait is my least preferred method of fishing, but we'll discuss it briefly here. Bass can be a fairly aggressive fish and can be taken on a variety of lures, so it is usually not necessary to fish with bait. Moreover, many fish caught on bait are deeply hooked, and it is difficult to release them (including sublegal-size fish), so I advocate using lures in casting and searching for bass.

Of course, live bait can be effective in the hands of a good fisherman. The key to success with it is the same as with any type of artificial lure: knowing the habits of the fish and selecting the right habitat in which to work your lure or bait. Live bait can be fished anywhere that lures can, including the perimeters of and underneath dense, matted vegetation.

The kinds of live bait that catch bass are the same as would be found naturally in their environment, as well as some that are not: worms, minnows, crayfish, large shiners (and occasionally shad or alewives), frogs, salamanders, leeches, water dogs, and a few other creatures. Sometimes it pays to select your bait in accordance with the type of food most prevalent in the particular habitat of the fish, such as minnows or crayfish. At other times the best bait may be creatures that are not abundant in that water or that do not constitute a major part of the bass's diet, such as earthworms and frogs. The choice depends on the availability of bait, its importance in the diet of bass, and especially where and how it is to be fished.

The tackle preference for live-bait fishing usually runs to spinning and spincasting equipment with the small- to medium-size bait offerings, since it is easier to cast and position them with this gear. Baitcasting tackle can be used with larger, heavier bait. A lot of bank fishermen and some boat anglers still use cane poles. Live bait is fished with a variety of hooks from No. 6 for smaller bait to 5/0 for the largest; although single hooks are usually used, sometimes treble hooks are preferred, particularly in open water. Split shot is needed with small bait to keep it at the proper level, and unless you're *livelining* the bait (letting it run freely), some type of float or bobber is necessary. Largemouth bass are not shy about snatching bait, so line size usually isn't critical as long as it isn't too heavy in relatively clear water. Smallmouths, however, are more finicky and are often found in much clearer, deeper water than largemouths, making lighter line for

bait-fishing a little more appropriate.

Live-bait fishing for smallmouths is considerably different than for largemouths. Smallmouths have a decided preference for crayfish. I witnessed a phenomenal exhibition of live-crayfish success with smallmouths a few years ago on Lake Ontario with charterboat captain Charlie DeNoto, who perfected a technique he calls *centerline drifting*. He fishes near-shore areas that have a softball-size-cobblestone bottom, in depths ranging from 20 to 30 feet. He baits his hooks with soft-shell crayfish (locally called "crabs"), which ring a smallmouth's dinner bell like no other form of food.

The key to his technique, besides using softshells and knowing the prime locales, is drifting a 40- to 50-pound weight along the bottom. DeNoto uses an iron or steel block that doesn't snag up, and secures it with heavy rope to the gunwale amidships, allowing the boat to drift sideways with the wind. The anchor drags bottom fairly close to the boat, stirring up rocks and leaving disturbed crayfish in its wake. A chum line of sorts is created, and DeNoto claims that smallmouths are not only attracted to the free chow but even follow the dragging anchor. He applies a No. 1 or 2 split shot about 18 inches above a No. 4 hook, uses light line, and drifts the softshell in the trail of the anchor.

Four of us fished DeNoto style one morning, and in 4½ hours we used 10 dozen softshells; for every one, a smallmouth was caught or stole the bait. There were several times when all of us had a fish on the line, and there were also times when a bass was hooked every time a crayfish was put out. It was remarkable smallmouth action, and since every fish was taken on 4- or 6-pound-test line, it was outstanding entertainment.

Just as remarkable as the fishing was the fact that we could not duplicate the results using any other method. DeNoto and I both caught bass on hair or grub jigs worked behind the anchor, but were outfished by the bait anglers. He says the success rate with jigs is about a quarter to a third of the rate with softshells. He also says that hardshell crayfish are quickly rejected in favor of softshells and that worms are half as effective and minnows even less so.

There's no doubt that live crayfish make excellent smallmouth bait. Softshells are hard to obtain, however, and in most areas fishermen use hardshells of varying sizes. When still-fishing, leave your bail open, hold the line in your free hand, and periodically give a light tug to the line to keep the crayfish from burrowing under rocks. In drift-fishing, close the bail and keep the rod tip high to detect a strike.

Peculiarities pop up everywhere, of course. For instance, live leeches are a popular small-mouth (and walleye) bait in the spring in the Upper Midwest, but I don't find fishermen using them extensively anywhere else. I regularly hear about fishermen who have tremendous success in Ontario lakes with live frogs, though I have no experience with such fishing.

An old axiom says that big baits catch big bass. That's certainly true for largemouths. In Florida, it's common to fish with 9- to 12-inch shiners for trophy-size (more than 10 pounds) bass. Remember that a largemouth has an enormous maw, capable of consuming fairly large prey. If you're using small minnows for panfish, you may catch small bass, but you'll probably have to move up in size to appeal to the heartier appetite of bigger bass. Smallmouths don't often succumb to very large baits; small or medium-size baits are likely to work with all sizes of smallmouth bass.

Live bait must act naturally to get the attention of bass. A crayfish that rolls instead of crawls or a minnow that doesn't swim lessens your chance of success. You can hook live bait in a variety of ways. Nightcrawlers and large angle-worms can be hooked singly through the collar; or through the collar, midsection, and tail. Smaller worms can be hooked together to form a squirming, tail-hanging gob. Minnows are best hooked through the back just in front of the dorsal fin, as are large shiners, though trolled baitfish are sometimes hooked through the lip. Frogs are best hooked in the forward, meaty part of the leg, salamanders in the forward part of the tail behind the rear legs, and crayfish through the forward part of the tail. For leech-

fishing, use a small hook (about size 6) through the head and tail sections. Crickets, too, have been known to catch an occasional bass, though usually while employed for panfish.

Bait must be lively to be productive. Bass aren't interested in dull or dead bait, so keep your bait as fresh and lively as possible. Change baits whenever the one in use seems to be losing vitality. If you can keep your bait cool and well aerated, it will stay in good condition.

When you're fishing with a float or bobber, it's easy to tell when a fish is mouthing your live offering. But when you're livelining, it's often hard to tell whether a fish has picked up your offering or if your bait is hung on brush, rock, or grass. Keep a light hold on your line to detect gentle strikes, and when in doubt, pull ever so gently on the line. If it moves off vigorously, you've got a fish.

Determining what depth to fish is an important aspect of bass angling, too, but getting your bait to that depth is just as critical. Most of the time you need to fish bait on or near the bottom, whether you're fishing a lake, pond, or river. You must be able to detect, by feel, when the bait has reached bottom. When still-fishing with a float or bobber and a sinker, allow for the distance between sinker and hooked bait when setting out your rig; the bait should be slightly above, not resting on, the bottom.

Don't be in a rush to set the hook when live-bait fishing. A bass needs time to consume his quarry. Often he takes the bait crosswise in his mouth and swims a short distance away with it before swallowing it. If you wait and don't put any tension on the line for a few moments, you stand a better chance of hooking the fish.

Live-bait anglers should realize that there's a good chance that a bass with a hook in it will survive. If you've hooked a bass you can't keep (perhaps because the season isn't open or the fish is under the minimum size limit) or that you don't want to keep, clip the line off above the hook. The hook will deteriorate within a few weeks unless it is stainless steel or cadmium-tin. If the fish is not bleeding profusely and if you have been careful to handle it as little as possible, it should survive.

6

BOATS

On most medium- and large-size boats, electric motors are mounted on the bow, and operated by remote or hand control to allow for instant positioning while fishing.

I've had the opportunity to fish from almost every type of craft imaginable, excepting sailboats and racers, and have owned many bass boats as well as other craft in 25 years of evaluating the merits of various boats for bass fishing.

There is really no such thing as a "bass boat." What we call a bass boat is simply a good fishing boat that is particularly useful where a lot of casting is required and where presentation and boat positioning are especially important. I have often used my so-called bass boats for muskie, pike, walleye, trout, salmon, shad, pickerel, panfish, and striped-bass fishing.

Almost any boat can be used for bass fishing. Your fishing conditions, interests, and budget should determine the type of boat you use. The most popular and useful boats for bass fishing are the fiberglass models, the aluminum V-bottom and flat-bottom rowboats, and canoes. At one time, I owned one of each and used them all in different ways.

I use a fiberglass or aluminum "bass" boat almost everywhere I can because they are well-outfitted, comfortable vessels with lots of room. A V-hull, fiberglass boat is especially suitable for large lakes, ponds, and rivers, where rough water dictates sturdy craft and where a big boat with a lot of engine muscle can help cover distance quickly. Aluminum bass boats can also be

used under these conditions, but the flat-bottomed models do not handle rough water well. Some of these boats, pounded by hard running through rough water, wind up with loose rivets, so bear this in mind. V-hull aluminum boats take rough water a little better, but still not as well as fiberglass boats. They sit up higher in the water, and because they are lighter, they are more readily blown about in the wind, making electric-motor control difficult. I use these large boats any place I can. With a four-wheel-drive truck, I can put them in most places, even where access is meager.

A smaller aluminum or flat-bottom boat is functional for bass fishing on small lakes, rivers, and ponds, where it isn't necessary to cover a lot of territory and where conditions are seldom adverse. I use a jonboat on small private water where either motors are not allowed or the sight of big boats might create ill feelings with local residents. Small aluminum V-bottom boats are less suitable than jonboats for fishing the shallow, rocky waters of small rivers because their deeper draft draws more water; they are more suitable for small- and medium-size lakes.

I seldom use a canoe for bass fishing. Canoes are unsteady and difficult to position; they are influenced by current, the force of wind, and even the working of some lures. If you fish by

The launching of a fully rigged bass boat is a common sight on most large bodies of water.

yourself in a canoe and toss out a deep-diving crankbait, watch what happens: the canoe pulls in the direction of your cast. Canoes become moderately useful for bass fishing only when you put an electric motor on them for positioning.

Selection

Think of your boat as a fishing tool. It has to get you where the fish are. It must weather a range of water conditions and features, and it must be reasonably comfortable, allowing you to put in long hours. It must be versatile, capable of handling a variety of angling pursuits. It must be designed or modified to allow you to fight and land fish, especially big bass. And it should have readily available fishing and boating accessories.

In considering a boat for bass fishing, ask yourself: Where will I be using my boat? What type of boat matches my needs and the place(s) in which I expect to use it? What does my bank account allow?

Most bass boats look pretty much alike to the average angler or would-be boat buyer. One may be lighter than another. One may be faster. And so forth. They all feature many options, and the manufacturers make assorted claims. Most folks are at a loss to evaluate the products they see, particularly if they have never before owned a fishing or pleasure boat.

Safety

As you might expect, safety is the most important consideration in buying a bass boat, especially since many of the latest high-powered craft can travel in excess of 60 (even 70+) miles per hour (mph). But speed is important primarily to tournament fishermen and race jockeys; I have no use for it. Even moderately powered bass boats will go 40 mph, and that's pretty fast. I suggest you disregard speed capabilities and concentrate on the other features of a boat in making your evaluations.

Upright flotation is required on all new boats so that the boat will stay afloat if capsized or swamped. Most boats manufactured prior to 1978 do not have this feature, and you should bear that in mind in case you are still hanging on to one of them.

All of a boat's unusable space, except the sump area, should be filled with foam flotation. Check it out. A boat without foam flotation, or with an insufficient amount of it, will be cheaper but unsafe. Not injecting foam into all areas saves money and lowers the cost of the boat, but possibly at the expense of safety. Ask the sales representative if a recognized, independent testing agency has verified the manufacturer's flotation claims.

(See page 93 for information about ignition safety cutoff switches.)

Construction

To check construction, look for reinforcement (with marine-grade plywood) of critical areas where weight will be applied, such as the bow, the gunwales (on fiberglass boats), compartment and livewell lids, the electric-motor support, and the console. In some cases you cannot see the material used, but you can knock on different places and determine any change by the resulting sound. A hollow sound might indicate a lack of plywood reinforcement where it's needed.

Areas that wobble or buckle when you apply pressure indicate that the material used there is too thin. Also, look for good-gauge wiring; often marine dealers have to replace the electric-motor wiring in bass boats to accommodate high-powered electrics. And check for workmanship by examining the finish, smoothness, and general appearance of decks, gunwale, and sides. Also check the screws, locks, and fasteners to see if they are made of good-quality material to withstand abuse.

In fiberglass boats, look for fiberglass reinforcement, especially around joints. In some boats you can see the woven cloth strands. They should be on the bottom and continue up the sides, but some boats have it only on the bottom.

Also, the storage compartment should be laminated to the hull. You can take a pocketknife and push the blade under the edge to determine this. Look to see if the upper corners of the livewell are completely sealed; if not, water will splash into the corners when the boat is running and the livewell is full, and will seep into the adjacent dry storage compartments.

Check to see if the storage areas are really going to be dry. If there is a pedestal seat base above a storage area, that compartment may get wet. When the bilge or sump is full, water can seep into a storage area if it isn't sealed off. Look for proper ventilation in the gas and battery compartment, and make sure that batteries and gas cans or tanks are (or can be) firmly secured so they don't bounce around on the water or on the trailer.

Every prospective buyer should look for a solid one-year (or better) warranty from the manufacturer. Also, look for a detailed owner's manual. It indicates that the manufacturer stands behind his product and wants the consumer to obtain maximum use and satisfaction from it. Many don't have them, however.

It's a good idea to go with brand names in bass boats. Once scores of companies built bass

Jonboats are excellent for relatively calm, small waters and streams.

boats, but a poor economy a few years back put many of them (including many of the lower-quality boat manufacturers) out of business. Ranger, one of the first in the bass-boat business, may currently be the largest fiberglass manufacturer and makes excellent fishing boats. I've owned seven Rangers and can attest to their quality. Skeeter, Hydra-Sports, Tracker, and Stratos bass boats also have good reputations.

It's a good idea to confer with owners of the brand or model of bass boat that you are considering. You can get a perspective on the good and bad points of the boat (motor and trailer, too) and the dealer who sells and services it. In the past, many dealers who sold runabouts and ski boats were not familiar enough with the needs of fishermen to adequately rig boats for serious angling. Problems in the installation of electric motors, electronics equipment, propellers, and the like were rampant. Today, most of the larger dealers and suppliers of the better-known products are pretty savvy when it comes to installation and rigging, and there are not as many problems as there used to be. However, you should thoroughly discuss installation and placement details with a dealer before any work is done to be sure you get things installed where and how you want them.

Anglers who did not do so account for much of the dissatisfaction with certain bass boats. It's important to make a complete and careful determination of your requirements before you buy. Many bass-boat owners started small and worked their way up to more elaborate, more sophisticated, and more costly equipment, when they needed it all along. If they had correctly assessed their wants and needs in the first place, they would have saved money and time with the correct initial purchases. On the other hand, many bass fishermen have far more boat and engine than is practical for their needs.

Be especially careful about trying to get a boat that will perform many functions. Sure, it's good to have a boat that the family can use for running around and skiing, but multipurpose boats seldom make anyone happy. Dual consoles, for

example, eat up important space, and you will surely find yourself cramped with people and gear in a bass boat with a passenger console.

Electric Motors

Of course, in addition to sonar (which is discussed in the following chapter), one of the most important and useful items for any boating bass fisherman is an electric motor. An electric motor, called a "trolling" motor by most of the angling fraternity, allows you to maneuver and position your boat at the proper angle for casting and presentation, all as quietly and carefully as possible. Electric motors essentially take the place of oars and sculling paddles, but they're quieter and interfere less with fishing activities.

All electric motors are battery powered. Some run off a single 12-volt battery; others run off 24 volts, requiring two 12-volt batteries; still others have the capability of running off either one or two 12-volt batteries. Not all electric motors are alike; some are more powerful and some more battery efficient. The amount of energy (designated as amperes, or amps) consumed per hour by electric motors varies, and this figure will tell you how many hours of continuous use you can get out of a battery at various speeds. The heavier your boat and boat load, the more power (designated in thrust pounds) you need. Another factor to consider is how much fishing you do in areas of substantial current or wind; both drain the reserves of a battery quicker than calm-condition operation.

On most fiberglass and on many aluminum bass boats, the electric motor is mounted permanently on the bow (see photo on page 92), with the bracket support installed port side of the bow to put a little weight on that side and counterbalance the console and driver weight on the starboard side. On small boats such as rowboats and jonboats, electric motors can be mounted on the front or back. I have used them both ways and recommend bow mounting. Boats move with greater ease when pulled rather than pushed, and with bow mounting you can see where you're headed and avoid objects in the water.

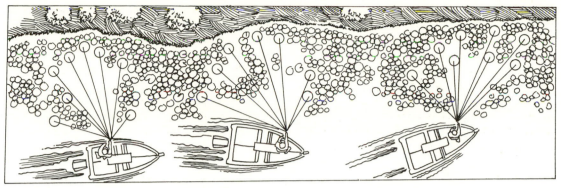

Perhaps more so than any other fishermen, bass anglers rely on electric motors to propel their boats for casting to likely bass hideouts. Electrics provide quiet maneuvering and positioning advantages so that anglers can spend most of their time placing their lures in the best possible spots, as depicted by this boat working a bed of lilies.

Small boats usually require only a single 12-volt electric motor, though you can employ more than one motor at a time. Some anglers who fish reservoirs where no outboards are allowed rig up two or three electrics simultaneously, and new electrics are available specifically for this application. I once had two small electrics of relatively low thrust on a jonboat, and they worked marvelously (each was hooked to its own battery). Small-boat electrics feature a turnscrew-clamp transom mount, which makes them adjustable and removable. With some, you can leave the bracket installed and remove the rest of the motor. Some of these models can also fit on the front of a small boat, but it pays to check out your boat first and then see if the motor you may buy will fit the design of your bow.

Permanent-mount electrics are used on conventional bass boats and large craft and can be operated manually or remotely, depending upon the unit. Most remote units are operated by a foot-control pedal on the bow deck; some have merely a long electric cord, and the newest models are totally remote controlled. Motor Guide's Lazer is one of them, and I've been using it for more than a year with excellent results. These motors are expensive, but they eliminate all the wires and cable that were a hindrance in the past.

Manual models do not have a foot-control pedal or cable running to the motor but are steered by foot or by hand. Many anglers prefer the manual type of electric and use their feet, hands, and arms to control positioning, because in the past they've experienced cable breakage with the remote-operated units. These days cables are much better, but you may have problems with the foot-control unit.

One feature to look for in an electric motor is a breakaway bracket, which allows the shaft of the motor to slip back if it collides with an immovable object, preventing bent shafts, damaged lower units, and extraordinary stress on the mounting bracket when objects are struck head on. For this to work, however, the motor has to be positioned dead on the bow.

Another important feature is a good armature and easy-release/take-up system for getting into and out of the water with minimum effort. Motors vary greatly in this regard. There are now some automatic devices for raising and lowering bow-mounted electric motors.

Batteries

With an electric motor you'll also need one or more batteries and a means of recharging them. An electric motor does not automatically recharge the power source, and in the course of a full day's fishing, you may drain the energy of a battery considerably. With pulse modulation,

The wave of the future for electric motors is totally remote-controlled operation, eliminating the need for a cable and hand or foot steering devices. The Motor Guide Lazer on the bow of this boat can be operated from any location.

good electric motors today don't drain a battery as much as they did in the past, and depending on the fishing circumstances, you may be able to get two or three days out of a battery without recharging it. But you'll still need a battery charger.

The best products for powering electric motors are deep-cycle batteries. Deep-cycle batteries are often called marine batteries, but not all marine batteries are deep cycle, so you should check to be sure yours are. They are constructed with special plates that allow them to be regularly drawn down and recharged; standard batteries are not meant to do that, when used for electric-motor operation, and do not have nearly the life of deep-cycle batteries. For maximum performance, your best bet is the highest-

amperage batteries you think you can use and a high-amp-capacity battery charger. For starting the outboard motor, you don't need a deep-cycle battery. A conventional automotive battery will do, but opt for a non-deep-cycle marine battery.

Remember that batteries are the lifeline to your boat's operation. Clean the terminals and connections regularly for good contact. Signs of a weak battery include low electric-motor propulsion, weak depthfinder or graph-recorder signals, low temperature-gauge readings, low tachometer and speedometer readings, and weak fuel-gauge indications.

Batteries on a full charge last longer, so keep your charge level high at all times, even through the winter. If you are charging directly to a battery, you can use the clamp-type terminal connectors, being sure to place the positive and negative wires properly and keeping the battery compartment ventilated. If your boat is wired for automatic charging, you need a three-prong adapter that is attached to your charger's lead wires and merely needs to be plugged into the boat receptacle with the system switched into the charging mode.

Accessories

One boating and bass-fishing accessory that I don't like to be without, but that many bass anglers don't have, is some type of temperature gauge. I have had many surface-temperature gauges on boats, or used sonar with a temperature-sensing option. I also carry a handheld pool thermometer. Temperature readings are particularly important in the spring and fall, when water temperatures are changing—sometimes on a daily basis—and when the surface temperature, particularly when it is rising, is a strong indication of where you might expect to find fish and what their activity level might be.

Bass fishermen who cast all day often stand up or sit in standard pedestal seats that are too low for them. Tall bicycle-butt rest seats are available from several sources; you can lean against them while standing up to take some pressure off your legs and back and be a little more comfortable.

Most bass anglers stand up when fishing, or lean on a pedestal seat, because they can see well and cast and retrieve better from a higher position.

Because safety is a top concern for every boater, your bass boat should have an ignition safety cutoff switch (all recent models do). Also known as a "kill switch," this device shuts the motor off if the operator is thrown out of the boat or away from the steering wheel. That can happen when you are traveling fast and strike an unseen obstacle that violently jerks the steering wheel out of your hand. It can also happen on that rare occasion when the steering wheel cable breaks while the boat is under high speed.

Another accessory that can be useful is a push pole. I carry a collapsible model with Y-shaped feet, which can be stored in the rod box or mounted along the gunwale or stern for easy access. It sometimes comes in handy for those exasperating moments when you get stuck on a sandbar or stump and can't rock the boat free. It's also useful at times for fishing in thick vegetation where electric-motor propellers get hopelessly bogged down.

Other boating accessories that should be carried for bass fishing, include spare fuses, engine oil, electrical tape, needlenose pliers, WD-40, and required boating paraphernalia. There should be a Type III (keeps an adult floating upright with head out of the water) life preserver for every person on board. The vestlike models are best and should always be worn when the boat is moving fast.

PRACTICAL

Courtesy of Lowrance Electronics

Sonar is the underwater eyes of fishermen. Second only to underwater diving, it gives you the best information about what is going on below.

BOAT AND SONAR USE

Very often the most crucial factor in your success or lack of it will be the way you use your boat and boating equipment to cope with the fishing conditions. What kind of boat you have is not as important as whether it suits your fishing needs and whether you can use it effectively.

Boat Positioning and Lure Presentation

One element of successful bass fishing is boat positioning—keeping your boat in the proper position for the time required to fish an area thoroughly. The most regularly fished area of a lake is the shoreline. When it's strewn with objects such as fallen trees, stumps, and rock piles, it is advantageous to position your boat 30 to 40 feet from shore and cast perpendicular to it. However, sharply sloping shorelines are better fished by casting forward over the bow of the boat, when the boat is positioned close to and parallel to the shore.

If two anglers are in the boat, both can cast forward, and their lures will be in the fish-catching zone more often than not. Once fish are located, it might pay to back out from shore and thoroughly work the area from all angles, especially by fishing meticulously with a plastic worm or jig. A shoreline edged with thick brush and grass and with an immediate drop-off of 3 or more feet should also be fished close. Jigs can be worked vertically in the brush as you move along, or floating/diving plugs can be "jiggered" zigzag fashion in, out, and around the shoreline with a long rod. This is effective and cannot be accomplished adequately by perpendicular positioning.

Keeping your boat close to shore and fishing outward is another tactic. Stump beds or rock piles or other objects that are far enough away from shore that they might be under the boat can usually be worked if you are positioned between them and the shore, especially if the water beyond them—away from shore—increases in depth. Deep-diving lures would probably be best here. Even if you don't see or locate underwater objects away from shore, it pays to cast deep-diving plugs out the other side of the boat occasionally.

If there are specific objects along the shore that can be seen and cast to, then fishing at right angles from a boat moving forward and parallel to the shore is acceptable. Where the shoreline does not have such obvious structure, but drops off at a good rate, you can "troll" plastic worms by working the boat in close and drifting or maneuvering with an electric motor to keep the

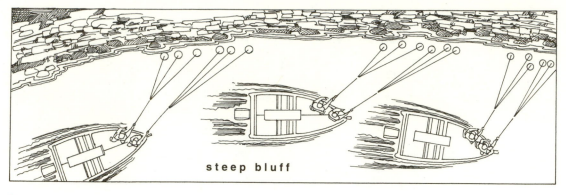

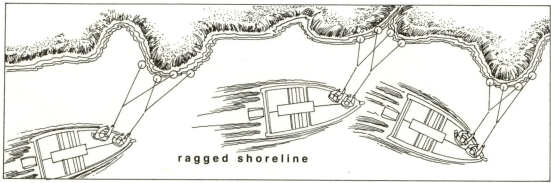

When working a shoreline that drops off quickly, it is sometimes best to position your boat close to shore and fish parallel, rather than perpendicular, to the bank. In a large boat, two anglers should cast from the bow, overlapping their casts. If that's not possible, set up the boat perpendicular to the bank, drift with the wind, and use your electric motor to maintain proper position.

worm bouncing along at the 10- to 15-foot zone. Rowboat anglers can do this quite well by drifting and occasionally working one of the oars to maintain position.

A visible straight line of grass beds is another place to fish close and parallel. When the grass is punctuated by cuts, channels, pockets, and the like, however, it's advisable to keep the boat out a bit and cast in, concentrating on irregular features and holes in the interior of the grass patches.

Points, always good fishing locations, should be fished more thoroughly than other areas. Three basic boat positions—on either side of the point and straight out from it—should be taken, and a range of casts should be made from each location. If you have sonar, you should watch it as you work around the point; concen-

trate on the break area where the point tapers off to deep water.

Sonar is a substantial aid to all bass fishermen anywhere on a lake, regardless of the type of boat. In most cases, proper boat positioning over areas likely to hold bass but not visible to fishermen can be accomplished only with sonar. By watching this instrument and following the contours of a promising spot (such as a mound, rock pile, or deep grass bed), you can keep your boat on the fringe of the likely area and your lures in the fish-catching zone.

Many fishermen fail to operate to maximum potential in bass habitat that is not readily identifiable. Take, for example, a deep weed line off a bar or point adjacent to deep water. Some anglers, intent on the immediate shoreline, may not discover the grass at all or may not work far enough out from shore. Others will give this spot only a few quick casts en route to other places. Since bass will hang in the deep weed line and at the end of points where they break to deep water, a prime location combining both of these attributes should be thoroughly worked—approached from all angles and covered with a range of lures. Keep watching the depthfinder while maneuvering the boat back and forth and in and out of such an area.

In many fish-holding locales like pilings, docks, fallen trees, bushes, and so forth, the important point to consider is how to present a lure most effectively and how to position yourself for thorough fishing.

The one element that thwarts the best positioning and presentation efforts of many bass fishermen is a strong wind. Casting into the wind is particularly difficult, strike detection and lure working are impaired, and effective boat positioning is seldom possible. Sometimes you can use the wind to carry you past the areas to be fished. More often you have to run the boat into the wind to maximize your time in desirable areas.

Sitting versus Standing

There is no doubt in my mind that you can see fish and fishing holes better, can cast better, can set the hook better, and can play a fish better while standing than you can while sitting down. It has been a time-honored safety practice to remain seated in small boats, and I admit that

These anglers are arriving at a rocky point, and are preparing to fish one side of it, then work around the tip of the point and fish the back side. When they're finished, they will have thoroughly cast around this likely bass habitat.

Bruce Holt

standing can be risky in cluttered boats, unstable craft, and in areas where a boat may collide with obstructions in the water. But in many boats, and especially the modern breed of bass boat, you can stand up reasonably comfortably and safely.

Because of their raised pedestal seats, sitting in most bass boats is akin to standing anyway. Sitting anglers, however, have a tendency to become complacent and lose their attention and concentration. Also, some lures require that you keep your rod nearly horizontal with the surface. If you fish these lures from a low point—seated in a jonboat, rowboat, or aluminum V-bottom—you may bang the side of the boat. The higher elevation afforded by standing or sitting in a raised seat gives you better vision and more freedom of movement.

I stand up while bass fishing in nearly every craft but canoes. I even stand up in small jonboats, provided my companion is careful about his movements and is not constantly fidgeting around. I don't, however, stand while river-fishing. In small boats I usually position my legs on either side of the seat and may lean a knee against the transom or gunwale for stability and support. I place a lot of importance on visibility, fishing position, and general awareness, and I think standing up enhances them. Standing, of course, is not for everybody, nor is it practical in many types of craft (small jonboats, pirogues, and folding boats, for example) or in rough water. Use your best judgment, and if you do stand up in dubious circumstances, wear a life preserver.

Fishing from the Back of the Boat

In my experience and observation, a fairly to moderately skilled bass angler fishing behind a good angler will not do as well during the course of a day as his companion. But a good angler fishing behind a fairly or moderately skilled angler will do as well as, if not better than, his companion. A good angler who fishes at a moderate pace will generally get first crack at most of the better bass cover. I believe the first cast to a likely bass hole is the most important one. That's why I emphasize the importance of accurate casting and good presentation. A good caster can conceivably hit every prime spot along a particular section of cover or shoreline. Where you are positioned in the boat is less important than your skill in casting and presentation.

The attitude of the boat operator and the attitude of his guest are pertinent to this discussion. If the operator, or forward angler, is incapable of precision boathandling and positioning, he can unintentionally make fishing more difficult for his companion. If his attitude is not one of fairness and fellowship, then he's likely to try to hog every fish-catching opportunity. When I have friends in the boat with me, I try to take into consideration their general fishing skill and their casting abilities. It's not necessary to tell good anglers what to do. When we work a shoreline, for instance, I'll cast to every other good spot, leaving my friend good fishing opportunities, which he recognizes. With other anglers, I may deliberately pass up the first cast to a good spot, pointing it out to them and giving them first crack at it. If you're friends and you're interested in a good time, fun fishing, and success for both of you, I think this is the way it should be.

If you're the guy in the back and you're not satisfied with the opportunities you're getting, say so. Simply ask to have the boat positioned the way you need it (closer to or farther from shore, for example). I've often been in this situation, and sometimes it's not a bad idea to give the guy in the bow a subtle message by casting up ahead of him or by going right up to the bow and casting shoulder to shoulder. Sometimes, in fact, such as when flipping in close quarters, it is best for both anglers to be in the bow, or the stern angler will never get a chance at the right spots. In my opinion, two anglers in a boat should work with, not against, each other. They can use different tactics and different lures to try to figure out where the fish are and what they'll take. This complementary approach can mean better fishing for both anglers.

Many times I'll invite someone to fish in the bow of my bass boat. Or I'll work the boat so he can have the proper angle for a cast at a particular spot. I expect he'd do the same for me. If someone wants to hog everything or complain all the time, then I won't fish with him.

A final point regarding how you work a shoreline, or weed-line edge, or in general follow a straight path along some type of cover from the back of the boat: the angler in the back should not fish parallel to or behind a moving boat. Let's say you're working parallel to the bank, bow on the left and stern on the right. You're in the stern and the boat is moving slowly down the shore in the direction the bow is facing. As you face the shore, you have a casting range that arcs roughly 180 degrees. Your best fishing chances, best presentation efforts, and best lure working occur in the first half of that arc. A lure cast up ahead will cover more ground than will one cast perpendicular to the boat or behind an imaginary perpendicular line; it will work more naturally. A lure cast behind a moving boat leans sideways and runs erratically. And a straight-ahead cast is generally more precise. This fact applies equally to anglers fishing in the front and the back, but for some reason back-of-the-boat anglers seem likely to ignore it.

Sonar

Sonar provides information that can greatly aid in your fish-finding and fish-catching efforts, particularly on an unfamiliar lake. Without sonar, you can determine the depth of the water you're fishing and then use the appropriate lures for that depth.

For example, suppose you're fishing a shoreline with a gradual drop-off where the water is obviously shallow close to shore. As you move down that shore, suddenly it is not so shallow any more against the bank, and you're not certain how deep it is. You could be 50 feet from shore and be in only 10 feet of water. You could also be in 60 feet of water. If you were tossing a crankbait that ran about 7 feet deep to that gradually sloping shoreline, your lure would not be in a bass zone throughout its retrieval because you could not hope to get the lure down to the fish along

this steep drop. Furthermore, you wouldn't know the drop-off existed unless you were using some type of sinking lure that you kept bouncing off the bottom, or unless you had a weight attached to line that you periodically dropped overboard to pinpoint the depth in various areas.

Sonar may be used to find fish, but in bass angling it is especially used to determine depth, to ascertain the characteristics of the bottom and anything between the bottom and the surface, and to guide you in learning the contours of any body of water so that you may locate suitable habitat.

The simplest type of sonar is a small portable unit, and those work well on small boats. You can

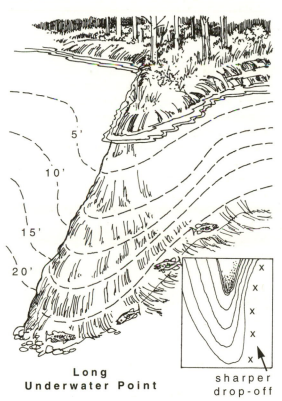

Long Underwater Point

sharper drop-off

This representation of an underwater point shows why it is necessary to approach such a location from several directions and to cast in many places. Points often taper off abruptly. Breaklines and sharper drop-offs (marked by an x) are the best locations when bass are deep, and they can be pinpointed with sonar.

use a bracketed or suction-cup transom mount or an electric-motor mount, whichever is most convenient for the type of transducer you have.

A permanent bow-mounted depthfinder is particularly helpful for bass fishermen, who spend much of their fishing time in the bow, casting and running the electric motor that takes them along likely fishing areas. You can get by with a bass boat equipped with only a console-mounted depthfinder, but you have to look back at it constantly to check the depth. You can flip the unit over to read it upside down from the front, or you can place it on an adjustable swivel (try Johnny Ray or Ultra Mount) to turn it toward the bow. A unit mounted on the bow, right in front of you, is clearly the most desirable alternative. Ideally, the transducer for this unit should be located on the bottom of your electric motor to give you readings directly below the front of the boat.

Sonar equipment is no substitute for angling savvy, skillful presentation, and knowledge of fish behavior and habits. But it can help. To use it well, it would be helpful to understand some basic operating principles.

Sound travels at 4,800 feet per second through the water, which is four times faster than it travels through air. Sonar instruments issue signals (pulses) at extremely swift rates. The greater the distance between transducer (the object that sends the pulses out and receives them) and bottom, the longer it takes for the pulses to bounce off it (or other objects between it and the bottom, including fish) and return. Nonetheless, the speed of operation is amazingly swift.

Transducers send out pulses in a three-dimensional cone-shaped wave. Cone angles range from narrow to extremely wide. The diameter of these cones influences how much detail will be seen. An 8-degree cone has a 2-foot diameter when the water is 15 feet deep; it has a 4-foot diameter at a depth of 30 feet. A 20-degree cone has a 6-foot diameter in 15 feet of water and a 12-foot diameter in 30 feet. A 45-degree cone has a 13.5-foot diameter at 15 feet and a 27-foot diameter at 30 feet.

On larger boats with two sonar units, the one at the bow is used most frequently, especially while you're running the electric motor and casting.

The transducers I've had ranged from providing the narrowest to the widest cone angles, and I've found that the narrowest cones are most useful in extremely deep water (150 feet or more). The widest cones enable you to see a lot more of what's beneath you, are especially useful for downrigger trolling and fishing directly below the boat, and work only at slow boat speeds. The medium-range cones are less specialized, have all-around functionality, and are best used in less than 100 feet of water. Most bass fishermen use a cone angle close to 20 degrees.

Although it is no longer made, I still use a Lowrance X-16 paper-chart recorder, which utilizes both 20- and 45-degree transducers. But I'm now primarily using a Lowrance 350A sonar, which has a 20-degree transducer, and also the latest Humminbird Wide View *liquid crystal display* (LCD) with dual 16- and 53-degree cones. The only drawback to the superwide cone angle is that it takes in so much information that you may trick yourself into thinking the fish it details are directly below the boat when they may be well off to the side. As long as you remember that your field of view is great when you're using the wider cone, you can switch back and forth. In *Fish ID* mode (fish symbols are displayed instead of dots or arches), however, the Humminbird Wide View distinguishes between fish under the boat and fish to the side.

Some units can look to the side as well as down, either with scanning transducers or fixed side-viewing transducers. Side-viewing sonar in principle is a great idea, especially for people who are searching large areas for schools of bait and predators. But I've had some experience with them and frankly am not convinced that they perform to expectations. I tested side-finding sonar on fish that were staked and positioned to the side of the boat, and the units didn't pick up the fish. Because I don't have great confidence in this technology, I'd recommend that if you're considering purchasing a side-viewing unit, you get together with someone who has one and watch it work in a reasonably controlled situation.

The entire sportfishing sonar field has changed radically over the past decade, and will become more sophisticated in the years ahead. Computer chips have given sonar phenomenal abilities, and the options available to anglers are incredible. Sonar evolved from flashers to paper-chart recorders to LCDs. Paper recorders are now obsolete and flashers are practically so. There's been a mild resurgence of interest in these flashers, but I suspect it's taking place among anglers who've tried inferior LCDs. Incidentally, since almost all sonar today features a liquid crystal display, and the industry now uses the terms *sonar* and *LCD* just about synonymously, I'll assume that you understand I'm referring to modern units when I use the term *sonar*.

Sonar today gives detail almost as good as did the best paper-chart sonar of old, and it's better in many ways than a flasher. I haven't used a flasher on my boats in years. My Lowrance X-16 paper unit sees duty from time to time because it is the Rolls Royce of sonar, but the results are virtually as good with my 1996-era sonar, which does not require paper and which has many

more options. What I miss about paper is the physical record. I used to save some remarkable paper records for later review and study, and you can't do that with the new sonar (although some day they'll have a memory and home-computer compatibility).

Many people have difficulty getting optimum results from their sonar and a lot of units are returned for service when there is really nothing wrong with them. Most problems are a result of operator misuse and improper transducer installation (which we'll discuss later).

Today's electronics are so sophisticated and the operations manuals are so thick, that they can be intimidating. Most of us want simply to turn the device on and be done with it. Certainly I do not look forward to reading the manual when I get a new unit. So a lot of people simply run their units in automatic mode and never get into the finer points of operation. I strongly recommend that you take the time to read every page of your manual. The place to do this is out on the water (not while fishing), so that you can go through the operations step by step, actually see the machine do what it's supposed to, and gain confidence in the unit. It's a good idea as well to bring your boat over shallow water near shore, where you know the depth, and check to see that the sonar reads accurately. Find a stump several feet down, and see how it registers on your machine. Go over a sandy bottom, a mud bottom, a rocky bottom.

While many units work adequately in automatic mode, you may get much better performance in the manual mode, where you control the sensitivity and range settings to get much finer detail. I use both modes on my machines and prefer manual, although it is not without drawbacks. Having to change the bottom setting when you get into deeper water, for example, is a minor nuisance.

A lot of operational troubles center around the control functions, particularly sensitivity and suppression. The sensitivity control, which used to be called *gain,* is akin to volume. Many inexperienced sonar users keep this turned down too low in older units, either because they are experiencing electrical interference or because they think a low setting is adequate. But if the sensitivity is too low, sonar may fail to register key bait, fish, or bottom readings. Modern units run on autopilot and don't usually have this problem. However, more detail can be observed with higher sensitivity settings. Some units cannot be adjusted in the auto mode, but if yours can (the Humminbird can), turn up the sensitivity for trolling. On the other hand, if you are merely looking for big fish and don't want to see every detail, then you might want to lower sensitivity.

If you turn sensitivity too high, you may clutter the screen with a lot of nonfish debris. I think the best marriage is a high-enough sensitivity to get a solid bottom reading with a distinct gray line, some surface clutter (minute matter in the upper layer of water), and a lot of detail in between. Sometimes I run sonar in the manual mode to get the best detail. If fish are holding tight to structure or the bottom, especially mud, the manual mode provides a better view.

If it's possible to adjust the scroll rate of your screen, crank that up, too. I think you get better detail with a fast screen (this is certainly so with paper sonar), and I like mine to move fast when I'm trolling, because I'm on the move as well. A slow speed sandwiches details. When you know what to expect, are continuously going over the same ground, or are interested only in depth, a slow speed might be adequate.

When it comes to range settings, I like to see as much on a screen as possible, which is why I hated the many small-screen sonars that were prevalent in the 80s and early 90s. By the time you studied the sonar the information was off the screen. I like wide (actual viewing area) screens and clear pictures. Sonar is sometimes really critical in bass fishing (to check deep-water structure, for example), so the better I see below, the better I fish.

The bottom range adjusts by itself in auto mode but has to be changed by the operator in manual mode. Here again, I prefer to see more on the screen rather than less, so I'm not happy with units that jump to a 60-foot scale when the boat moves into 31 feet of water, so that half the

Abe Cuanang photo

This Fish I. D. mode of a sonar shows three sizes of fish. Most anglers operate their sonar in this mode because it shows only the fish; better detail can be had in the manual pixel-character mode.

screen is occupied by the bottom. Depending on the unit, you may be able to work around this by using the manual mode, by zooming, or by splitting the screen for two different views. In automatic mode, some units keep the same general area of the screen (the upper two-thirds) no matter how the bottom depth changes.

Modern sonar has many other features, so let's briefly look at the key ones for bass fishing. Most sonar today can show fish symbols in the Fish ID mode. In standard mode, sonar identifies fish as a series of dots *(pixels)* in a line or arched. It also identifies surface clutter, temperature variations, minute particles, and thoroughly indistinguishable "stuff." I prefer standard operation, again, because of the sophisticated level of detail and because it enables me to determine for myself what I'm seeing. Many operators prefer the Fish ID mode, however, in which only fish (in theory) are targeted; all other information is filtered out by the machine, and several sizes of symbols are used to correspond to the fish.

All units now have fish and bottom alarms. I never use the fish alarm because the chirping is such a nuisance. The bottom alarm, however, can be practical for high-speed navigation.

Interpreting what you see on the screen is a challenge. Which signals represent fish, what kind of fish are they, how big are they? These are the big questions.

Fish signals should appear as an arch unless the fish are very small, the scroll speed is very slow, or the boat is moving very fast because a fish is first picked up on the outer edge of the cone, then directly underneath it (the strongest pulse area), then on the outer edge as the boat passes over it. The strongest reading of the fish is seen as the center part of the arch. A partial arch means that a fish was moving either in or out of the cone when you passed by. A school of bait shows up as a big pod, which may be vertical or horizontal depending on the species.

It is difficult to tell the specific size of fish detected with sonar because the representation you see on the screen varies according to the species, boat speed, scroll speed, and the sensitivity setting. If you catch a fish out of a school that you've just marked on a flasher or graph,

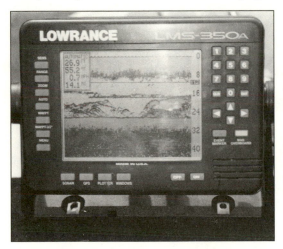

This shows what the latest sonar can offer. A corner window provides programmable information—in this case depth, surface temperature, speed, and distance traveled. The main screen depicts a massive school of baitfish, large individual fish, and a trolled downrigger weight. This unit, mounted on the author's boat console, also features GPS, a navigational device used by some bass fishermen on huge bodies of water.

you may have some idea how fish size compares to signal size, but if any of those factors change as you continue fishing, it's a new ball game. Sonar cannot identify species, but an angler's educated guess, based on extensive experience and knowledge of individual species' behavior and habitat, can be accurate.

One item used frequently in conjunction with sonar equipment is a marker buoy. Many fishermen find them helpful. When you come upon a place you would like to fish more thoroughly or to boat over to and examine more closely, you can pinpoint it by using one or more marker buoys. You can make your own, but good products in bright colors are available from several sources. They are nothing more than plastic floats and heavy weights, with strong line attached to these weights. Get a flat, square marker rather than the round, barbell version because the former is more resistant to the effects of current, wind, and waves; it doesn't drift off. Round markers can get blown quite a distance from the specific site they were supposed to identify. Incidentally, you might want to put your name on these buoys with a dark indelible marking pen; some of mine have been picked up by curious pleasure boaters and sailors.

Transducer Installation

Improper transducer installation leads to poor sonar readings that can hamper your fishing efforts. If you don't want to install it yourself, take the sonar and transducer to a boat dealer with extensive experience rigging fishing boats.

If you're purchasing a new fiberglass boat, the absolute best thing to do is purchase the sonar before the boat is manufactured, send the transducer to the factory, and have them hand-lay it into the fiberglass when they are setting up the hull. Some transducers done this way shoot through the hull (but the results can be imprecise if there is air in the fiberglass or resin). Some companies mount the transducer face flush with the hull, and you can't even tell where it's located.

Otherwise you'll have to mount the trans-

Most bass fishermen use a bow-mounted sonar with a transducer attached to the lower unit of the electric motor to get precise readings of the depth below the front of their boat. For precise definition at that depth, and for following a depth contour and edges such as submerged weed lines, the transducer should be positioned on the lower unit of the bow electric motor.

to the centerline of the hull, the better. If there are heavy bubbles below a transducer, you'll get no readings. Generally, however, to get the best readings of fish, the transducer should be level and its face pointed straight down. Units that aren't straight down will display only a partial arch when going over fish.

Finally, remember that the location and installation of the actual sonar unit and electrical and transducer wires should be well thought out. Wires and other electronics often interfere with sonar, causing dots or lines to appear on the sonar screen. One of my present sonar units interferes with my VHF radio; the wires and the antenna are too close together. Rerouting wires may be necessary if you're experiencing problems caused by other electrical instruments.

Maps

Every angler who fishes a large or unfamiliar body of water should have a good map of that place with him and use it in conjunction with his sonar. Maps, especially those that show underwater contours and hydrographic features, will help you navigate without getting lost or possibly running into obstructions, and will help you find areas that may provide good fishing. By pinpointing the location of islands, mounds, shoals, reefs, drop-offs, roadbeds, channels, river- and creekbeds, and other forms of structure, you can fish the particular places that are most likely to harbor bass.

The nice thing about such maps is that, days before an outing, they enable you to devise in your own home a plan of attack for fishing an unfamiliar lake. Once you have acquired the knack of reading an underwater contour map or a navigational chart that details bottom features, you are certain to find some areas where bass are located.

Underwater contour (hydrographic) maps and navigational charts denote water depth and the location of reefs, rocks, shallows, and such, while topographic maps seldom do. Underwater contour maps are available for many lakes and can be particularly useful because their high

ducer to the transom exterior. Be sure to read and closely follow the manufacturer's installation instructions. On aluminum boats be sure to install transom-mount transducers midway between the hull strakes to minimize the effects of turbulence when the boat is under way, and don't tighten the kick-up bracket so much that it will not push back if you strike an obstruction.

Position a transom-mount transducer so that no air bubbles will trail below it. Strakes, weld lines, and rivets, among other things, give off a bubble trail, especially at high speed. Find a location that permits clear water to flow below the face of the transducer, such as between strakes on an aluminum hull. The closer you are

level of detail pinpoints important hydrographic features. When used in conjunction with a compass or a GPS, they help you maintain course, especially in fog, in low light, or at night.

Topographic maps and navigational charts are produced by American and Canadian federal agencies and are available at some sporting goods stores, marinas, and in maps stores in major cities, and cost a few dollars apiece. Dealers usually stock local area maps and can order others for you.

Keep in mind when you're buying or ordering maps that the larger the scale, the greater the detail. And get your maps together long before you expect to depart on a trip. Other maps of big waters may be available from jurisdictional agencies such as the Corps of Engineers and the TVA, although their maps are rarely detailed enough to give you more than general information.

Maps supplied by private firms are often geared to fishermen's interests and provide a good deal of underwater contour information. Their size and scale will determine how helpful they are as boating and fishing aids. Many good ones are available at tackle shops, sporting goods stores, and marinas near popular waterways. In addition, check with state fisheries agencies. They often have contour maps (ranging from large scale to an 8½-x-11 reduction) particularly for smaller lakes and ponds.

Lake maps may not be perfectly accurate, and underwater contour maps or navigational charts may not indicate every structure you find in the water. But for fishermen who know bass habitat and behavior, the maps can identify areas likely to be productive. This is particularly helpful on big lakes, where it would take an inordinate amount of time to explore for bass and bass habitat. These maps not only help you find your way around, but also help you locate the types of seasonally preferred habitats discussed earlier in this book. Moreover, you can refer to your map to search out areas similar to those in which you've already found bass.

The symbols for the features shown on a map are easily deciphered once you've read the symbols chart. Look for features that indicate habitat in the water you're fishing at the time of year you're there. One spring I used a contour map of Truman Lake in Missouri to direct me to feeder creeks. I fished a few, and found that bass were nearly ready to spawn in the backs of coves and feeder creeks, and caught some nice fish shallow along sharply sloped banks adjacent to deep water. Then I used the map to point me to other creeks and coves with similar features and started exploring. In summer or fall, I would have been looking for a different situation.

It's a good idea, incidentally, to waterproof maps or store them in a large, clear, sealable plastic pouch to help them last in marine environments. Color-coding the different contour levels or marking certain areas with indelible markers is also worthwhile.

THE

Here's a classic flipping situation: flooded timber, especially a fallen tree, in murky water.

FINE
POINTS

Most of the fine points of tackle usage and angling technique are understood but not often expressed by experienced anglers, and they tend to be lost in the usual fundamental reviews of bass-fishing information. These are the pivotal details passed on by the veterans. They are based on years of trial and error and the insight that comes with experience. If you appreciate their value and use them well, you'll become a better bass fisherman. Remember that how you use your tackle is as important to your success as which tackle you use—often more important.

Practical Casting Techniques

All anglers should fully master casting technique. Most fishermen know basic casting procedures, but the finer points of casting, as related to bass fishing, often need sharpening.

The first cast to a likely bass hole is often the most important one, so it pays to make each cast count. That requires practice, but it also helps to use fish sense while casting. Every cast should have a purpose; it should be directed at a likely bass hideout, and that spot should be fished in a deliberate manner. If, for example, you are fishing crankbaits along a rocky shoreline that drops off dramatically, you won't have success if

your lure consistently lands 6 feet out from shore. No matter how deep your lure dives, it will have missed a prime area right from the start, whether the fish are hugging the bank or 12 feet down on the bottom.

Make every cast count by knowing what visible cover bass prefer and then by casting to the position likely to do the most good. Make casts to all sides of likely places. And learn how to feather your casts so that the lure doesn't come crashing down on the water's surface like a bomb. With spinning tackle most people use their index finger to control the cast and water entry. You might try the technique used by professional casting demonstrator and master bass angler Stan Fagerstrom; he takes the bail off a spinning reel, puts his noncasting hand on the spool and uses the forefinger of that hand to feather the line as it comes off the spool. With baitcasting gear you achieve accuracy with delicate thumb control on the reel spool. Raising your rod tip at the last moment helps soften lure impact, but is not reliable as a means of controlling accuracy. Sidearm or underhand loop casting, where it can be accomplished, is an effective method of making a soft presentation.

Forget about long-range casts for most bass fishing, with the exception of certain crankbait-fishing. Short- and medium-distance casts are probably better much of the time. Most long casts waste time because they require you to make a retrieve over a lot of barren water. If the bass are within the first 15 feet of shore, don't sit 100 feet out banging away unless the water is especially clear and the fish are spooky.

By covering a lot of water through most of the retrieve, you ultimately squander a lot of fishing time during the day. You also risk losing a fish that strikes your lure at long distances, because distance and line stretch (more of a factor with nylon monofilament than with braided or fused super line) may keep you from setting the hook properly or controlling the fight.

Many times I've been asked to move the boat out from shore or from grass or weed patches by anglers who are so used to making 70-foot over-head casts with spinning tackle that they can't cope with 30-foot flips into brushy, weedy spots. But you have much more control over a fish on a short line than on a long one.

As in all forms of angling, the basic casts in bass fishing are the overhead, sidearm, and underhand casts. In other types of fishing, the overhead cast is used perhaps 75 percent of the time, while the other two casts are seldom used. In bass fishing, however, because of the nature of the cover in which these species are found and because of the necessity for accurate lure placement, there is a regular need to use all three casts. Therefore, you must become proficient enough with them to make accurate, quiet lure presentations.

The overhead cast is the most common cast in bass fishing. Here, the wrist and forearm do all the work, using the top section of the rod for thrust. The cast begins with the rod low and pointed at the target. Bring the rod up crisply to a point slightly beyond vertical position, where flex in the rod tip will carry it back; then, without hesitating, start the forward motion sharply, releasing the lure halfway between the rod's vertical and horizontal positions. The entire casting action should be a smooth, flowing motion; you are doing more than just hauling back and heaving.

The sidearm cast is similar in motion to the

When fishing any isolated object, such as a stump, don't aim your cast to land directly on or in front of it; that usually spooks a bass. Make your first cast beyond and away from the stump, a tactic that may draw out a fish. Make the next one beyond it also, but bring the lure as close to the object as is feasible, even bumping it. Make sure that you and your partner have covered all angles.

overhead, except that the movement is horizontal rather than vertical. The sidearm cast can be dangerous if performed next to another angler in a small boat, so you must be mindful of the position of your companions at all times.

To cast underhand, hold the rod waist high, halfway between the vertical and horizontal positions. The rod must be flexed up, then down, then up again to gain momentum for the lure through the flex. Many rods are too stiff to permit this kind of casting.

Another cast that I use in tight quarters or for short ranges is a *flip cast,* which is something of a cross between the sidearm and underhand casts (different from flipping). Start with the rod horizontal to your side, but bring it backward only a short distance and then make a loop with the tip so that the tip springs around in a 270-degree arc and flips the lure straight out and low. This cast is used for short-distance (under 20 feet) work in areas where you can't bring your rod up or back for a conventional cast. This cast is almost impossible to accomplish if you're sitting down in a boat.

Setting the Drag

I've met so many anglers who have told me exciting but woeful tales of losing monster bass—in some cases, surely world records— because the fish broke the line, that I have identified the same pattern in nearly every experience. It amazes me how many 8-pounders break 17-pound line, how many 12- and 15-pounders break 30- (even 40!) pound line, and that the hapless and harried victim doesn't recognize the incongruity here and doesn't realize that it was his own fault.

Let's be honest; a 10-pound bass swimming at maximum speed can't possibly apply 30 pounds of pressure to your tackle. Technically, on a dead-weight basis you should be able to hang that 10-pounder from 12-pound or stronger line without the line breaking. So why does that fish break it in the water while fighting to get free? Let's analyze the possibilities.

First, you could have bad line, weak in spots. That's possible, and anglers always blame the line first. Seldom, though, is this blame deserved, particularly if the line was a premium-grade product from a recognized manufacturer. Second, the line could have been cut or frayed or poorly knotted. This is a more likely explanation, especially if you're angling in areas with many abrasive obstructions and you don't check your line periodically. Cut or frayed sections may be only half as strong as the undamaged portions. If the knot slipped or didn't hold up, you should be able to tell by examining the line. If the line is curled, then your knot slipped out; portions of a broken knot may still remain on the line. Third, the line might have broken because it took more pressure than it could absorb, even if it was strong line. This is often the main reason for breakage; however, it is not due to the brute force or sheer weight of the fish so much as to the angler's failure to properly

employ one of the primary features of his fishing reel—the drag.

The purpose of the drag is to let line slip from the reel at varying pressures when force is applied to the line. It serves as a shock absorber, or clutch. The looser it is set, the less force is required to strip line off. If the drag is set properly, a strong fish may be able to take line from the spool by applying less pressure than would be required to break the line or knot (this is determined by the breaking strength of your line and the efficiency of your knot, as detailed in Chapter 4). Thus, the drag acts as insurance, as a buffer between you and the fish. Properly set line drag is most useful when you're playing strong, hard-fighting fish, using light line, and reacting to sudden surges by the fish. Such surges may occur at the beginning of the fight and especially as you bring a still-green fish alongside the boat, and they are crucial times in playing a fish.

The reason so many big bass are lost due to line breakage is that the angler tightened the drag so there would be no slippage. In effect, he did not use the drag. When the big fish made a sudden surge, there was no shock absorption (other than line stretch if he was using monofilament). The impact of the rush was more than the line could withstand, so either the line or the knot broke.

In defense of anglers who use tight drags, it should be noted that most do so because of the habitat in which they are fishing. Thick grass, hyacinths, timber, and stump fields leave little margin for error when you hook a big bass among them. The fish usually tries to get to cover, where he may break off or pull free, and you have to muscle him away from it. This can't be accomplished easily with light line or a loose drag, so you have to compromise in these situations.

The most accurate way to set the drag is to bring line off the spool through the rod guides and attach it to a reliable spring scale. Keep the rod up as if you were fighting a fish and have someone pull on the scale as you watch the dial to see at what amount of pressure the drag began to slip. Lighten or increase tension accordingly. I set the drag tension at between 30 and 50 percent of the breaking strength of the line for normal bass-fishing conditions. In heavy cover I'll raise the tension to roughly 75 percent. If you think about drag tension in terms of the breaking strength of your line, you'll realize that 50 percent of 12-pound line is still 6 pounds of pressure, and few fishermen exert 6 or more pounds of pressure even when setting the hook. I think most anglers would be fooled if they were to pull line off their drag and guess the tension setting.

An important point to realize about drag tension is that the less line you have on your spool, the greater the tension will be. As the diameter of the spool gets smaller, more force is required to pull line from it. In bass fishing, as I've mentioned, line capacity is seldom much of a factor, so this item about drag doesn't usually come into play. Nonetheless, if you use your tackle for other species of fish, such as striped bass, that may take a lot of line, you need to be aware of this and to compensate accordingly by not having too tight a drag at the outset.

With a lot of experience, you can set the drag by hand, adjusting the drag control and pulling line off by hand until you reach what feels like a good tension setting. That's what I do, but it is imprecise. Another, better technique is to catch your lure or bait hook on some solid object, like the underside of an oarlock or a handrail, and pull back on your rod to approximate the surge of a fish. Adjust the drag while doing this to find what feels like a suitable setting.

I like to set the drag somewhat loose when using light and ultralight tackle and particularly when fishing for smallmouth bass, though not so loose that line slips when I set the hook (which impairs hook-setting efficiency). In open water a loose drag gives the fish a little more of a fighting chance and adds to the fun. And you can apply extra drag tension if need be. By cupping the palm of your hand over a spinning-reel spool or by putting your thumb on a baitcasting-reel spool, you can apply some additional tension to what your drag is applying.

Be aware of the importance of using the reel drag properly and check the drag periodically. It has been known to freeze when stored too tight for long periods (it's usually hard to free initially, and the flow of line is jerky), so keep the drag pressure loose when storing a reel and adjust it at the start of each day's fishing.

Mastering the Retrieve

The art of retrieving may be the most underrated element of bass fishing. Working the lure is an intrinsic part of the fishing process. We detailed specific retrieval methods in each lure category in Chapter 5, but there are some fine points to cover that are basic to all types of lures.

Most of the time, plastic worms are fished in and around cover and on the bottom. A worm should be retrieved slowly, crawled along the bottom, and lifted and dropped over stumps, limbs, and other obstructions.

The keys to successful retrieval of most lures are depth control, action, and speed, all of which vary in importance depending on the situation and the lure. It should be obvious to most anglers that achieving the proper depth is perhaps the most important factor, since you can't hope to catch fish unless you get your offering down to the fish's level. Only an extremely aggressive bass will go far to catch bait not in its area.

If you are not catching bass, it may be because you are not fishing deep enough, even though you're fishing in the right territory. One of the reasons that plastic worms are the single most effective type of largemouth-bass bait is that they are almost always fished on the bottom. On the bottom, whether it is in 2 feet of water or 12, is where the bass usually are.

The ability to achieve a certain depth is a function of the design of the lure and the way in which you use it. A plastic worm or jig must weigh enough to maintain contact with the bottom for the length of the distance covered in the retrieve, when it is used in such a manner and not (as in the case of a jig) fished vertically in open water. But, of course, you first have to let that bait hit the bottom and not retrieve it too fast.

Don't rely on the diving ability of plugs as stated in the manufacturer's packaging. You can easily test this feature yourself by tying on a lure and casting it over a known depth. When you retrieve it a few times, if it doesn't scratch the bottom where you're fishing, bouncing off obstacles and making the rod tip pulsate as it contacts the underwater terrain, then that lure is not diving deep enough for you. And if a new plug was on the bottom, you should be able to see the scuff marks on its bill or lip.

Another factor related to depth and diving lures is your line. A plug will dive deeper on light line than it will on heavy line. Light or thin lines have a smaller diameter and offer less water resistance, allowing the lure to reach greater depth. Sometimes the difference is minute, but the difference between a diver retrieved on standard 20-pound-test line versus one retrieved on standard 10-pound-test might be enough (1 to 3 feet) to bring success.

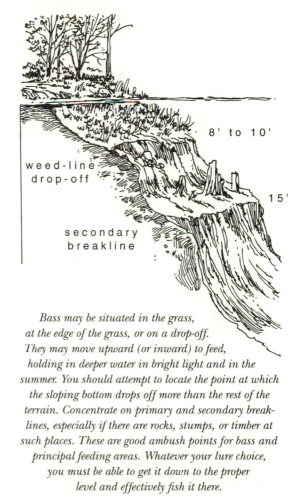

Bass may be situated in the grass, at the edge of the grass, or on a drop-off. They may move upward (or inward) to feed, holding in deeper water in bright light and in the summer. You should attempt to locate the point at which the sloping bottom drops off more than the rest of the terrain. Concentrate on primary and secondary breaklines, especially if there are rocks, stumps, or timber at such places. These are good ambush points for bass and principal feeding areas. Whatever your lure choice, you must be able to get it down to the proper level and effectively fish it there.

Many reels have a high-speed retrieve, which enables you to bring in some lures rapidly and to gain line quickly when fighting a fish. You retrieve a greater amount of line for each turn of the reel handle than with a slow-speed reel, which requires more effort on your part to retrieve the same amount of line. In some fishing situations an angler with the right lure but a slow-retrieve reel is at a disadvantage to another angler with the same lure but a higher retrieval speed. When the fish are sluggish, however, the reverse may be true. A high-speed reel lulls some anglers into retrieving too fast, dwelling more on fast fishing and covering a lot of territory than on proper presentation.

To some extent, speed is a factor in the retrieval of all lures. Moderate speed for plugs catches the least fish, with more succumbing to high- or low-speed retrieves. Some lures can be retrieved too fast, at which point they lose their tight action and run to the side.

Fishing Deep

Exactly what is "deep"? It varies between lakes and between fishermen. Anything more than 10 feet is relatively deep in bass fishing. In Florida, few lakes are more than 15 feet deep. In northern lakes, most of the water is more than 20 feet deep; bass have been caught as deep as 80 to 100 feet in some places. Getting your offering down to these fish is often more of a problem than getting them to strike. Here are some considerations for fishing deep.

A lot of attention has been given by manufacturers in the past decade to plugs that will dive more than 12 feet. Most smaller crankbaits will not go deeper than 12 feet on a normal cast-and-retrieve. There are plugs that dive 15 to 20 feet on a cast-and-retrieve, but to get them to work at that depth for a good period of time you usually have to make a pretty long cast, keep your rod tip down (or maybe in the water), and crank at moderate instead of fast speed. I have had some really good bass fishing with super-deep-diving plugs, in 15 to 25 feet of water, by both casting and trolling. You must be sure that

the plug is bumping along the bottom, and you should work it slowly, sometimes with a quick stop-and-go, for best results.

Remember that line diameter affects the depth your lure will attain and the way it will work. The bigger and heavier a jig, the faster it will fall. In really deep water, most jigging is done straight below the boat. In less deep, shoreline areas, jigs can be retrieved to cover a lot of bottom terrain. Worms, too, will go as deep as you like, but they are best fished on the cast-and-retrieve, rather than vertically, and are of limited value beyond 20 feet.

Any lure that sinks, of course, will achieve the depth you desire. The drawback here is that it takes time to get it to the desired depth. You can determine the sinking depth by counting until your lure reaches the bottom (as signified by slack line), trying to maintain a drop of 1 foot per count.

Using weights is another way to get lures deep. Sometimes small weights, such as split-shot or rubber-core sinkers, will be enough of an aid, though they may influence lure action. A good weight for river trollers is a bead-chain sinker; a good weight for drifting or trolling is a bottom bouncer. With both, a leader of 18 to 48 inches connects the weight to the lure. A good use for these weights is in casting or trolling small crankbaits, so that the lures will reach a depth they couldn't reach unaided. I use bottom bouncers occasionally to catch small-

To get crankbaits deep you have to use the right plug, make a fairly long cast, keep your rod tip down, and reel at a moderate, steady pace.

mouths in 20 to 25 feet of water, primarily floating/diving minnow- imitation plugs or shallow- to medium-depth crankbaits in crayfish and shad patterns.

In places where trolling is appropriate, people used to troll for bass, but today largemouth and smallmouth bass are pursued almost entirely by casting. Sometimes, however, trolling is a way to get deep and catch fish when other methods fail. I've done it and caught big bass that way. The open-minded bass angler ought to know about trolling.

The most successful and functional lure for bass trolling is a crankbait. Although earlier models were rather bulbous in shape, newer ones are smaller in length and girth and have longer lips that allow for deep diving and more built-in action through a tighter, better-controlled wiggling pattern. Usually, the larger the lip, the greater the trolling depth. The exceptions to this are lures that sink immediately to

the bottom because they aren't designed to float. They, too, may have smallish lips, but it is their weight, the size and amount of line you have out, and your boat speed that determine their working depth.

One critically important aspect of crankbait-fishing overlooked by many bass anglers, particularly if they're unaccustomed to trolling crankbaits, is the diving ability of the lure. Because you must fish near-bottom structure for bass, you must know how deep any diving plug runs to be effective with it. Diving abilities depend on the lure, the strength of your line, and the speed of your boat.

Spoons and spinners make their trolling mark, too. The average diehard bass caster won't have a spoon in his tackle box appropriate for trolling. One-eighth to ¼-ounce thick-bodied spoons up to 3 inches long can be cast or trolled, and lighter, thin-metal spoons up to a similar length are strictly for trolling. These

How you fish is often as important as what you fish with, and getting down to the level of the bass is crucial for success, especially in summer on large lakes and reservoirs. Watch your sonar and use the right lure to get deep.

are the same types of spoons used for trout trolling. In fact, smallmouth bass are often caught accidentally on spoons trolled for trout in two-story lakes hosting warm-water and cold-water species of fish.

Spoons and spinners sink, of course, and this poses problems for trollers when they momentarily stop, because the lure sinks quickly to the bottom and invites a hangup. Trolling spoons are better fished on downriggers in deep or intermediate-depth waters. Thin spoons don't achieve any depth when trolled, so they really must be fished behind a downrigger weight or some weighted-line system. Heavier spoons will achieve some depth, but it is much harder to discern diving depths with such a lure when it is flatlined than it is with a plug. When bass are relatively shallow, flatlining a spoon can have merit, but for deeper trolling, you need

a more controlled method of presentation at specific depths.

Although it is by no means a standard tool for bass fishermen, a downrigger certainly can be used for bass, particularly smallmouths. One of the best pieces of graph-recorder paper that I ever ran was on Lake Ontario one summer while smallmouth-bass fishing with downriggers. We trolled small crayfish plugs and spoons at 30 feet over a cobblestone bottom and watched smallmouths come up from the rocks, look at the downrigger weights, and strike the lures that were trailing a short distance behind.

Spinners are not usually thought of as a bass lure by many anglers today, particularly by those who chase largemouths exclusively or who never fish streams, but spinners are one of the most popular lure types in the world. A favorite in-line spinner for bait fishermen is the so-called June

This bass angler is trying some trolling with a downrigger to get deep in a reservoir. Trolling for bass is not common, but it can be effective.

Bug, which features a long-shank hook and a single rotating blade with beads along the shaft. Variations of this, especially the Erie Dearie, are popular lures for smallmouth bass and walleye.

One of the best times to fish spinners for smallmouths in lakes is just before spawning (provided the season is open) and in the fall, when bass are just off rocky shorelines in 5 to 8 feet of water. Fish them slowly, but fast enough to keep the blade turning and the lure from hanging up on the bottom constantly. This is essentially flatline trolling, although line is often weighted with split shot to help keep a trolled spinner down.

Whether fishermen cast or troll for bass, when they are unsuccessful, it is often because they fail to get their offerings down to the level of the fish. Accomplishing that is often more of a problem than getting bass to strike. When trolling for bass, always be cognizant of the bottom depth, the level at which you believe bass are located, and the level that your trolled lure is actually working.

Fishing Close

Quiet presentations and close-to-cover fishing can be productive for largemouth bass, and they require specialized methods. One such old-time method of sneak presentations in shallow areas is *jiggerpoling*. Few anglers try it anymore. To jiggerpole, you attach a minnow-shaped floating plug or a hooked piece of fish belly or pork strip to the tip of a long cane pole with a short line. A fisherman sits in the bow of a boat (a pirogue or small jonboat), prowls shallow cover, and jiggers or dapples the lure in and around grassy banks and stumps. In another method, called *yo-yoing* or *doodlesocking*, a small clearing is made (with a pole or paddle) in a clump of thick moss, milfoil, or other grass, and a jig or worm dropped into it.

Flipping

Without question the premier close-to-cover bass-fishing technique today is *flipping*. Some form of flipping has been around for years and

was called *dabbling* or *pitching* until the marketing wizards latched onto it.

Flipping is a fairly simple, controlled, short-casting technique used in close quarters for presenting a moderately heavy jig or plastic worm quietly and accurately to cover that cannot be properly worked by a lure cast from a long distance.

Imagine that you're looking at a bank with a sharply sloping shoreline. Within half a foot of the bank are some bushes, the base of which may be in 2 feet of water. Any plug pitched at such a target will land directly in front of it and will be on its way without getting very near the fish. A worm might do the trick, but the first cast would have to be extremely accurate; most likely the worm would fall too far in front of the bush to entice the bass out. But when flipping, you could position your boat 15 to 18 feet from the bush and use a long rod to swing a jig or worm so that it lands in the most opportune place without smashing down noisily on the water's surface. A lot of bass inhabit thick cover, and flipping is a surefire way of getting your bait literally in front of their mouths.

At a time when bass are probably more attuned to the ways of man and more skittish than before, flipping is a good technique to use with such cover as brush, standing timber and stumps, logjams or debris-filled flotsam, heavy lily-pad and vegetation clusters, steep craggy ledges, docks, and boathouses. Flipping will reach the bass holding close to such cover.

The tackle required is a long rod, heavy line, and a jig or worm. The rod should be 7 to 8 feet long, with a long, straight handle. It must be stout, because bass are often violently jerked out of heavy cover on a short length of line, and the bigger the bass, the greater the line stress and the greater the degree of difficulty. Flipping rods are one-piece, with an upper section that telescopes down into the handle for easy transportation and storage. Most flipping is done with baitcasting tackle, but some anglers prefer spinning gear. The same rod features, however, are applicable to both. Flipping takes a toll on your arm muscles if you do it for a long time, so a graphite rod, weighing considerably less than a fiberglass rod, is beneficial.

The reel used on a flipping rod can be the same that you use for other bass-fishing applications, but it is best if it's light and has a narrow spool (line capacity is not a factor). It should also have a clear sideplate (no knobs sticking out to catch line). A reel that allows one-handed operation is a big plus. A so-called *flipping feature,* which allows the line to be stripped out without your having to disengage and reengage the freespool is convenient, as you often have to strip off more line but don't have to take time to crank the handle to engage the gears.

Most flippers have used 25- to 30- pound-test nylon monofilament line because of the lack of stretch, greater abrasion resistance (you often fish in abrasive areas), and greater line strength (to horse big fish out of thick cover). You can use lighter line, but you have to be sensible. Braided and fused super lines, with their high strength and low diameter, are good candidates for flipping. Their low stretch improves strike detection, but because of the close sudden struggles that characterize flipping, you'll have to be careful that you don't overload your rod.

Black or brown jigs, primarily ½-ounce size, but also a little lighter and a little heavier, are the most popular flipping baits. They should have fiber weedguards when used in all but rocky ledge areas and sport a "living rubber" skirt and a large hook. They are adorned with all manner of enticements, including worms, curl-tail grubs, pork strips, and the like, but pork chunks (No. 11 Uncle Josh in black or brown) are the most popular.

I prefer to flip a plastic worm, however, and usually do until someone fishing with me proves that jigs are doing it and worms are not. I use a 7- to 8-inch worm on a 5/0 hook for this, and a heavy (⅜- or ½-ounce) slip sinker that is pegged to prevent it from sliding up the line. This seems to get hung up less frequently than a jig, and when you have a strike you can hesitate for the slightest moment to get a firm hookset. Try a worm with a paddle or beaver tail when flipping, although curl tails work also if they aren't so

To flip, let out about 7 to 9 feet of line from rod tip to lure; strip line off the reel and hold it in your left hand (1). Point the rod tip up and out and swing the jig forward (2). The bait will come back toward you, and when it reaches the top of its pendulumlike swing, direct it toward the target (3). Lower the rod tip, and let line flow through your free hand; extend your rod arm if necessary to reach the target, and keep the line in your hand (4).

sinewy that they grab onto every limb.

To flip properly, remember that your goal is to make a pinpoint bait presentation to a particular object within 10 to 20 feet of your boat and to do so in a quiet, splash-free manner. Seldom are you able to flip while sitting down; this is a technique that requires stand-up work, occasionally with two fishermen close together in the bow of a boat (as when working every nook and cranny of a stump- and blowdown-filled stretch of shoreline). To begin flipping, let out about 7 to 9 feet of line from rod tip to lure. Strip line off the reel until your free hand and rod hand are fully extended away from each other; this will give you 5 to 7 feet of line in your free hand. Considering the length of line out and the length of your rod, you're now able to reach a target 20 to 22 feet away (a few more if you count the length of your arm).

To flip your bait out, raise the rod tip and swing the jig back toward you under the rod. The motion demands wrist action, not elbow or shoulder movement. The bait swings back toward you, and when it reaches the top of its pendulumlike swing, flick your rod-holding wrist to direct the lure toward its target. Lower the rod tip, and let line flow through your free hand. Extend your rod arm if necessary to reach the target, and keep the line in your hand until it reaches the target. When you retrieve the lure to move it to another spot, lower the rod tip and point it toward the lure, grab the line between reel and first guide with your free hand and strip it back while lifting up on your rod (similar to the hauling technique used by fly casters). Swing the lure out and back and send it forward again to the next object.

When the lure is in the water, you may jig it up and down or crawl it along after it has fallen freely to the bottom. Climb it up, over, and through all the cover. Closely watch the line for the slightest movement, and be attentive to the softest strike. Don't keep the lure in any one place long, and try to nudge it through cover instead of ripping it. When you set the hook, you may do so in the conventional manner, with one hand on the reel handle and the other on the rod handle, and play the fish out of the cover (easier done with a worm). Often, however, a strike occurs when you're holding line in your free hand and the rod in your other hand and there isn't time to grab the tackle conventionally, so you strip the free line back, jerk the rod tip up sharply, and hope you not only have gotten hook penetration but can yank the fish out, all in the same motion. It doesn't always happen, and a lot of good-size fish are lost with flipping, so you have to work fast and try to outmuscle the fish through the cover as best you can. At times you'll stick a small fish and yank him clear out of the cover

and over the boat, but when you hook a big bass in thick cover while flipping, you'll have an excitingly fast and furious bulldog scrap.

Tuning Crankbaits

Considering the advanced state of manufacturing technology, as well as the hefty retail purchase price, it would seem that crankbaits should be fishable right out of the box. Alas, 'tis not so. Not every lure can be freed from its wrappings, knotted on your line, and run true, cast after bass-catching cast. Some need extensive modification, and, unfortunately, a few never run well at all. Many manufacturers have refined their quality-control methods and are producing lures that essentially run true out of the box (a few, such as Rapalas, are all tank-tested and tuned at the plant before distribution). Nonetheless, even good-tracking lures can run awry after catching fish, so you need to know what to do to get the best action out of these products.

Most crankbaits have clear plastic bills of various lengths and shapes for diving. Line-tie screws are attached to these bills, and all running problems center on these little screws. When a crankbait runs awry, it is the fault of the line-tie. The line-tie screw must be placed vertical to the mean horizontal plane of the lure's bill, but since this screw eye is positioned partially by hand at the manufacturing plant, the element of human error can be introduced. And occasionally an assembler misaligns the screw. If it is placed a fraction of an inch out of position, the lure will not run perfectly true and will need tuning.

A well-designed crankbait should have a good wiggling action. Some lures have a tight action, and some have more of a wide wobble. Whichever action it exhibits, a swimming or diving lure should come back to you in a straight line. The body of the lure should be vertical, not canted off to either side. It's important to get the lure running perfectly true; if it runs even a little bit off, it has an unnatural action that will probably cost you fish. It's a good idea to check each plug before you fish it; tie it on your line, drop a few feet of line from the tip of the rod to the lure,

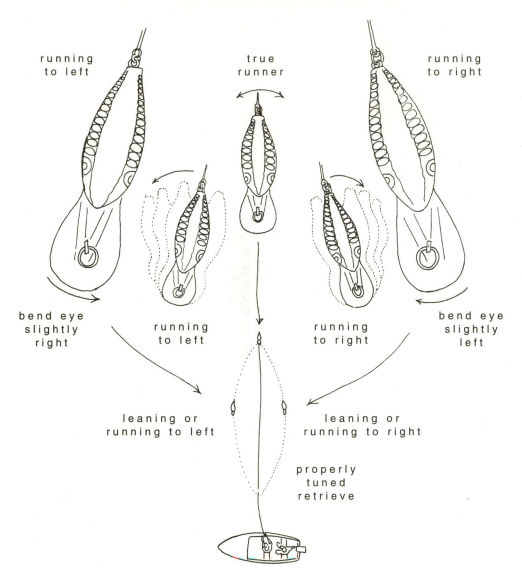

To tune a crankbait to run properly, bend the line-tie in the opposite direction from which the lure is running astray. Don't twist the line-tie, which may loosen it, but bend it with a pair of needlenose pliers. Do this in increments until you get the crankbait running straight ahead with a good side-to-side wobble.

then run the lure through the water a few times next to you. If it doesn't run properly, adjust it immediately.

To adjust a crankbait, you need only a pair of pliers, preferably needlenose, to bend the line-tie screw. If, as you watch the path of retrieve head-on, the lure is running to your right, you must bend the line-tie screw to the left (again, looking at it head-on). If the lure runs left, bend the screw right. Adjust the screw in stages, bending it slightly, then casting and retrieving once to see the change. Keep adjusting and changing until the lure runs true. In extreme cases you may have to bend the line-tie screw far from its original position. When bending the line-tie screw, be careful that you do not loosen it, which may render the plug unusable.

Before you tune a lure that seems to run awry, make sure you are not retrieving it too fast. All plugs have a top working speed, beyond which they will not run properly, and it's not the same for all lures. With today's high-speed-retrieve reels, you could be reeling your lures faster than they will run effectively. And, make sure you're not working the lure against the movement of the boat, which will also cause it to run improperly. Check it when the boat is not moving, or put the lure in the water next to the boat and watch its action.

Most crankbaits will not run well if a tight knot is tied directly to the screw eye. For this reason, it is best to use a split ring or rounded snap (not snap swivel) and tie your knot to that. (Most crankbaits come with split rings or snaps.) Snap swivels may alter the action of these plugs, making perfect tuning a difficult task. A lure that is already tuned to work without a snap swivel may have to be retuned to work with it. And a snap swivel is one more thing that can go wrong when you're fighting a fish. The only advantages to using a snap swivel are that it facilitates lure changing and prevents twist. But crankbaits don't induce twist, and snaps will ease the job of lure changing. However, few avid anglers, myself included, use snaps for bass fishing, preferring to tie the line directly to the split ring on the lure. In a rush, I can tie a knot to a crankbait in about 30 seconds, which is seldom a significant loss. Moreover, a foot or so of line above the lure is sure to get abraded with a bit of use, necessitating regular line inspection, clipping, and reknotting.

Sometimes crankbaits can be sensitive to the slightest adornment. If you pull a plug through weeds and get a tiny confetti trailer on your hooks or line-tie, you'll feel the action of the lure change. Tie a new knot on a bait that was running fine, and the action may be off due to the position of the knot. This is corrected by changing the knot's position and realigning it or by retying the knot and snugging it tight. You may also find that some crankbaits (deep-diving minnow-shaped plugs and some surface lures) work best if you use a loop knot.

Some crankbaits seem to need more frequent tuning than others, and some small lures need more frequent tuning than large ones. Some never get tuned exactly right. It is not uncommon to make many casts and retrieves and modifications of a new lure before you get it running to your satisfaction. So when you have a finely tuned, fish-catching crankbait, you should treat it with respect and give it a special place in your tackle box.

Ideally, you should tune all your lures before they are put to the ultimate fishing test. When I don't want to waste time tuning lures on a fishing trip, I go to a lake beforehand to check the action of every crankbait I plan to bring along. You can do that if you have a pool or beach area in which to work leisurely. A swimming pool is especially good because you can see how the lure works and how deep it dives. If you want to observe action and depth of retrieve, don goggles and get into the water while a friend casts. Close-up observation of a working lure provides reliable information you can't get any other way.

Preparation and Versatility

With all the emphasis these days on fishing techniques, habitat identification, and fisheries knowledge, too often the simple, practical matters are neglected.

Many fishermen do not prepare any of their tackle before starting the day—a big oversight. For most bass fishermen, especially the occasional angler, and particularly during summer months, the early morning is a productive time. Every moment you lose then is a vital one. Don't be readying equipment at lakeside when you could be fishing. Rig your tackle, even to the point of tying on a lure you expect to use, the night before you go fishing. You can always retie a hook or lure for the conditions in the morning. Get all your lures and accessory equipment shipshape beforehand, too. When the sun peeks over the trees and the mist rises off the water, you should be out there fishing, not running line through guides and tying knots onto hooks and lures.

A well-organized tackle box (or boxes) is a step in the right direction. It allows you to group lures by types and categories, yet avoid the extremely annoying entanglement that results when several treble-hook lures are placed in the same compartment. You ought to organize your lures in such a way that when you need something, you know where it is, and you can get it out and tie it on fast.

Having several fishing outfits on hand and ready to use on any given outing adds to your preparedness and versatility as well. But having one or more additional rods prepared for fishing is even better. A lure of a different type, style, and color for each rod makes sense.

Having several rods at the ready is not a sign of overeagerness. It makes good fishing sense. I fish with four or five rods in the boat most of the time. I use only one at a time, of course, but I can switch instantly if necessary. This pays off most when a bass strikes but misses a lure. Often the fish will not come after the same lure a second time, but if you pick up another bait immediately and throw it out, he'll probably hit that one.

Several rods are also a benefit when a feeding fish or school of bass surfaces nearby; you can drop the rod you are fishing with, pick up another with a surface lure on it, and whip out a cast to the action spot. Also, having rods with different strengths of line can be of immense value if you have to go to heavier or lighter tackle than originally planned.

Some words about versatility: fishing conditions can change from day to day and lake to lake. The most consistently successful bass fishermen are those who can adapt to these changes. This necessitates proficiency with a variety of tackle, fishing techniques, and lure

presentations. The one-lure fisherman is in for a number of fishless days.

Aside from tackle and tackle-related equipment, lack of boat readiness is another factor that hampers efficient fishing operations. Fueling up in the morning is probably the worst offense (though better to do this than run out of gas halfway across the lake).

If you are new to a lake or will fish it for the first time, you'll save a lot of fishing time if you find out as much as possible about it beforehand. Trading stories on the dock; tinkering with boat, motor, accessories, or tackle on the water; running needlessly back and forth over the lake; and spending too much time in unproductive areas or in repetitive situations will also squander your fishing time. Do your best to minimize those possibilities. One of the hallmarks of better fishermen is that they have an uncanny knack of knowing when to change, when to do something different, when to go to a new locale. Adaptability, versatility, and preparedness are good traits to cultivate.

Confidence

Some anglers are more astute than others; some are just plain luckier; some are blessed with more natural talent. But every angler can improve his skills if he desires to do so and is willing to make the effort. Confidence is earned through experience. It can't be bought in the tackle shop or acquired from a successful and experienced compatriot. It is earned through experience.

You acquire confidence by doing and learning, by developing an understanding of the habits and habitat of your quarry, by mastering the intricacies of your tackle, and by slowly putting together the pieces of the bass-fishing jigsaw puzzle. I hope this book helps to upgrade your fishing skills so your confidence will soar.

Just going out and catching a couple of bass is a big boost to the neophyte's confidence. So is having and knowing how to use good equipment. When I first started getting seriously involved in fishing, I got a top-quality spinning rod and reel. It was one of the best outfits then available, and the mere possession of that equipment gave me confidence. Sure, that's a psychological ploy, but for some people it works—the fact that they have good equipment instills in them the desire to achieve and the motivation to learn and become more skillful.

I also remember how frustrated I was back then on days when I caught little or nothing. And there were many. I used to wonder when I'd catch more than two keepers each outing. Then I wondered if I'd ever catch a limit. Eventually I was wondering about a big-fish limit. But I stopped wondering a long time ago. And catching a limit isn't as important as having a good time anyway. As you learn and as your abilities grow, your level of bass-fishing competence rises, and you become more successful. Success breeds confidence, which in turn may foster greater success.

Every move that a good bass fisherman makes is related to confidence: in selecting a lure, selecting an area to fish, placing casts; judging when to stay in, or leave, a particular spot; deciding on the appropriate retrieve; and so on. Because he is confident, he concentrates harder on what he is doing and is generally more attentive to the nuances of bass fishing. At the same time, he realizes that not every cast will produce a fish, nor will every day be a good one. He realizes that bass are unpredictable creatures, and he can't always figure them out, which is probably why he likes the sport in the first place. Yet, every top-notch bass angler I know is convinced that there's a bass hiding by the nearest ambush point and that he's going to catch it. That's confidence.

Don't overlook the effects of feeling positive about your abilities and about your understanding of the world of bass fishing. Well-placed confidence may be the best your most valuable equipment.

9   PLAYING,

Keep bass in the water, out of a net, and off the floor of the boat if you plan on releasing them.

LANDING, AND RELEASING BASS

The pleasures of preparation and anticipation, the enjoyment of the outdoors, the pursuit of the unseen, and the challenge of outwitting a game quarry are among the joys of bass fishing. The ultimate thrill for most anglers, however, is hooking and fighting the fish. Therefore, knowing how to play, land, and handle bass and how to care for those that you keep is especially important.

Playing and Landing Bass

With heavy tackle and relatively small bass, what you do to bring that fish to net doesn't matter too much, because the odds are in your favor. But when you match your tackle to the quarry, making the fight more balanced, or when you latch onto a particularly strong or large bass, your skill at handling that fish from hooking to netting will be tested. Choreographing the fight with a fish under these conditions is critical and can be mastered through experience, provided you understand the fundamentals.

The first step in fighting a bass is to be prepared for what is about to happen. Start by keeping your rod tip down during the retrieve. With the tip down, you're in the best position to respond to a strike. If there is little or no slack in the line, you can make a forceful sweep up or

back when you set the hook and then be in immediate control of the bass to begin playing it. (When working a jig or plastic worm, however, it is necessary to keep the rod tip up to feel the lure and readily detect a strike.) When setting the hook, you can compensate for a high rod position by bowing the rod slightly toward the fish while reeling up slack; this enables you to get a positive sweep and be in the proper position for the beginning of the fight.

Hook-setting is always a quickly accomplished maneuver. When a bass hits, the angler reacts reflexively, bringing his rod back and up sharply while holding the reel handle and reeling the instant he feels the fish. The position of the rod is important. The butt is jammed into the stomach or midchest area, and the full arc and power of the rod are brought into play.

Throughout the fight, keep the rod tip up and maintain pressure on the fish. The position of the rod butt remains unchanged. Reel the line in while lowering the rod; then pressure the fish as you bring the rod back up. This technique is used for all but the smallest fish; often referred to as *pumping*, it is most effective when you're fighting a large bass or using light line.

Often, a fish remains energetic even by the time you've worked it fairly close to you. Continue to keep the rod high. This is a time to be directing the fish. If you are in a boat and the fish streaks toward it (perhaps to swim under it), you could be at a disadvantage, particularly with light tackle. You must reel as fast as possible to prevent slack. If the fish gets under the boat, stick the rod tip well into the water to keep the line away from objects that might break it.

You should anticipate that a bass will rush the boat, so be prepared to head it around the stem or bow. In some cases, a companion can manipulate the boat (especially with an electric motor) to help swing the stern or bow away from a fish, a smart maneuver that can aid the playing of a large and energetic bass. If possible, go toward the bow or stern to better follow or control the fish. Don't get into a tug-of-war with a large, strong fish; use finesse rather than muscle.

When a fish swims around your boat, keep the rod up (sometimes out, too) and apply pressure to force its head up and to steer it clear of motors and propellers.

Eventually the fish is next to you and may be ready for landing. If it still has a last burst of energy, however, this will be a crucial time. Because of the short distance between you and the fish, a lot of stress will be placed on your tackle. You must act swiftly when the fish makes its last bolt for freedom. As it surges away, don't pressure it. Let it go. Point the rod at the fish at the critical moment so there is no rod pressure. A large bass will peel line off the drag, which, if set properly (and does not stick), will keep tension on the fish within the tolerance of the line's strength and provide the least amount of pressure. As the surge tapers, lift up the rod and work the fish.

If you're alone and without a net, be careful when landing the fish. Keep a taut line, extend the rod well back behind and over your head, and reach for the fish with your other hand. In this position, you are able to maintain some control over the fish, even if it is still active, and avoid creating the momentary line slack that may give the bass its freedom.

Remember that fish-playing maneuvers take place within a brief time span and the action is often fast. Your reactions must be swift and instinctive, and your tackle, particularly line and

reel drag, should be in top condition.

Unfortunately a lot of big bass are lost at or near the boat through the fault of the fisherman. Probably the greatest sin of new anglers is their reliance on muscle. They reel the fish right up to the tip of the rod when the catch is at boatside, as if they were going to spear it; and they apply too much pressure on a green fish near the boat. Finesse, common sense, and anticipation are the keys to landing bass.

Small to medium-size bass that are well hooked and caught on tackle that is sturdy enough to permit it, can be boated simply by

Bass fishermen are known for muscling in their quarry, often because the tackle they use is fairly heavy for the average size of the fish caught. A lot of anglers land their bass by swinging them into the boat, as this angler is doing, although crashing to the floor of the boat is not good for the fish.

Land a bass by grasping it with your thumb just inside the lower jaw, which immobilizes the fish and allows for secure handling when you remove the hook. Bass are particularly well suited to the lip hold.

being lifted aboard with the rod and then grabbed. However, some people haul the fish in and then let it fall to the floor of the boat, where it flops for a while before they can grab it. This is bad for the fish.

Landing fish by hand is a tricky maneuver with some species but a practical and desirable method for bass in most instances. Small fish that are to be released immediately should be unhooked to minimize handling.

You can unhook or land a bass by grasping its lower lip, if the fish is tired out before you try it. Simply insert your thumb over the lower lip, with your other fingers outside and underneath immobilizing the fish. Be careful not to plant your thumb on the hooks of the lure.

Large bass and very active fish can be netted. Yet many avid and successful bass fishermen rarely have a net in their boat and are unaccus-

tomed to using one when the need arises.

Here are some netting tips: Keep the net solidly in hand, at the ready, either motionless or out of sight, until a fish is almost within reach. Ideally, the fish should be headed for you so that it must continue forward or can be cut off by the net if it turns. As a general rule, I don't try to net a fish unless its head is on the surface or just breaking to the surface. If you try to net a fish that isn't headed for the net, a multihook lure will get snagged on the mesh or webbing of the net bag. That's one of the surest ways to lose a fish and one reason to be sure your net is the appropriate size.

Releasing Bass

Because bass are so popular, fishing pressure in many areas is intense. The "good old days" of ready limits and big fish catches are gone. Size and creel limits have become more restrictive, and slot limits have been increasingly instituted—all helping to provide better bass fishing in many lakes. For these reasons and more, it is important—indeed, it is a tenet of good sportsmanship—that anglers be concerned with the treatment of fish they do not keep. Those bass are more than just potential trophies; they are the fish that will help guarantee angling tomorrows.

On the face of it, releasing bass seems simple enough; unhook 'em and toss 'em back. From the moment it's hooked until well past its release, a bass is affected by many variables, all of which play a role in its survival.

The actual catching, landing, and physical handling during release are the most obvious ones. Luckily, bass are a reasonably hardy fish and are not too disturbed by moderately respectful handling. They can be grasped without harm to fish or fisherman, but always avoid excessive handling.

The manner in which bait or plastic-worm fishermen set the hook in a bass is one factor in that fish's survival after release. The longer you wait for a bass to swallow your offering, the greater the probability that the fish will be gut- or gill-hooked. There is no question that fish caught on artificial lures are less severely hooked than those caught on bait. Treble-hook lures, furthermore, are every bit as practical as single-hook lures, not only for hooking bass, but for ensuring their harmless release. They rarely are caught in the fish's stomach or gills, and usually hook the bass in the edge of the mouth.

Deep hooking poses problems because the hook can penetrate vital organs, either when swallowed or through the angler's effort to extricate it. Bass are seldom hooked deeply on lures, but commonly so on bait and occasionally on plastic worms, so it is critical that bait anglers understand what to do with a sublegal-size bass.

A small fish that is deeply hooked has a much greater chance of surviving if the hook is left in the stomach and the line is clipped off. Some studies show that line clipping can give a deeply hooked fish a 300-percent-greater chance of survival than one with the hook removed. Strong

stomach acids will dissolve a bronze or nickle hook over time. But stainless steel and cadmium-tin hooks do not break down in freshwater, so you should not use them in bass fishing.

Most fish that are gill-hooked will bleed. And if a bass is bleeding, its chances of survival decrease drastically. The gill, a delicate organ in all fish, should not be touched. If you have a bleeding bass that is of legal size, keep it and eat it. Release another, healthier fish that you may have already caught, or may catch later, in its stead.

Infection, bodily damage, and suffocation are the principal dangers of landing and handling a bass. All fish have a slimy, mucuslike coating over their bodies that protects them from bacterial infections. If a portion of this coating is removed, the fish's resistance to disease is lowered, a condition that may be fatal.

Netting can also remove some of the mucous coating—and scales—from a fish. Often a plug-caught fish gets enmeshed in a net because some of the loose hooks catch in the webbing. As the bass thrashes around and pulls against the stuck plug, it can bend the hooks or tear its mouth. Never drop a netted bass into the boat; hold it aloft and reach into the net to grab it by the mouth, so the hooks can be freed without undue damage to the fish. I net few of my bass, reserving the net for really big bass or for ensuring that a companion's fish will be landed.

If you intend to release the fish, don't let it flop around on the floor of your boat. This, too, results in mucous-coating and scale removal, and puts the fish in contact with substances on the bottom of your boat that are probably harmful.

Fishermen often grasp small bass tightly around their midsections to prevent movement during the unhooking process, and this can cause internal bleeding and organ damage. (Such handling, of course, is entirely acceptable for a fish that will be kept.)

The best technique for landing bass that are to be released is the lip hold, already described. It provides minimal physical contact and does the least damage. There are few other species of fish that can be grasped so handily, either because they have sharp teeth along their lower lip (which a bass does not) or because their mouths are too small for easy thumb insertion. But the lip hold requires caution, since a bass is usually hooked in some corner of the mouth, and the hooks are often exposed. If the lure has many hooks, the bass should be well subdued for your own safety before a lip-handling attempt is made.

Your hand should be wet before you touch the fish, to help prevent loss of mucous coating or scales. It is also best not to take the fish out of the water. Besides decreasing harmful physical contact, you avoid exposing the fish to the trauma of out-of-water breathing. The longer a fish is held out of its environment for unhooking, photographing, and so on, the lower its odds of survival. Almost any fish can be released without being touched at all if you hold your rod high enough to keep the fish's head up and use a pair of needlenose pliers to unhook the fish. This is a technique I often use for slimy, toothy fish such as pickerel and northern pike. As a general practice, however, I don't recommend it: if the fish thrashes and the hook pulls out, it could rocket back at you.

The best way to release a bass is technically not to catch it. This sounds like facetious advice, but it refers to shaking off a hooked fish at boatside. Sometimes you can bring a bass to the boat and use your rod and line to jiggle the lure free of the fish, especially if the fish is hooked lightly on a single hook or if your lure has barbless hooks (which it won't unless you've crimped the barbs down or filed them off). You have to be careful that you don't break light line or tear the mouth of the fish when heavy line is used, but sometimes gentle jiggling of the lure while the fish is lying passively near you will permit the hook to slip out. This gives you the satisfaction of hooking and playing a bass without having to touch it at all.

Besides handling, the two most important factors in the survival of released bass are water temperature and how the fish is played. A tired fish is much more susceptible to harm than a fairly vigorous one. Though bass are reasonably able fighters, they do not have to be played for extended periods, unless you are fishing with light tackle and the fish is exceptionally large. Bass have a better survival rate if they are played forcefully (not manhandled, but not coddled either), brought to the boat, and released as quickly as possible. If they do seem severely stressed, as they might be if you had a difficult time removing the hooks, hold them gently in the water and lead them around by the lip to force water and oxygen through the gills and into the respiratory system. Move them forward only, not back and forth.

Released fish are least likely to survive in late spring, summer, and early fall. Because the water temperature is warm then, the fish are either more stressed by the whole experience or less

If a bass is too lethargic to swim off on its own, which it might be if it is large and has been stressed in hot weather, you can put it into a well-aerated livewell for a short while till it regains its strength. When you put a tired fish back in the water, lead it around headfirst to get oxygen through its gill rakers.

metabolically suited to recovery. In spring and fall, when the water is cool, bass do much better.

Don't get the impression that bass are fragile fish. They are no more fragile than others and are hardier than most (largemouths even more so than smallmouths). Good handling, adequate water temperature, and ample oxygen are keys to the survival of hooked and landed bass. Proper care of the fish you release will go a long way toward perpetuating the sport, and will mark you as an angler of high caliber.

Retaining Bass

The only reasons to keep captured bass alive for any period of time are to keep them fresh till you get them home to be cleaned or to release the fish at the end of the day in a tournament. The only good way to keep bass alive and reasonably fit is with some type of aerated livewell. Bass kept on stringers and dragged around for a long time are seldom suitable for release, even though they may still be alive. It is because of tournaments and their bonus weight allowances for live fish that livewells became a standard feature in conventional bass boats.

Livewells are good for keeping a few bass alive, but most are not designed to hold many fish or to hold really big bass. There is some serious opposition to the daylong holding of bass in this environment. After all, bass kept in a livewell not only have been hooked, played, landed, and handled, but have also suffered long- or short-term captivity in a restricted place, bouncing around during travel, confinement with other fish, and then release at a later time in a foreign place. Some bass will make it; many won't. To keep fish in a livewell for consumption is fine; to keep them for grandstanding at the end of the day and then making a heroic release is false sport.

There are two types of aerated livewells: plastic, metal, or fiberglass versions built into bass boats; and coolers set up with some type of aeration system. Some boats have two small livewells; others have a single large one with a divider. I prefer the large one and use it without the divider so the fish have more room.

Most bass-boat livewells have cutoff valves that prevent water from entering or exiting. I leave this valve shut most of the time to keep water out of the livewells because when they are full, there is a lot more weight in the boat (water weighs roughly 8 pounds to the gallon). When I catch a bass to be kept, I then open the valve to allow water in. When you have a bass in the livewell, you should shut the valves (or plug the drain), since the livewell water will drain out and the fish will be dry if you have to travel any distance. If you have to fill a bass-boat livewell quickly, open the valve or plug, put the engine in reverse, and drive backward. This forces water in and fills the livewells.

Make sure that your aerator-system lines are clean and free of debris for maximum performance. Be careful about using livewells for storage of small baitfish. I've found this to be more trouble than it's worth—the fish get into drain lines and clog up the aerator. It's a good idea to clean your livewell once in awhile, to remove the dirt and scum that accumulate if you use it enough. You can wash out the drain lines with a garden hose.

You can also fashion a livewell from a food and beverage cooler, if you have a bilge pump for aeration and a battery to power it.

Two keys to keeping bass alive are the amount of aeration they receive and the temperature of the water in the livewell. Bass need to be in reasonably well oxygenated, cold water. If I expect to keep bass alive in warm weather, I sometimes put one or two small blocks of ice in my cooler or livewell. That keeps the water temperature suitable for a short while.

Chemical formulas are a big help in keeping bass in good condition in a livewell. Some contain a mild tranquilizing agent that sedates fish and keeps them from banging around, an antifungal agent that prevents bacterial infection, and other active ingredients meant to keep bass from requiring more oxygen than normal.

When using these formulas, however, you must keep your livewell plugged so that water will not escape, or you'll find that you have to add the chemicals to it regularly, as treated water will disperse through the overflow line or out the drain when you move quickly.

Bass on a stringer are traumatized and seldom fit for release at the end of the day. Of course, if your intention is to eat the fish, putting them on a stringer is fine. Once you put them on a stringer, however, they should stay on it—don't release one in place of a bigger bass you catch later, in order to comply with your state bag limit.

Stringers are made of metal, nylon, and rope, and may have metal or plastic hook snaps. With hook snaps each bass can be well secured, and the hooks are spaced far enough apart that the fish are relatively unrestricted in the water. The best way to fasten a bass to a stringer is to run the hook snap through both lips. To accomplish this, bring the point of the open hook snap up from underneath the lower jaw, through the soft tissue, then up from underneath the upper jaw and through it before closing the snap.

Make sure that the snaps are well secured and won't pop open after you've hooked a bass on them. Check the strength of the O-rings or connectors that affix the snap to the stringer; some won't handle much weight and may need to be replaced.

10

EARLY

As the weather warms in spring, bass fishing begins to improve; fish move shallower and nearer shore, and they become more aggressive. Tributaries, including creeks and small rivers, warm up before the main body of water, and may remain several degrees warmer. This prespawn bass was caught on a spinnerbait up the creek arm of a large lake.

IN THE SEASON

Spring was created especially for bass fishing. Bass are as accessible and agreeable at this time as they are likely to be all year. Anglers become imbued with the promise and freshness of this season. And opportunity equaled with optimism is always a potent mixture.

Though you shouldn't expect to have miraculous one-fish-every-other-cast angling in the spring (and indeed the fishing can sometimes be disappointing and uncomfortable), you can experience regular action and catch trophy-size bass if you are well versed in the vagaries of springtime angling. Fishing techniques and bass behavior during this season are heavily influenced by natural factors. Understanding nature's calendar will help you focus on the where, when, and how of catching bass.

The most obvious influence on bass behavior in the spring is a gradual warming of the water. In southerly areas this may be gradual and extend for a considerable period of time, while in northern locales it may be of much shorter duration. If you were a vagabond angler wishing to sample the best spring fishing available, you might start your journey in early to mid-March in southern Florida or Texas and work north to end up in New England or at the Minnesota-Ontario boundary in mid- to late June. I have experienced fishing in Florida in late March that was quite similar to fishing in Missouri in late April, to Pennsylvania in late May, and to New Hampshire in late June.

Weather in the winter and spring further influences the timetable. A severe winter puts spring conditions two to three weeks behind normal patterns. An unusually warm spring hastens them up. Severe spring weather fluctuations disturb the behavioral patterns of fish and can lead to poor fishing. Because peculiar weather seems to be the norm these days, be prepared to adapt to or capitalize on changing developments in seasons and fish behavior.

Water Temperature

Comfortable water conditions, preferably in a location that offers security and feeding opportunities, are important for bass at any season, but especially in the spring. Because cold water slows their metabolism in the winter, bass are relatively inactive then and require little food. But as the water warms, temperature holds a key to bass activity.

All bodies of water behave similarly in the spring. The surface layer and shallows warm first. Bass begin to move out of deep sanctuaries, becoming more active as the temperature rises. Though bass can be caught in water colder than

50 degrees F, it is my experience that when temperatures reach that point, bass are most likely to have shaken their winter behavior. When the water warms up enough, 60 to 65 degrees F for largemouths and 58 to 62 for smallmouths, they spawn. This warm-up may occur from late March to late June, depending on locale, species (largemouth or smallmouth), and water conditions. Eventually, the water will become too warm in the shallow and upper layers, driving fish deeper or farther into thick cover, where their comfort, food, and security requirements can be met.

Checking water temperature can help you find places that are especially productive for largemouth bass. It's one of the best things that a spring bass angler can do. I installed a surface-temperature gauge on my bass boat and refer to it constantly. In other boats I use a pool thermometer hung over the side.

There are some interesting spring phenomena at work in each body of water. Small lakes and ponds that are generally shallow throughout are the first to warm up and are often best for early-spring fishing. A shallow pond will warm up weeks ahead of a deep lake even if they are side by side. In the beginning of spring, I would focus on the pond first.

Small lakes may warm up entirely by several degrees per day during a spring warm spell. A sustained period of warm weather will activate the fish in this environment. A cool spell, however, will drop the temperature and confuse the fish. Cool nights and mornings have a negative effect on spring fishing, which is countered only by sunlight and mild evening weather.

The surface temperature of large lakes, reservoirs, and small deep lakes doesn't rise as dramatically in a given day, but temperature can vary in different areas of the lake. Shallow flats, coves, feeder creeks, and tributaries are generally much warmer than the main body of the lake, and are prime locales when the rest of the lake is still too cold to induce significant fish activity. Northern and northwestern sectors of a lake, particularly the coves and bays, warm up slightly ahead of other areas, as they are exposed to more sunlight.

Regardless of lake type, afternoon fishing is often best in early spring. Water temperature in shallow lakes and in shallow areas of larger lakes can rise several degrees during a sunny day. Fish that have been subdued by cool nights and cool shallow-water temperatures respond to the afternoon warmth and become more aggressive in chasing bait.

A heavy warm rain is especially desirable in the spring, and bass fishing will pick up shortly thereafter. Large rivers and navigable tributaries that enter a big lake will have significantly higher temperatures than the main portion of the lake. The area of the lake nearest the tributary will benefit from a warm rain, too. Tributaries that drain a large watershed may not warm up until two or three days after the rain. But in small lakes with small inlet creeks, the temperature rises the day after it rains. In large lakes you may notice a difference in water temperature from one area to another if there has been a strong wind that could push warm surface water to one side of the lake. That may spur bass-feeding activities for a while until temperatures level out.

You can't rely exclusively on water temperature to guide you to good spring bass fishing, however. If you aren't catching fish in the shallows at a time when water conditions suggest bass should be there, it could be an indication that the fish are still holding in deeper water. If a harsh winter or cold early spring delayed bass activity, even if followed by a sudden warm spell that brought water temperatures up, bass will probably remain less active than usual for the time of year.

Temperature and Bass Behavior

If your area were to receive a sudden early-spring warm spell, sending surface and shallow-water temperatures up into a range where they are suitable for bass, it wouldn't necessarily mean that the bass would rush into the shallows. Their own biology is another important factor. If their eggs aren't ripe and they are not ready to spawn, they will not enter their prespawn stages, regardless of the temperature. They may, however, be holding in deep water near the expected spawning areas.

Not all bass in a lake will be in the same stage

at any given time. Some bass may still be relatively immobile in cold, deep water while others have reacted to the early signs of warmth and have moved toward shallower water. Of those that have moved, some will be in a spawning mode; others will be in a prespawn mode. Bass in a prespawn stage will feed and may be caught more readily than spawning bass. They may feed in deep water on the fringes of the shallows or come into the shallows for a short while and return to deeper water.

Immediately after spawning, bass seem somewhat spent and listless for a short while, and it's a relatively unproductive angling time. Many bass caught then have reddish and split tails, and bruises and sores on their body owing to the hardships of nest-building and mating. When bass recover from that stressful period, they are hungry. They will be aggressive in shallow-water areas that are warming and providing a host of feeding opportunities.

By now the fry of many fish species, including bass, pickerel, pike, perch, and walleye, have hatched. Small bass and intermediate-size fish will prey on this fry, and bass in turn will prey on all small and intermediate-size forage. Their metabolism is in gear and they are starting to exhibit their standard behavior patterns, locating near cover, bottom, and objects, and utilizing them as ambush points to prey on other fish or crayfish. Their willingness to strike a lure now is motivated as much by hunger as instinctive aggressiveness.

Lures and Bait

Nearly all lures have merit at some time during the spring season, but crankbaits and spinnerbaits are the most productive throughout this period and throughout the forthcoming stages of lake development and bass behavior.

Crankbaits

Crankbaits are terrific for scouring the bottom in relatively shallow water. Eight feet or less in

A shallow flat with plenty of cover can be a great place to find active largemouth bass in the spring.

the spring and 12 feet or less thereafter can be considered shallow water. Speed of retrieval is particularly important, and it varies through the spring. Generally, the colder the water, the slower the retrieval speed. That's not to say that in warm weather you should blaze the lure along, but for very cold early-spring conditions, you often can't reel a crankbait slowly enough. In the first part of the season, bass won't expend the energy required to chase a fast-moving crankbait. They usually ignore it. The slowest action that gets the built-in wiggling motion out of a lure is just right in cold water.

It pays to watch your lure as it comes back to the boat at this time. If, as often happens, bass swirl after a lure near the boat or take half-hearted swipes at it, or if they are poorly hooked or impaled by one barb of the rear treble of a crankbait, it could mean that you are retrieving your lure too fast, that the bass are only vaguely interested in feeding, or that they are trying to stun their prey before consuming it. Perhaps all these factors are at work. A slow, steady retrieve or a slow stop-and-go retrieve may be the answer.

Whether you should use a shallow-, intermediate-, or deep-diving crankbait depends on water temperature and depth and cover type. If the water is very cold, you'll probably have to use a lure that gets down 5 to 10 feet and works on points, steeply sloping banks, and shores with breaklines at the 5- to 10-foot level. In shallow lakes that have a lot of stumps, flats with cover (though cover is barely starting to emerge when the water is still cold), and the like, a shallow- or intermediate-running crankbait is probably best. As the water warms and the cover, which may be grass, milfoil, or cabbage weeds, begins to grow, the same crankbaits can be used to skim the edges and tops, but you may have to vary the retrieval speed.

By late spring, in shallow lakes with a lot of grass and pad cover, crankbaits will have become impossible to use because they hang up so often on the vegetation. Shallow-running crankbaits can still be effective at this time, however, if they are worked in a stop-and-go manner over the top of this cover. Minnow-imitation plugs can be worked effectively in a straight or erratic retrieve over this cover as well.

Crankbaits are particularly productive in large lakes with a lot of deep water, where there is usually no vegetative cover. Largemouth and smallmouth bass begin their spring movement along rocky bluffs and riprap or craggy shorelines that slope steeply into deep water. Here, crankbaits worked parallel to the shore can be the ticket for early fishing success. Crankbaits can also be hot in lakes with stump fields, timber flats, timbered coves, and the like. Bass get into these areas in the spring before and after spawning. The point where the outside bend of a submerged creek or river channel meets the shore (often by a bluff) can be a choice crankbait locale, too.

Don't overlook the importance of rocks to

Fish crankbaits along riprap or rocky banks in the spring. Some bass will be close to the rocky shoreline, and others will be in deeper water. Use the appropriate type of diver for each depth.

Shallow rocky areas, near shore or around islands and shoals, produce excellent smallmouth-bass action in the spring.

early-season bass. In addition to providing ambush points and feeding locales, rocks in shallow water retain heat. Bass may use those rocks to help stimulate the development of their eggs and milt. Or the rocks may provide security. Smallmouths, of course, are known to congregate around rocky shores, gravelly areas, rocky shoals, and the like, but largemouths may inhabit such areas as well.

Crayfish dwell in rocky areas, which also explains why bass are there. Crayfish are a staple of smallmouth bass through all seasons and are one of many food items for largemouths, depending on their availability. But in the spring, when other forage is not yet abundant near shore, crayfish become especially important in a bass's diet.

To some extent, crankbaits imitate crayfish as well as small baitfish, particularly when they are rooting along the bottom and scouring through the sand, rocks, and gravel. Colors or patterns that imitate crayfish are prime smallmouth

catchers in extremely rocky areas and in other areas with good crayfish populations.

In places with large shad or alewife populations, where crayfish are not part of the diet, or where small minnows make up the bulk of early-season bass food, white and silver crankbaits are especially effective. Most of the time these colors are referred to by manufacturers and anglers alike as "shad."

Other colors that may have merit, especially for largemouth bass, are bone, chartreuse, gold, and chrome. Color choice in lures has a lot to do with the color of the water being fished. For instance, a light-colored crayfish-patterned crankbait may work better than a dark one in muddy or tea-colored water (which occurs a lot in rivers and in large reservoirs fed by rivers, due to runoff). Light-colored crankbaits that have flash are good in the same waters. Chartreuse is a good color in blue-green water. Gold and chrome are good in dark, tannin-stained lakes.

Natural-finish plugs don't necessarily have

more fish appeal than lures with standard finishes and colors, since action, vibration, and diving ability are the primary attributes of plugs. There are times, however, when lures that resemble certain bass forage in nearly every detail are especially successful fish catchers. In northern lakes where perch and walleye are abundant and where small individuals of these species are available and eager to prey on bass fry in early to midspring, shallow-running crankbaits with perch or walleye finishes are good largemouth baits. The same can be true for bluegill and catfish imitators.

Spinnerbaits

Though spinnerbaits don't represent an identifiable food source, they certainly appeal to the instinctive nature of bass and are highly effective spring lures. Spinnerbaits are substantial and tempting morsels, offering the visual elements of good action and motion (the swimming skirt and spinning blades) as well as vibration. They are used primarily on largemouth bass but can be effective for smallmouths as well. (They are also devastating on pickerel in the spring and on northern pike, and the smallest models are suitable for various panfish species.)

Spinnerbaits can be fished deep, but they are most effective in the shallows, preferably within sight. Spinnerbaits don't become principal spring bass lures until the water warms enough to stabilize fish behavior and keep bass in the shallows. These lures are not productive when the water is cold; crankbaits are best then.

Though retrieval speed is not as critical with spinnerbaits as with crankbaits, spinnerbaits can be worked too fast. When bass are striking short and nipping rather than nailing lures, it is time to slow your retrieve.

Watch a spinnerbait closely when you fish it shallow. In the spring, bass commonly take a stab at this lure, yet miss it. Sometimes you can catch these fish by casting the spinnerbait again, though bass usually spurn it the second time around. Tossing a different lure (such as a floating surface plug, crankbait, or plastic worm) in

the appropriate spot is a better strategy. I've experienced frustrating spring trips, catching only a few bass, although many swiped at a spinnerbait, swirled on it, or chased it momentarily near the boat. But whether you catch bass or not, at least you know they're present and what kind of mood they're in.

A trailer hook is an indispensable spinnerbait addition in the spring, as long as it can be used without causing the lure to foul when worked through cover. A lot of short strikers can be caught on trailer hooks, and if you're not catching many fish this way, it may be a good idea to slow retrieval speed.

I'm partial to tandem-blade spinnerbaits in the spring because they can be worked slowly and near the surface, and produce a lot of flash. If you have an assortment of silver- and nickel-blade spinnerbaits, with chartreuse, white, and chartreuse-and-black (or -blue) bodies, you are well equipped for spring bass fishing. White is good in dark, tannin-colored water and in muddy or milky runoff. Chartreuse is better in blue-green environments and in some clear lakes.

One of the attributes of spinnerbaits is that they are relatively snag- and weed-free and can be fished in nearly all types of cover. In the spring, vegetation such as moss, pads, weeds, and grass is almost nonexistent early in the season but thick by the end of the season. Spinnerbaits are effective here until such cover becomes impenetrable.

Other forms of largemouth cover, particularly stumps, timbered flats or fields, fallen trees, and brush, are ideal places to work a spinnerbait. The trick is to cast beyond the target and bring the lure by it, sometimes nicking or bumping the object. An especially productive tactic is to retrieve the lure up to a stump or log from behind, then let it fall over the object and flutter down in front of it before continuing the retrieve. This technique, called *slow-rolling*, works best with a large single-blade spinnerbait.

Smallmouths don't inhabit vegetation or much of the nonrocky cover that largemouths prefer. They may be taken with spinnerbaits

*Timbered flats are good places to fish a spinnerbait in the spring. Bump the stumps with the lure,
roll it slowly over downed logs, and flutter it beside tree stumps in deeper water.*

when they are in shallow rocky environments close to shore, when they are on shoals to feed, and when they are on beds in sparsely covered terrain. Although I have caught some big-lake smallmouths on spinnerbaits fished along rock- and boulder-studded shores, I have also found them slow to hit these lures under similar conditions on other lakes. I know one excellent spring lake where small in-line spinners will take bronzebacks that refuse spinnerbaits, and another where shallow bass occasionally strike a plug and quickly take a jig, but repeatedly pass up a spinnerbait. So it pays to be adaptable.

Surface Lures

Spinnerbaits and crankbaits, of course, aren't the only lures that catch early-season bass. Shallow-running floating/diving minnow imitations in single and jointed models are effective for both largemouths and smallmouths. These lures can be worked as swimming plugs or crankbaits in shallow water on a steady retrieve or in a stop-and-go manner. They are productive surface lures, worked in a pull-pause twitching action, and are the primary spring surface bait for bass. The colder the water, the less likely bass are to strike any surface lure, but in early to mid-spring a slowly worked, fairly noiseless plug such as this is more likely to gain results than other surface plugs.

As the water warms further, other surface lures become effective. Among them are minnow plugs with fore and aft (or just aft) propellers, stickbaits, and wobblers. Buzzbaits are ineffective until the water temperature hits the low 60s, though shallow lakes that warm quickly may produce buzzbait action earlier in the season than you might anticipate. Spinnerbaits can be run just under the surface to create a wake, and work as well as a buzzbait although they're quieter.

Jigs and Worms

Spring bass often won't rise for surface lures. If they also won't move for a crankbait or spinnerbait, you may need to go to jigs or worms. Though the tendency is to think of jigs as lures for mid- to deep-water fishing, they can be effective spring bass lures, especially for smallmouths. One-eighth- to ¼-ounce jigs, with bucktail, grub, or curl-tail soft-plastic bodies, work when the fish are in mid-depth, near-shore water prior to spawning; when they are on shoals or reefs to feed; and when they are on spawning beds. Smallmouths guarding the nest after spawning are also susceptible to jigs. The male guardians may swim away from crankbaits or spinnerbaits, but evidently can't resist a slowly worked jig bouncing through the nesting area.

Brown and black work well for hair-bodied jigs; purple, gray, and green are good in soft-plastic bodies. Though my experience with white and yellow jigs for smallmouths has not been noteworthy, some folks swear by those colors.

Plastic worms are essentially for largemouth bass, though a small worm, fished on a jig head, may be suitable smallmouth fare. Worms don't have much appeal to bass in cold water. I've had little success with this bait when the water was below 55 degrees F. A worm is especially good in the spring for catching bedded bass; when flipped into heavy cover; and as a secondary lure to throw back at a fish that has struck but missed a crankbait, spinnerbait, or surface plug.

Live Bait

Some spring fishing is done with live bait, including worms, crayfish, hellgrammites, shin-ers, and assorted minnows and other small bait-fish. Live bait undoubtedly catches fish better than artificials in cold, early-spring conditions. The key to success with live bait, as with artificials, is to put the offering in the most likely areas and at the proper depths.

Though a still-fishing live-bait angler should have success, an experienced lure fisherman who covers a lot of ground in the spring has the upper hand. If bass behavior has stabilized, a lure angler can put his wares before a lot of fish, many of which are likely to be aggressive. Moreover, it's easier for the lure angler to release small or unwanted fish without harm. When bass are spawning, however, live bait may amount to an offer that cannot be refused.

A floating/diving minnow plug, which caught this smallmouth, is a good lure for spring bass when the water warms up and the fish are shallow.

When spawning bass strike a lure or bait, they don't do so to consume it. They merely want to get it away from the nest. They'll grab it sideways and swim off with it a few feet, then release it. It's difficult to hook bass that do that. I've had spawning smallmouths hit a surface lure four or five times before they finally got hooked. They are usually hooked lightly, however, on the corner of the mouth or in the jaw on the outside of the mouth.

A plastic worm is often carted off by the tail. A double-hook rig, with the second hook buried close to the tail and connected to the first with strong line, helps hook spawners. You can also use a standard single hook and thread the shank through the worm so the point can be embedded far back.

Spawning bass are often able to avoid being hooked by jigs, too. If you don't have a good feel for detecting strikes, a smallmouth may pick up, move with, and drop a jig before you react. Many a smallmouth is missed this way or is so lightly hooked that the jig is thrown the minute the bass takes to the air.

You'll lose a lot of fish in the spring, but you'll also catch a lot. With plenty of action, no hot weather, no water-skiers, few boaters, and nature coming alive, it's a great time to be bass fishing.

11

LATER

Early-morning fishing is often good in summer and fall.

IN THE SEASON

When the lake water eventually turns as warm and stultifying as the water in a hot tub, and the season is replete with thunderstorms, tornadoes, snakes, and sunburn, you will fondly remember cooler days earlier in the year. Some call the summer period the *doldrums*. Indeed, the fish can be uncooperative, and some fishermen have an excuse for every tray in their tackle box. The water's too hot. The lake's too busy. The fish have been pressured too often. There's too much bait for them to eat. They've gone deep. They've gone into thick cover. They've . . . shut down.

This is the time to do some practical thinking and to play the odds. Do not fish where and when you did earlier in the year. Focus on the comfort zones of the fish and think about where their major food source would be. Fish have to eat. And you can be absolutely sure that they *are* eating, even in the warmth of summer. Bass don't choose July and August to become weight watchers. Since they have to eat, they'll be active. Activity means there's more of a chance that you can catch them than there would be if they were dormant.

Of course, you have to deal with practicalities. Unless you visit lightly fished private waters with plenty of unsophisticated bass, you have to knuckle down for most summer fishing. You can't expect maximum results with minimum effort, without paying attention to such impor-

tant matters as the cover fish use for shade and forage, or the depths they seek for optimum temperature. In other words, in a game plan for summer fishing you must, as always, consider the habits of bass, their likely habitats, and the availability of food. Where these elements converge is where you want to be fishing.

Water Temperature

By midsummer the surface water is hot everywhere, and bass prefer the comfort of shade or cool depths.

In reservoirs with little vegetative cover but enough depth for a thermocline, most of the bass will be in deeper, cooler water. In shallow lakes, the fish can't go deep for colder temperatures. But they can find more comfort in the pads, weeds, moss, hydrilla, and other cover offering shade and food. Some small waters contain springs with considerably cooler water. If you've ever been swimming and felt the temperature drop as you passed through a spot, you've probably encountered a spring. Fish like such places, too.

In a broader context, the water is much cooler in the summer in the North than in the South, and if you're on a fishing vacation you might want to try, say, the Michigan latitude.

Shorter growing seasons in the North make for somewhat smaller bass on average compared to southern bass, but cooler nights make for generally cooler waters and bass that are within reach throughout the summer.

Actually, bass are seldom out of reach no matter how deep they may go, but fishing effectively for them when they're very deep is not as easy as we'd like it to be. Most of us just aren't adept at it or don't like that type of fishing. That's why you might fish smaller bodies of water.

Small Waters and Uncrowded Areas

For most people, the more accessible the fish are, the more catchable they are. Bass anglers are primarily casters, who enjoy tossing lures to specific places where fish may be hiding and practicing the art of retrieving and manipulating their lures. They are most adept at this, have the most confidence with it, and are therefore more effective when they're fishing this way. If you know what you like and what you don't, play to your strengths if you can. In midsummer, small lakes and ponds can provide better fishing for the average angler because bass have fewer hideouts, they are relatively shallow and accessible, and the angler can use his best skills most advantageously and most enjoyably.

If you don't have the opportunity to fish small bodies of water, you might try fishing where and when it's not crowded. A major impediment to successful midsummer fishing is competition from other people. They may use speedboats, sailboats, or personal watercraft, or simply be swimming; but the end result is noise, waves, and roiled-up water. When this commotion is at a minimum, you may have an advantage for midsummer fishing. That would be early in the day, at dusk, at night, at midweek, and when the weather is cool, cloudy, or rainy.

If you have to fish in the middle of a bright, hot Saturday or Sunday, then you might try the places that are least attractive to other watersports fans: backwaters, stumpy rivers, where there is flooded timber, where there are rocky

reefs and shoals—places where it's difficult to do anything but fish. This is no guarantee that the bass will be eager for your lures, but you stand a better chance of a hookup. And it is true that the slightly cooler water, reduced traffic, and better karma of fishing early, late in the day, and at night (more on this shortly) are a good bet for maximum enjoyment and productivity.

Light Tackle

And when midsummer bass fishing is tough, you can also increase your productivity by exercising a little more finesse and fishing light tackle. Not in heavy cover, of course. Nor in dingy water. But for deep fishing, angling in clear water, and using small lures, light is right.

Natural presentations, more strikes, and better depth are among the benefits of light-tackle

Bass are generally in deeper water in the summer and fall; a good lure to reach them then is a deep-diving crankbait.

angling. By midsummer, bass have been subjected to a lot of fishing pressure, so a fine-diameter line can be important. Four- to 8-pound strengths are good for jigs, small plastic worms, some spoons, spinners, small crankbaits, and minnow-imitating surface plugs. You can use spinning tackle for some of these lures and baitcasting tackle for others. Just pick your times and places carefully and fish the right lures in the right places at the right times.

Lures

It's unrealistic to expect to catch bass on a surface lure in the shallows in the middle of a hot sunny day, unless a school of baitfish has been herded there. Surface, shallow-plug fishing is a low-light proposition in midsummer. Under low light you can not only catch bass that are temporarily shallow, but also get them to come up for your lure. When bass are deep, you have to get down to them. What's deep? Depends on the situation, but generally over 10 to 12 feet. The terrain, the cover, and the situation dictate the tactic.

What you use to catch the bass, and how you use it, of course, become especially critical. Motivating fish to choose your offering over seasonally abundant natural forage can be a tough, but not insurmountable, problem. Start by limiting your lure choices to those that are productive throughout the summer.

Surface lures, for example, are everyone's favorites. But with surface lures you often waste most of the daylight hours trying to coax topwater strikes. In summer, surface lures are good for fishing in shallow, cover-laden environments on dark, overcast days, or working weedless lures through slop and matted vegetation such as milfoil or moss. Generally, low-light conditions (early and late in the day, for example) offer the best opportunities for surface-lure success. Be smart enough to know when to quit fishing them.

Crankbaits can catch summer bass, but they're not among the top producers because many anglers fish them too fast. Summer bass have much food available and are great at ambushing, so they don't have to expend lots of energy for

the mere possibility of a meal when the intended victim seems to be healthy and swims pretty quickly. If you can get deep-running plugs down to the proper depth and suspend them, swim them in a stop-and-go manner, or give them an erratic, injured, jerking retrieve, then you might have a full-time summer fish catcher. However, if you find bass concentrated or in bait-chasing schools, a crankbait is always a good lure to have handy. Remember that in summer it can be important to match the size of your lure to the forage. Bass anglers tend to use large lures. That's okay some of the time. But when fishing is tough, you might try matching the size of your plugs more closely to the size of the most abundant midsummer forage, usually 2 to 3 inches long.

One disappointing summer lure is a spinnerbait. Most anglers are accustomed to fishing them in murky shallow water for visible strikes. But in the summer heat, the shallows may be steamy, with few adult bass waiting to be poached. In really warm locations, shallow sight-fishing with spinnerbaits does not produce well. However, single-blade spinnerbaits, fished in a lift-and-drop manner along steep shorelines and tumbled over submerged ledges and drop-offs, are a possibility.

The all-time choice among summer lures for bass and fishermen, of course, is a plastic worm, which includes the traditional Texas-rigged bottom crawler, Carolina-style floating rig, and jerkform soft plastics. The key to their effectiveness in the hot months is simply that they are unobtrusive and vulnerable, and they're fished slowly and deep in the bass's lair. There's a message here: other lures would catch summer bass as well as soft plastics if they could be fished as slowly and as tantalizingly in the same places.

Rubber-legged jigs with a pork or plastic trailer come close. Though bulkier and often heavier, in some situations they have advantages similar to those of plastic worms. And they tend to produce good-size fish. Also, grub- and bucktail-style jigs have merit in less cover-laden water for smallmouth bass, provided you don't have to fish them too deep.

And don't dismiss the possibility of using a jigging spoon for deep-dwelling bass. Because

The plastic worm is the top bass producer later in the season. This worm-caught bass came from a deep-water hump, but worms fished in heavy cover are also effective.

approaches are called for, particularly in bays and coves, near shore, and in small waters. Most bass waters are a frantic sea of activity during summer months, and even the backwater spots that don't host skiers, personal watercraft, and pleasure cruisers, see activity. Electric motors get plucked up and down, departing fishermen crank up megahorsepower outboards, stuff gets clanked around in aluminum boats, electric motors whine at high speeds, and so forth.

Fishermen would do well to have more respect for their quarry's ability to make a negative association with an outside presence. It is, after all, adaptive survival. You might increase your odds if you practice stealth. Approach likely fishing spots as quietly as possible, without using the big engine. Leave them silently, too. Be nei-

this requires some deft underwater probing, a lot of anglers pass it up. Indeed, it's not my favorite method, but we're not talking favorites; we're talking catching fish. And in many lakes and reservoirs where bass go into deep water, fishing vertically with spoons is one way to do it.

Other Considerations

There are some practical considerations to keep in mind, especially for summer bass angling and especially if the fish are uncooperative.

For example, are you making enough of an effort to minimize your presence? Quiet, subtle

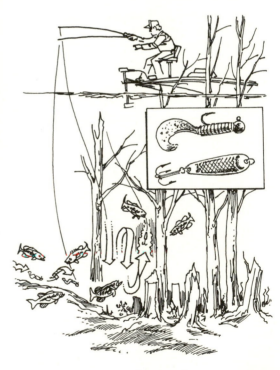

Casting toward shore and jigging a lure back along the bottom is a standard tactic and it may prove useful in summer. But it may be more appropriate to move farther from shore and vertically fish a jig on or just slightly above bottom or structure.

ther seen nor heard. Try using your electric motor on a low speed, and sparingly. Turn off your sonar for a while. Be quiet in your boat. These measures cannot *hurt* your efforts. As another means of minimizing your presence, try fishing with smaller lures and thin-diameter line.

At the same time, try s-l-o-w-i-n-g down. Bass may be eating well in the summer but that doesn't mean they're ravenously swimming around, mouths agape, chasing bait. For the most part, bass are opportunistic feeders. They have lots of forage opportunities in the summer and don't have to chase a lure unless it's extraordinarily tempting. So slow down your retrieves, get your lures to work temptingly, and keep that temptation in the strike zone.

In some waters it pays a great deal to be observant. When fishing is tough, the splash of a baitfish may tell you where a feeding bass is located. You might just catch the best (or only) fish of the day by working the area where you spied that splash. In some places, largemouth bass chase schools of shad or other baitfish in late summer and early fall, and you can have some of the best action in all of bass fishing if you can get in on that. On lakes, where it's common, local anglers

On many bodies of water, especially large lakes and reservoirs, it may be necessary to move away from the bank and search open water for deep structure that could attract feeding bass. Put a marker buoy out on a likely spot, and then work around the entire area with jigs, jigging spoons, deep-diving plugs, or plastic worms.

know where and when it most frequently occurs. By being observant and watching and listening for splashes under light-wind conditions, you may be able to get in some quick action. This also happens, though less frantically, in backwater areas at times. So, again, pay attention to what's happening elsewhere on the water.

When all else fails, dig deep into your bag of tricks and start doing something different. Try really noisy lures if you've been trying slow-and-subtle for hours to no avail. Maybe try trolling, as unpopular as that is with many of the modern bass-fishing crowd. Trollers cover a lot of water; with deep-diving plugs they get their lures down, often to the depths that other anglers are not scouring with cast-and-retrieve or jigging methods. This can work if it puts you into territory (an open-water hump, for example) that holds more fish and that can be fished effectively by other methods.

Perhaps you need to reevaluate the places where you've been fishing during the heat of summer. Maybe the bass are deep in heavy moss and your lures are only probing the edges and the surface, not really getting to the heart of the matter. Time to change tactics. Maybe you've been fishing the first breakline of steep points when the bass are farther out and deep on the point.

Study your sonar carefully. When the going gets tough, the better you can read your sonar (you thought those lumps on a level bottom were rocks; are they really rocks, or might they be fish?), the better chance you have of finding opportunities to exploit.

Finally, many bass fishermen make a big mistake by not thoroughly exploring places where they have had success. They might be casting along a particular shore, for example, and catch a small bass, release it, and then keep plunking along the shore, then picking up and moving to another locale. But if fishing is tough, fish could also be concentrated. And places that yield one fish can sometimes produce two or three or more, from the same spot or nearby.

Don't be in a hurry to move on after you've caught a bass. It's probably telling you something.

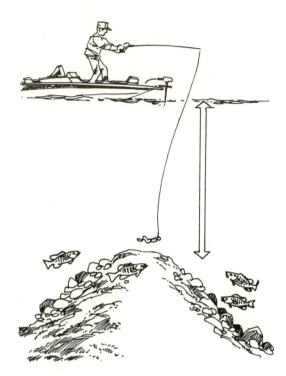

In the heat of midsummer you may find, by studying your sonar, some underwater humps or reefs away from shore and overlooked by other anglers. Bass may move there to feed and then move back to deeper water. You can fish a jigging spoon in these places, a crankbait if the water isn't too deep, or a heavy jig or plastic worm.

Fishing at Night

Bass fishing at night is seldom uneventful. A pond or lake after dark is markedly different than in the daytime. Frogs croak. Bats, bugs, and mosquitoes fly freely. Fish splash loudly in the shallows. The air is cool, sometimes chilling. Familiar places and objects seem foreign. Shore lights and moonlight occasionally play tricks on your mind. Every sound, every action is accentuated.

In many places, night-fishing for bass in midsummer is consistently more effective than daytime-fishing, in part because of all the daytime activity on the water. The lakes that suffer the heaviest traffic during the day are often the best night producers. I concentrate most of my night-fishing on small lakes and ponds, many of which are ringed entirely or partially by residential communities, youth camps, or bungalow colonies, and which host a lot of daytime activity. These places are generally shallow and often blessed with an abundance of cover. The beach area, boathouses, coves, docks, weedy or rocky points, and shallow lily-pad and weed areas are prime nighttime bass haunts. Ponds and small lakes also benefit more from cool summer evenings, too, because their temperature drops, often stimulating fish activity. You needn't fish deep either.

Though there are exceptions, most night bass fishing is done in the shallows, in depths of 6 feet or less. This is ideal for surface and shallow-water lures and tactics. Deeper fishing can also be successful at times, particularly in large lakes and reservoirs.

Surface-fishing is the most stimulating form of night bass angling. Because you can't see your lure working and can't see a fish strike, you work primarily by hearing and feeling. It's a special thrill to hear the telltale slurp of a bass inhaling your lure, then feel it on the end of the line. Actually, listening to some surface lures, like a popper or a wobbling surface plug, and anticipating a strike, has its own entertainment value. Surface lures are likely to catch some of the biggest bass, too.

To be successful at night surface lures have to create a commotion. Noise is often paramount in good night-fishing. Wobbling surface plugs are tops, particularly in large sizes. The almost monotonous "plop-plop" of these plugs is a come-hither call to nearby bass. At night, bass respond best to and are more likely to be caught on a slow, steady retrieve.

In night-fishing, you often miss hits, and striking fish often miss the bait. On dark nights a surface lure offers little, if any, visual stimulation; the bass respond primarily to the vibrations. A regular retrieval rate can give a bass a more accurate fix on the precise location and directional movement of a lure, so that when the bass strikes, it has a better chance of connecting.

Sometimes it's worthwhile to stagger the retrieval cadence or to use a popping plug retrieved with intermittent jerks, but this is not nearly as reliable as continuous wobbling and is more prone to draw errant strikes.

Missed strikes are one of the chief peculiarities of night bass angling. They have two common causes. One, because the bass are primarily guided by vibrations, a lot of them miss the intended target, whether it is moving continuously or irregularly. Occasionally, a fish will hit a missed bait a second time, but you'll have a better chance to score if you have a different lure on another rod to toss at it. Shallow-running crankbaits or spinnerbaits could be good lures then because of their detectable vibrations. Two, the fisherman also is usually working by sound. Very often he'll hear a strike before seeing or feeling it and in his eagerness, he simply sets the hook too soon. It's a hard technique to master, but a momentary delay in hook-setting is advantageous at night. Then, when you actually feel the fish with the lure, set the hook.

If a bass misses the bait and you haven't yanked it out of the water, but kept it coming, he may zero in on it again. Bass are aggressive at night and when they strike, it's with gusto. They don't daintily suck in a bait—they smash it. When they are right on target, you'll know it and you'll have a hookup. Perhaps some anglers will find themselves (as I often do) turning an ear in the direction of the lure to hear better and leaning forward to be ready. It's not necessary. Anticipation is the downfall of many a nighttime angler.

Perhaps equally as effective on the surface as wobbling plugs are buzzbaits. They are best in ⅜-ounce and larger sizes for night use. Another after-dark surface lure is a propellered stickbait. But instead of retrieving it in the normal pull-pause, tantalizing action, speed up the retrieve to a quicker, more direct pace. This lure, in particular, gives the impression of slashing, feeding fish and, used in combination with a partner's lure, can prove to be interesting.

Surface lures don't work all the time, of course, so don't stick with them if results aren't encouraging. Shallow-running crankbaits, spinnerbaits, jigs, and worms all have merit for night bass fishing. I'm most partial to spinnerbaits for fishing in and around grass and pad coverings, along shore, and in shallow water. The spinner blades make vibrations in the water, enhancing the lure's detectability. Worms, though not good for covering a lot of territory in the dark, are great for fishing specific locations, and since they are rigged to be fished weedless, don't invite many hangups. (Getting snagged, on either an object in the water or a bush or tree limb on the bank, is the bane of all night bass anglers.)

In small ponds, crankbaits prove more of a burden than a blessing because of the abundance of cover and opportunities to get snagged. The shallowest-running crankbaits, including floating/diving minnow imitators, have some merit over submerged weed beds and along the edges of vegetation and other shallow cover, and hold a lot of promise around rocky environs in locales where crayfish (which are nocturnal) are found.

I like sturdy tackle for night-fishing, since you never know what you may encounter. I use only baitcasting gear for lure-fishing at night, generally with 12-pound-test line, and heavier line in large-bass and snag-infested waters. Usually, you don't know what obstacles are between you and a hooked fish; with stout tackle you can apply a lot of pressure and get the fish to the boat fast. You can also pull your unseen lure free of most weed and pad tangles. Medium-heavy spinning gear will do, of course, and some may find it preferable because a severe overrun on a baitcasting reel is big trouble in the dark, especially if it occurs during prime time.

And when is it prime? Some folks say two hours after sunset. Some say after midnight. Some say just before and after a full moon. My experiences have been best on dark, moonless or cloudy nights. I have also had exceptional success just before and after sunset. The 2½-hour period from 7:30 P.M. to 10 P.M. (in midsummer) has been consistently good, with action often nonexistent thereafter. Many other anglers, however, don't do well until after midnight, fishing from then till daylight. You should try to establish a night-activity pattern by being on the water as often as possible after dark. The more you fish each particular water, the more attuned you'll become to its fish activity.

A few other points about night-fishing for bass: Be quiet. Noise from the banging of oars, shifting of tackle boxes, dropping of rods, coughing, loud talking is magnified at night; and bass are sensitive to it. They like noisy plugs, not noisy fishermen.

It's also a good idea to wear a hat. A hat at night, for me at least, is like a security blanket. Everywhere I've ever fished at night, bats were abundant. I've hit them with the top of my rod; they've bumped my line and darted after a cast lure. They sometimes come a lot closer than you'd like, and a hat may make you feel a little more comfortable.

Bass are often caught in the evening or at night during the summer. Surface lures are favorites at this time, but other lures are effective as well.

You should also use an electric motor if you have one, keeping it on low power. Keep the shaft down far enough into the water so that you don't churn up the surface with your start-up, and use a weedguard or weedless propeller to ease navigation through unseen vegetation.

Keep light use at night to a minimum. Don't flash your light around looking for the shore or for your lost lure. In the dark, that's usually enough to alert the fish. If you need a light to find a lure or tie a knot, use it discretely, low in the boat, preferably masking most of the beam. You'll be surprised, though, how well your eyes adapt to the dark and how much you can see without a light. However, you might look for bright lights on docks, piers, or boathouses. They attract bugs, and if a lot of bugs fall into the water, they will attract small fish, and in turn larger ones. Bright light may also attract small baitfish, bringing bass in with them.

One of the hardships of night bass fishing is tying knots. Holding a lure up to the moon or the feeble light of the stars to help guide the line through an eyelet is exasperating. Tying a knot in the dark can be done by feel if you're adept, but some folks need light for that, too. Using a snap will aid lure changing, but some lures don't work well with snaps. (I prefer not to use them at all.) A black light might help with night tying,

especially if you use fluorescent line.

Be prepared with your tackle when night-fishing. An extra rod or two, prerigged with a lure and ready to use at a moment's notice, is valuable when the action is fast and you get snagged or some other problem arises.

Using boats at night has disadvantages, one being the difficulty of launching in ponds or small lakes, most of which have no, or poor, access locations. With my four-wheel drive I can put a bass boat, jonboat, or canoe into almost any locale. I may stumble around a bit in the dark, pushing boats off trailers or winching them on, but it's usually worth the effort. You may want to install a pair of rear spotlights on the back of your vehicle to illuminate the launch or trailer area and help you see what you're doing.

Watch how you handle fish at night. I once caught what I thought was a bass on a surface plug, brought it to the boat, reached over to lip-land it, and found my fingers about to grasp a well-barbed bullhead. Use of a net, on the other hand, can be problematic at night when multi-hook lures get tangled in the mesh. With sturdy tackle you can swing a medium-size fish on board and grasp it by the lip. Make sure that your bass are well played out before landing them by hand. Think about what you're doing, and be careful in the dark.

12

WORKING

Bass are often very deep in thick vegetation. Sometimes it's difficult to get into these spots and to fish them effectively.

THE VEGETATION

Largemouth bass are particularly attracted to aquatic vegetation because it offers them security, food, suitable water temperature, and appropriate oxygen and light conditions. Remember that baitfish require food as well as protection from predators, and they, too, find this in the vegetation, so it is natural for bass to frequent such areas.

Deep in the recesses of lily pads, milfoil, moss, hyacinths, and other masses of aquatic salad, the environs are protected and cooled to a tolerable level for largemouths. They live there, they feed there, and they can be caught there. Vegetation, particularly at moderate depths (from 3 to 10 feet), is a reliable place to locate bass in the summer and fall and should be considered by all largemouth-bass fishermen, especially those with limited deep-water angling acumen and limited time.

The characteristics of vegetation vary. Most forms are obvious, but others are not—submerged grass and weed beds are common in many places. The concentrations of vegetation also vary from sparse to thick to unbearable. All of it can be fished, though you can't get your boat through the worst of it except by poling. Some types of vegetation, such as grass, can be found extending through and covering the surface, as well as submerged several feet, and sub-

merged grass can be shallow or deep. You have to adjust to the peculiarities of each situation, but some patterns hold true for all vegetation.

I believe that in any lake from spring through fall, there are some bass in the grass at all times. Once you have acknowledged that bass will reside in even the thickest clumps of vegetation, you must figure out how to catch them there. That's easier said than done, and there is no simple, surefire solution to this problem. Nonetheless, certain aspects of vegetation-fishing are common to all its varieties, and point the way to specific patterns and lure types.

Vegetation Types and Appropriate Tactics

The most obvious, most common, and easiest way to locate bass in vegetation is to work the edges. In large, fairly thick concentrations of grass, for example, bass stick close to the outside line, most likely because they can see and ambush prey there, and especially if the grass is so congested that you can't work any type of lure across the surface.

Milfoil beds are a prime example of this type of cover. Here, you may have to work the edges with a plastic worm, dropping the worm on top

Bass go with grass like butter goes with toast. You can be sure that wherever you find vegetation, some bass, especially largemouths, will be in the neighborhood.

of the milfoil just inside the edge, then slithering it off and letting it drop vertically along the edge. Most strikes will occur within a foot or two of the edge. Any irregularity in the weed line, such as a protrusion or pocket, may be particularly productive.

In sparse grass, frequently the key is to fish small, thick isolated clumps. (They may be inside the main body of vegetation as well as outside.) Identify and fish every one of them until you find a spot that is more worthwhile than the others. Then zero in on it and work it thoroughly. When sparse vegetation is also partly submerged, you won't be able to identify isolated clumps, but you may be able to identify edges, as well as drop-offs or holes, by traveling across the area first, using your sonar.

If the vegetation—either emergent or submerged—is thick and contains visible pockets or holes, start casting. Clearings in the grass are prime fishing locations, and they are easier to fish than the thick spots.

In the case of emergent grass, a worm can be

worked in the same manner as in fishing the edges, but in submerged vegetation the chore becomes a little tougher. If the vegetation is too deep to see, you'll have to locate pockets by feel; an experienced worm chunker can tell when his worm passes through the grass into a small clearing and then back into the grass again.

Submerged grass at the delicate see/no-see level is also a problem, particularly for the sight angler who's better off if he can watch what he's casting to and fishing. I've fished in areas where the only openings in submerged vegetation were created by large flat rocks. You can find those openings only by hunting and pecking, and watching the sonar. Then you drop marker buoys and fish a plastic worm on the edges of the openings.

Lures

It is a curious fact that many anglers pass up the best summer fishing locales in the lake—thick pads or grass—in favor of shoreline plunking or

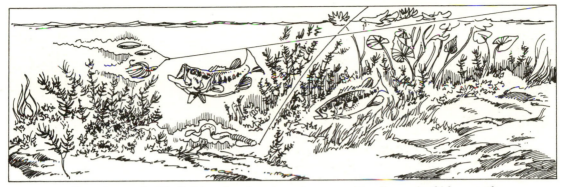

Vegetation can be fished with various lures in various ways, depending on its thickness and whether it is submerged or emergent. Surface lures are popularly fished over submerged grass, and spinnerbaits can be worked in areas that aren't too thick. Worms and weedless jigs produce a lot of fish, too.

deep prospecting. And I suspect it's because they haven't developed adequate continuous weed-fishing techniques. Vegetation-fishing calls for a weed-free, or so-called *weedless,* presentation and, naturally, your lure plays the lead role here.

Undoubtedly, you've seen claims about the snag-free capabilities of completely weedless lures. It's been my experience that the claims are not entirely true. I've found that if a lure has a hook, if it has some weight, and if it is fished in thick cover, it cannot be 100 percent tangle-free. There are relative degrees of weedlessness, but there is no guaranteed-never-to-get-stuck bass-fishing lure.

The plastic worm can be one of the most tangle-free lures and is the most acclaimed and successful vegetation-fishing lure. But plastic worms get snagged occasionally in thick cover. If the hook actually gets stuck, it is because the hook point pulled through the soft-plastic neck of the worm, or because the point was embedded too deep; perhaps the body has been used too often and is incapable of holding another hook. More often the sinker is the culprit, snagged on or wedged into impenetrable vegetation instead of riding over it.

Some folks like to fish a plastic worm without a slip sinker in shallow vegetation, but I almost always use a bullet-shaped sinker. I'm not the patient type who can wait all day for the bait to

Not all vegetation is emergent and visible. The weeds wrapped around this worm-caught largemouth were submerged.

get down to working level. The key to fishing a slip sinker is to use the lightest one you can possibly toss and that will still get the worm down adequately, and to peg it with a toothpick. A free-sliding slip sinker often pulls off an underwater object, leaving the worm behind. You need to have the two working close together to effect a proper, natural presentation. A slip sinker pegged with a toothpick (see page 76) to keep it from sliding does the job. An alternative is to use a weedless jig head or a plain jig with the hook embedded in the worm.

When bass don't go for a worm, you need to give them a more enticing movement, with a flash of metal, to get a strike. Combinations of spoon and pork chunk, or spoon and plastic skirt, work then.

The weedless spoon and pork rind has justifiably been a longtime favorite of grass and pad fishermen. In moderately heavy cover it is fairly tangle-free, and its action is reasonably good when it's drawn into open pockets from the clustered vegetation. The Johnson Silver Minnow is the foremost such bait. Weedless spoons are available in different sizes, and it is good to have a selection of colors on hand. There are times when a black spoon is far more productive than a silver or gold one. Putting a light-colored strip of pork behind these spoons adds to their appeal, as does a single- or twin-tail, curly soft-plastic trailer.

Sometimes, though, you'll find that these spoons, despite their good swimming action, do not muster enough flash appeal to interest a bass that passes up or strikes short on a spoon-and-pork combo or a worm. Thus, another popular combination for fishing the green stuff incorporates an in-line spinner, a spoon, and a skirt. This is rather like the old and still popular Snagless Sally (Hildebrandt). The flash of the spinner on this bait is like the whipped cream on the parfait.

An offshoot of this arrangement is a spoon-and-skirt rig with the blade from an in-line buzzbait placed ahead of it. It gives you a noisy surface bait that is essentially snagless, but it doesn't have the flash appeal of the in-line spinner arrangement. There are some relatively weed-

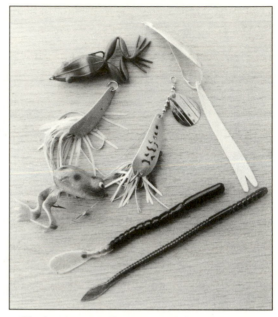

Plastic worms, weedless spoons, and weedless surface baits are the top lures for extracting bass from of the vegetation.

less buzzbaits on the market that incorporate a buzzer with a spoon, or spoonlike body, though I can't say I've had great success with them.

For good measure, you can also add a trailer hook to both of those arrangements. The trailer will mean more hooked fish, though it also means more snagging on pad stems, grass clumps, and the like; you have to be willing to make the trade-off. If you put on a trailer, be attentive to which hook actually gets the bass you catch. If it is the main hook, the fish are hitting the lure well and you probably don't need the trailer. But if most of the fish come on the trailer, they are swiping at the lure or hitting it short, and you'll have to continue to put up with snags in order to catch bass.

In addition to these lures, spinnerbaits can be highly effective near vegetation. When pads and grass are not too thick, in the spring or early summer, a spinnerbait is the best lure to use. For thicker grass and pads, a spinnerbait can be productive when worked on the edges, either fished parallel along them or fluttered down vertically along the breakline. Only when you fish deep in thick vegetation must a spinnerbait yield to other lures.

Keep in mind that bass are sometimes very deep in matted grass or pads or hyacinth and hydrilla beds, if the water is reasonably deep. In Florida, where hyacinths may be so thick that you can't possibly get a lure through them, and where ample water extends far back under the matted surface debris, anglers liveline big shiners so that they will run back under the vegetation. Live-shiner fishing is hugely popular and successful there.

When edges don't produce around vegetation so thick it looks as though you could walk

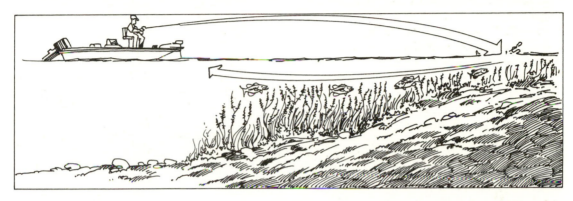

When fishing submerged weeds, you can work the lure above them, or drop the lure into a pocket, or work the weed line and drop-off to deeper waters.

across it, you've encountered the most demanding vegetation-fishing situation of all. Fishing effectively is only the second half of the problem. Getting your boat in there and maneuvering it adequately is the first half. You can hardly row through it, and you can't run an electric motor. Poling is about all that works, and you spend more time poling than fishing. Using an outboard motor is usually impossible (and harmful to the engine; if the water intake becomes clogged, the engine overheats).

Sometimes there are small holes in the mass that can be readily fished, but more often than not you wind up making your own hole and

Be sure to work the edges of weeds and the area near deeper water, and try retrieving your lure in several different ways.

dunking your bait in it. You may even have to use your rod or an oar to poke the hole. There's no casting involved here. The angler reaches over the hole with a long (7-foot-plus) rod, drops the bait (usually a weedless jig, jig-and-eel combo, jig-and-pork-chunk combo, or spoon-and-pork-chunk combo), slowly works it up and down, and then reaches for the next spot. When bass are concentrated in or under thickly matted vegetation, and you probe stealthily and patiently, this technique works.

A few other types of lures are also suitable for vegetation-fishing, particularly over sparse or submerged grass. Spinnerbaits and buzzbaits can be effective here, as can shallow-running minnow imitations, which can be worked on the surface or beneath it, though retrieved slowly. This type of plug is excellent for determining whether fish are present in such vegetation and for locating pockets that might contain concentrations of fish. Such underwater pockets can then be probed more thoroughly and slowly with a plastic worm.

Surface lures are everybody's favorite in areas where they can be properly worked. If bass are actively feeding in submerged grass, surface plugs can be dynamite. Fore-and-aft-propellered stickbaits; stickbaits without propellers, such as the Zara Spook; and wobbling surface plugs will catch bass here.

"Weedless" soft-plastic lures also have their place. Some of the best are frog imitations, including the Snag-Proof Frog and Harrison-Hoge Superfrog. These come as close to true weed-free fishing as possible. They look realistic, have good maneuverability through the salad,

and catch fish. The same can be said for the so-called weedless rats, most of which are soft plastic. It's often hard to hook fish with most weedless lures, however; they can be frustrating.

Tackle

Vegetation-fishing generally requires stout tackle. Depending on the conditions and the maximum size of bass that might be caught, you'll have to be the judge of what is adequate. Where big bass and thick vegetation are common, most old hands use no less than 17- or 20-pound line, and some use still heavier line. But even with heavy tackle, there are times when a good-size bass throws itself behind a thick mass of cover and you have to hurriedly bring the boat over to it, keep rod pressure constantly on, and hope you can reach down with your hand and scoop out the fish. (You often lose it.)

After you've been vegetation-fishing for a while, you'll find that it seems to be more productive in low light than in bright daylight. Brightness drives bass deeper and farther into the vegetation, where they are harder to reach effectively. Dawn, dusk, and overcast days offer the best conditions for vegetation-fishing. Nighttime is good as well.

Keep in mind the features to look for in trying to establish a bass-catching pattern in vegetation. Edges, pockets, irregular breaks, and isolated patches all have potential. If there is current in the lake, seek out the areas most affected by it. And if the going is tough and the bass have to be pursued in the thickest vegetation, so be it. Get in there after them.

13 CATCHING

A big smallmouth bass like this is probably harder to deliberately target than a big largemouth.

BIG BASS

Experience has convinced me that trophy bass are the most pursued, most revered prize in freshwater. There are more trophies in a given body of water than we suspect. Many die of natural causes, but anglers take their share, too, and not always by mere coincidence. You can catch big bass on purpose.

A bass that's "big" in California may not be in Texas or Pennsylvania. Generally, though, a fish is big if it's well above the normal size wherever you're fishing. A 4-pound smallmouth is a good fish everywhere; 5 pounds or more is a trophy. A 5-pound largemouth is a respectable fish everywhere, but though it's a trophy to some in northern states, it's merely a good one in southern locales. Any bass over 7 pounds, however, is special in almost any body of water.

Size is relative to fish population, fishing pressure, and especially to geography and length of growing season. For instance, on the average, a 7- to 8-year-old bass in New York would weigh 5 pounds, whereas in South Carolina that fish would be about 2 pounds heavier.

The number of big bass in any water is generally low in comparison to the size of the entire bass population. But anglers tend to estimate the numbers even lower because relatively few big bass are taken from most lakes. Many so-called "fished-out" lakes, however, produce a good number of cagey old giants.

For me, the prime season for catching big bass is spring. They can be caught in summer and fall, but overall, spring seems to offer the best opportunity for landing a big one, particularly a smallmouth (which prefers a deeper and more lightly covered habitat than a largemouth throughout the season). For most of the spring, bass are in the shallows and fairly accessible to anglers. And just before or during spring spawning, big female bass laden with eggs weigh considerably more than they will after spawning.

In contrast, some good anglers I know, particularly several in Florida's lunker country, land more big bass and in the summer than in any other season. This may be peculiar to Florida, because it has predominantly shallower lakes than other parts of the country, and perhaps their fish are more vulnerable than deeper and warier fish in other climes. In the big bass spots in the San Diego region, the largest lunkers generally come in late winter and early spring, and are often taken deep.

Regardless of season, you stand a better chance of duping big bass if you use large lures. I've caught big bass, especially smallmouths, on diminutive lures, but, in general, if you want a trophy, feed it a mouthful. There are six different types of lures that I consider big-bass baits.

Big lures tend to catch big bass a great deal of the time. Although not a particularly huge largemouth, this fish took a big jointed plug, one of the better lures for targeting big bass.

When fished in the appropriate places, they can tempt trophies as well as just larger-than-average (slightly bigger than the standard keeper) bass.

Lures

A big plastic worm is the most effective lunker largemouth catcher throughout the seasons. I thought I knew something about using big

worms until I fished a few lakes in Cuba several years ago. In these waters, 12- to 18-inch eels were a major bass forage and the principal bait of local fishermen. Also, 12- to 14-inch worms were the ticket for big and little bass alike, and though smaller worms did catch some fish, they were not as effective.

On our side of the Caribbean, largemouths don't often see such giant forage, so 7- to 9-inch plastic imitations are ample throughout the United States, though larger ones are occasionally fished in Florida and other places where water snakes are prevalent. Worms are most effective for big bass from mid- to late spring through midfall.

The same period is also prime time for stickbaits. These are my favorite surface bass lures and the most dynamic and predictable of all big bass catchers in the hands of skilled retrievers. These 4½- to 6-inch-long stickbaits appeal to the streetfighter side of a bass's nature. No other lures can match them for sheer trickery or ability to elicit angry, electrifying strikes. A lake with a lot of stumps, brush, and vegetation in shallow water is a top candidate for stickbait-fishing on calm days.

A buzzbait is another excellent big-bass surface lure. Primarily effective in warm water, on cloudy days, and when the surface is calm or only lightly rippled, a buzzbait appeals to the reflexive nature of a bass. For big bass, the best bet is a large buzzbait with a trailer hook equal in size to the main hook. I use a trailer hook most of the time, but the largest bass usually hammer the bait and get impaled on the main hook anyway. The most effective buzzbaits are those that can be worked the instant they hit the water and slowly fished below the surface. They also make a distinctively loud clicking sound as the buzzing blade rotates.

Perhaps most realistic of the big-bass lures are floating/diving minnow plugs. I favor the wooden plugs for their added buoyancy. But one big, old tarnished plastic Rebel that I found, repainted, and put new hooks on has proven to be a treasured bass getter. These big minnow baits work best in spring and fall. They can be fished on a slow, steady retrieve, an erratic stop-and-go subsurface retrieve, or strictly as a surface plug in the manner of a stickbait. My better fish have yielded to the latter two techniques.

Spinnerbaits and jig-and-pork combos may be the most versatile big-bass lures. There are all kinds of spinnerbaits available, but the larger ones, such as Nos. 5 to 7 single-blade or tandem models, with a rubber skirt and a trailer, are most effective for big bass. A curled, twin-tail white or chartreuse plastic trailer is a lethal spinnerbait addition that adds enticing action and substance to the lure.

Although spinnerbaits can produce big bass through standard retrieves in assorted types of cover, slow-rolling is the next best thing to using an electric shocker. (Slow-rolling, you'll recall, is the technique of bringing a spinnerbait up to a stump, log, fallen tree, or bush, easing it over the object, then fluttering it down in front of an unsuspecting bass.)

Like spinnerbaits, jig-and-pork combinations—in the form of a jig-and-eel, jig-and-worm, jig-and-pork chunk, or jig-and-frog—have application throughout the fishing season. They, too, will catch bass of all sizes, but have a better-than-average track record on bigger bass. They are effective when flipped into close cover, jigged in deep water, or worked slowly in the edges or pockets of vegetation.

All of these lures appeal to the feeding, reflexive, or pugnacious instincts of large fish, and all have their moments for big bass. But most are at their best when fished in and around thick cover. Remember, though, that trophy bass are generally not as aggressive as the smaller, more eager members of their species. This is not to say they are docile; when they want something, they'll go for it. But big bass are not accustomed to expending a lot of energy to get their food. You have to show them something easily taken but worth the effort, something irresistible.

"X" Marks the Spot

Most fishermen who catch a big bass have a tendency to move off from the place where they caught it. Or they eliminate the possibility of catching more bass from the same spot by drifting over it or making a big commotion. Some people get so excited when they hook a big bass that they don't think of anything except that fish and that fight. The angler who keeps a cool head is able to work the fish properly while also noting exactly where it came from and adjusting the position of the boat with the electric motor to stay away from the spot, keeping down boat noises and otherwise minimizing disturbance, in case the area turns out to be a haven for big fish or a cafeteria for bass on a feeding frenzy. Some of the best short-haul catches I've made have come from a single locale late on a spring day, when bass had turned on in the warm shallow waters.

A lot of fishermen forget where they've seen, caught, or lost big bass. They forget the exact location—the specific stump along a row or the particular bush on a brushy bank, for example. It's important to know, to the most precise detail, where you encountered a good fish so you can return to that spot. It's not a bad idea to mark those spots in some way if they are near shore.

I fish a lot of unfamiliar water each year and see all kinds of markers in the form of cans, ribbons, glow-in-the-dark cloth, and so forth. Some of them mark trotlines, nets, or brush piles, but I suspect some mark particularly desirable fishing spots. Stakes, poles, and other objects driven into the bottom also serve as markers. In the Arctic, Inuits traditionally place rock piles along lakeshores to mark good fishing places. (A tip on marking big-bass locales: Don't mark the exact spot. Place a marker a certain distance to the side of the exact spot, so it's more difficult for others to find.) Such marking is particularly useful in lakes that experience water-level fluctuations.

Don't get the impression that big bass are found only near the shore. In deep lakes without thick shoreline cover, in heavily pressured lakes, and in shallow lakes with good cover throughout, you're just as apt to find the monsters in deep or open water, so check the terrain on all sides of the boat.

Go Ahead, Try It!

You shouldn't be timid about trying something out of the ordinary when seeking big bass. I once had a letter from someone who caught a 7½-pound smallmouth on half a cricket he'd been using for crappies, which shows that anything is possible (and that luck or circumstance often plays as big a role in catching big bass as skill and technique). A few years ago I was fishing a Cuban lake for big bass, and it occurred to me that if giant bass will take 12-inch shiners in Florida, wouldn't these bass hit a properly presented big crankbait? Fishing with a 5-inch deep-diving muskie plug seemed weird to my companions, and I'll admit I felt a bit awkward doing it, but I landed an 8-pounder and lost a bigger fish when it leaped and broke off. Yes, those fish may have been a bit naive, not having had much hardware tossed their way, but who's to say this sort of experimentation wouldn't work elsewhere?

On another occasion in a Florida phosphate pit, I was fishing a small pit from shore near a sluice pipe that was dumping out water from another pit and creating a lot of current in the immediate locale. I tried fishing with a Bagley DB3 crankbait, but thought I needed to get deeper and replaced it with a 5-inch deep-diving Bagley Bang-O-Lure (a muskie and saltwater bait). On my first cast I landed a 4-pound largemouth. A few casts later, in the same spot, I took a 6-pounder. I know that few people would think of using such a big crankbait for bass, yet I've seen big bass (including smallmouths) hit a big bait meant for stripers or muskies or pike, and while I admit it doesn't happen often, occasionally going outside the norm and trying a different kind and size of lure might hook that big bass.

The One That Got Away

Hooking is one thing; catching is another. There may be twice as many big fish hooked each year as landed. Everyone loses big bass, though some seem to do so with more frequency than others. The fishermen who see only one or two big bass

Courtesy of Daiwa

A fish like this, or just a few ounces heavier, is what most bass anglers would love to tie into. This is a replica of a released California bass that weighed 22 pounds 1 ounce, just 3 ounces shy of the long-standing all-time world record. Unfortunately, many big bass are lost by anglers for a variety of reasons.

a year are the ones who get my condolences when they lose a good one. Most big bass are lost because the line was too light for the conditions, the hook was not set properly, the drag was too loose or too tight, the tackle was inadequate (usually too limber), the angler didn't play the fish properly, or he didn't know how to net a fish. Many fish are lost when they jump, although some would-be jumpers can be duped into not jumping if you thrust your rod tip into the water and change the angle of pull.

I don't subscribe to the theory that a big bass should be thoroughly played out before you land it. Play the fish as hard as your tackle and the conditions will allow, and land it as soon as you're able. This increases your chances of catching it and reduces your chances of injuring the fish. Under ordinary circumstances, the less pressure you apply and the longer a big fish is in the water, the more can go wrong and the greater your chances of losing it. If you do lose a fish, it will rarely hit again without having rested. However, it's possible that you can return to the same spot and catch the same fish, if not the same day, then the following day or a few days later.

It's also important to pay attention to places where you've seen big bass strike and miss, or boil after a lure but never feel a hook. Sometimes these fish can be caught immediately on a subsequent cast with a different lure. A plastic worm is the best secondary lure in this situation, but a spinnerbait or minnow plug is also effective.

Some anglers can spend many hours casting one type of bait or lure in selected places, and though they don't fill the boat with fish, they do manage to catch big bass with enviable regularity. Confidence, patience, and determination are major assets to the trophy-bass seeker. I'm not patient, but at times—on lakes I'm intimately familiar with—I can psych myself into capturing a big bass. I may deliberately pretend that a real trophy lies in every spot. When a big one does hit, I'm so ready that it hardly stands a chance.

Fishing for big bass is a worthy challenge, provided you don't do it strictly for show and do release most of your fish unharmed. It's a pursuit that sets you apart from the average bass angler. Trophy bass don't come easy, but, as someone once cryptically observed, "Anybody can catch small bass."

INDEX